IN THE
NATIONAL
INTEREST

Beyond Boundaries:
Canadian Defence and Strategic Studies Series
Rob Huebert, Series Editor

ISSN 1716-2645 (Print)   ISSN 1925-2919 (Online)

Canada's role in international military and strategic studies ranges from peacebuilding and Arctic sovereignty to unconventional warfare and domestic security. This series provides narratives and analyses of the Canadian military from both an historical and a contemporary perspective.

No. 1·   **The Generals: The Canadian Army's Senior Commanders in the Second World War** J.L. Granatstein

No. 2·   **Art and Memorial: The Forgotten History of Canada's War Art** Laura Brandon

No. 3·   **In the National Interest: Canadian Foreign Policy and the Department of Foreign Affairs and International Trade, 1909–2009** Edited by Greg Donaghy & Michael K. Carroll

UNIVERSITY OF CALGARY PRESS

Canadian Foreign Policy and the Department of Foreign Affairs and International Trade, 1909–2009

Greg Donaghy and Michael K. Carroll, Editors

Beyond Boundaries:
Canadian Defence and Strategic Studies Series

ISSN 1716-2645 (Print)   ISSN 1925-2919 (Online)

© 2011 Greg Donaghy and Michael K. Carroll

University of Calgary Press
2500 University Drive NW
Calgary, Alberta
Canada T2N 1N4
www.uofcpress.com

LIBRARY AND ARCHIVES CANADA CATALOGUING IN PUBLICATION

In the national interest : Canadian foreign policy and the Department of Foreign Affairs and International Trade, 1909-2009 / Greg Donaghy and Michael K. Carroll, editors.

(Beyond boundaries, Canadian defence and strategic studies series, 1716-2645 ; 3)
Includes bibliographical references and index.
Also issued in electronic formats.
ISBN 978-1-55238-538-8

1. Canada—Foreign relations. 2. Canada. Dept. of Foreign Affairs and International Trade—History. I. Donaghy, Greg II. Carroll, Michael Kiernan III. Series: Beyond boundaries ; 3

FC242.S47 2011   327.71   C2011-901458-0

The University of Calgary Press acknowledges the support of the Alberta Foundation for the Arts for our publications. We acknowledge the financial support of the Government of Canada through the Canada Book Fund for our publishing activities. We acknowledge the financial support of the Canada Council for the Arts for our publishing program.

This book has been published with support from the Centre for Military and Strategic Studies at the University of Calgary.

Cover image: Image #13348650 by B. ARANOB (istockphoto.com)
Cover design, page design, and typesetting by Melina Cusano

For Mary Donaghy and Tara Scheurwater

Table of Contents

Acknowledgments — xi

Introduction
    Greg Donaghy and Michael K. Carroll — 1

Chapter 1
National Independence and the National Interest: O.D. Skelton's Department of External Affairs in the 1920s
    Norman Hillmer — 11

Chapter 2
"Behaving as Adults": External Affairs and North American Security in the 1930s
    Galen Roger Perras — 27

Chapter 3
National Identity, Public Opinion, and the Department of External Affairs, 1935–1939
    Heather Metcalfe — 51

Chapter 4
When the Department of External Affairs Mattered – And When it Shouldn't Have
    J.L. Granatstein — 69

Chapter 5
The Department of External Affairs and the United Nations Idea, 1943–1965
    Adam Chapnick — 81

CHAPTER 6

Sovereignty and Security: Canadian Diplomacy, the United States, and the Arctic, 1943–1968

    P. Whitney Lackenbauer and Peter Kikkert   101

CHAPTER 7

Advancing the National Interest: Marcel Cadieux, Jules Léger, and Canadian Participation in the Francophone Community, 1964–1972

    Robin S. Gendron   121

CHAPTER 8

External Affairs and Canadian External Trade Policy, 1945–1982

    Michael Hart   137

CHAPTER 9

Conflicting Visions: Pierre Trudeau, External Affairs, and Energy Policy

    Tammy Nemeth   155

CHAPTER 10

Setting the Canadian Foreign Policy Agenda, 1984–2009: Prime Ministers as Prime Actors?

    Nelson Michaud   181

CHAPTER 11

Engaging the United States: The Department of Foreign Affairs and U.S. Policy, 1982–2005
  Stephen J. Randall — 207

CHAPTER 12

The Department of Foreign Affairs and International Trade: Interdepartmental Leadership and the Beijing Conference on Women
  Elizabeth Riddell-Dixon — 229

Bibliography — 245
Contributors — 263
Index — 265

ACKNOWLEDGMENTS

This volume and the conference that gave rise to it have benefited from the strong support of a number of people and institutions. The Department of Foreign Affairs and International Trade and the Centre for Military and Strategic Studies at the University of Calgary have encouraged the editors from the start. Professor David Bercuson, Director of the Centre for Military and Strategic Studies, was a genial and stimulating host who helped us refine our themes and select our contributors. He was ably assisted by the redoubtable Nancy Pearson Mackie, who provided outstanding assistance "on the ground" in Calgary. We thank them both.

The success of our conference owed much to the efforts of the individuals who chaired its sessions: Patrick Lennox, Duane Bratt, Gordon Houlden, Brig.-Gen. Robert S. Millar, Terry Terriff, and Ariel Delouya. They carried out their duties with the requisite combination of firmness, good-humour, and wisdom. Two exceptional public servants and diplomats, Mel Cappe and Don Campbell, enlivened the proceedings with frank reflections on their own efforts to define and pursue Canada's national interest.

Several individuals with a strong interest in Canada's foreign policy and its rich past were also very helpful in bringing this volume together. The following individuals deserve our special thanks: Jean Bourassa, Weldon Epp, John Ferris, Mary Halloran, and Philippe Lagassé.

INTRODUCTION

Greg Donaghy
and Michael K. Carroll

Over the last two decades, Canadian foreign policy has benefited from an exceptionally rich and vigorous, as well as polarized, discussion of Canada's national interest. The contours of that debate emerged sharply in the mid-1990s, when the end of the Cold War still seemed likely to liberate global politics in general, and Canadian foreign policy in particular, from the traditional constraints of empire, alliance, and power. Canada's Liberal foreign minister at the time, Lloyd Axworthy, certainly thought so, and he embraced an ambitious "human security" agenda that placed individual – not state – welfare at the centre of the global agenda. His high-profile campaigns against landmines and for an international criminal court inspired a generation of progressive Canadians, convinced that their country's national interest lay in pursuit of a new world order.[1]

His critics were legion and vocal. They denounced Axworthy and his allies for engaging in a cheap "pulpit diplomacy" and attacked the minister for his "intrusive internationalism."[2] In the aftermath of the terrorist attacks of 11 September 2001, his critics wielded realist notions of the national interest with considerable effect. In his unlikely bestseller, *While Canada Slept: How We Lost Our Place in the World*, Andrew Cohen fretted about Ottawa's declining foreign policy assets and its fading influence abroad.³ Cohen's lament echoed among the think-tanks, where defining the national interest quickly became an *idée fixe*,⁴ and along the corridors of power. Liberal prime minister Paul Martin got the message and promised in February 2004 to "see Canada's place of pride and influence in the world restored."⁵ So too did his successor, Conservative prime minister Stephen Harper, who assured the House of Commons in October 2007 that "Canadian foreign policy must promote our values and defend our interests."⁶ For better or worse, discussions of contemporary Canadian foreign policy are firmly centred on frank assessments of competing definitions of the national interest.

As the Department of Foreign Affairs and International Trade contemplated celebrating its 100th anniversary in 2009, it was difficult to avoid the echoes of this debate. Indeed, the Centre for Military and Strategic Studies at the University of Calgary and the department thought it appropriate to convene a conference using the national interest as a theme for exploring the evolution of the Canada's foreign and trade ministry over the past century. The workshop brought together former diplomats and public servants with scholars from different disciplines and backgrounds to explore Canada's national interests and the department's changing role in defining and pursuing them. This volume, which brings together a variety of historical perspectives on the department's place in the debate over interests and values in Canadian foreign policy, is the result.

When the Department of External Affairs was established in June 1909, tucked into pokey offices above a barber shop at the corner of Queen and Bank streets in downtown Ottawa, few would have predicted its eventual importance. "It is not intended it shall be a very numerous department," Prime Minister Wilfrid Laurier reassured cost-conscious parliamentarians, or "a very heavy department."⁷ Tory to the core and convinced that Canada's national interests were best served within the comforting embrace of the British Empire, Sir Joseph Pope, the department's first under-secretary, had only modest ambitions for his new ministry. Under Pope and the two Conservative prime ministers he served, Robert Borden and Arthur Meighen, the department operated as a colonial "post office" and an archive for state papers. When they wanted advice, Borden and Meighen turned, not to Pope or his small staff, but to Loring Christie, who became the department's first legal advisor in 1913. With Christie's help,

Borden and Meighen led Canada through the First World War and into the new League of Nations, seeking Canada's advantage in new forms of unity within the British connection.[8]

Meighen's Liberal successor, Prime Minister W.L. Mackenzie King, had different objectives. Elected in 1921, King was haunted by the memory of the Conscription Crisis of 1917 and convinced that the preservation of Canadian unity was the country's principal national interest. He was suspicious of imperial entanglements that might limit Canada's freedom to manoeuvre and tear at its national unity. Determined to wrest greater freedom from London, he recruited the dean of arts at Queen's University in Kingston, O.D. Skelton, to help. Like King, Skelton, as historian Norman Hillmer argues in our opening chapter, was sure of the national interest, and he set out in the mid-1920s to build a foreign ministry that was both an "instrument and expression of Canadian interests." This meant a department that reflected Canada's bicultural heritage, a theme that reverberates through several chapters, and a ministry that provided for distinctive representation abroad. Most important, placing "Canada first" meant policies that severed its imperial ties with Britain and embraced Canada's destiny as a North American nation.

Canada during the interwar period was a post-colonial state of uncertain identities and fluid loyalties, where the national interest was especially tough to define. However compelling in theory, the case for embracing Canada's North American destiny was studded with doubts. The point is made forcefully in Galen Perras's chapter on bilateral defence cooperation in the 1930s. American uncertainty about Canada's very nature and Washington's maladroit diplomacy reinforced concerns on both sides of the border about the value of closer bilateral cooperation. These factors and the strong, emotional attachment felt by many Canadians to Britain and its imperial values rendered progress along "the American road" slower and more uncertain than its supporters might have liked. Seemingly so clear in Skelton's mind and in the department he built in his image, the national interest proved indeed, in Hillmer's phrase, "a slippery beast."

This ought not to be surprising, and several of the chapters in this collection underline the close but complicated, even treacherous, relationship between popular opinion and the national interest. This is especially true of the chapter by Heather Metcalfe, who is preoccupied with questions of public opinion and national identity. Armed with the kind of toolkit found among cultural historians, she links the national interest with "national" identity, a truth that Skelton and many of his younger colleagues in External Affairs intuitively understood. As Metcalfe points out, however, there were profound structural barriers to understanding popular opinion and knowing how to harness it in prewar Canada, barriers which often left elites and intellectuals frustrated by their inability either to understand or influence popular sentiment.

The outbreak of the Second World War in September 1939 changed both the parameters of the debate over Canada's national interests and the department's role in that discussion. The war swept away the inward-looking "little Canada" of the pre-war era, replacing it with a more mature and united nation that was inclined to define its national interests in more international terms. As Lester B. Pearson, who played a vital role in that transformation as both civil servant and politician, later recalled, "passive isolation and disinterest" gave way to "active participation and commitment."[9]

The war also transformed the Department of External Affairs and its policy-making capacity. Forced to embrace new allies, to seek markets in unfamiliar corners of the world, and to build a system for postwar global governance, the department's reach was suddenly global. By 1946, Canada had 26 missions abroad, up from 7 in 1939; by 1956, the total had reached 64.[10] At home, the department took on new responsibilities, for instance, overseeing trade in strategic goods and intelligence gathering. With Skelton's death in 1941, the way was clear to re-organize the department and bring younger and bolder leaders to the top. In 1946, the department regained its own minister for the first time since 1912 when Louis St. Laurent became secretary of state for external affairs, before becoming prime minister in 1948. Serving under him was Pearson, first as undersecretary and then as secretary of state for external affairs. Both men, and the diplomats they managed, were committed to responsible and active internationalism.

Striking the right balance between obvious national interests, for instance, Cold War defence or arctic sovereignty, and broader international interests and values was rarely easy. Jack Granatstein, who gave the conference's keynote address, makes this point in his chapter by contrasting

Skelton's focus on advancing ties with the United States with the quixotic campaign of his successor, Norman Robertson, for nuclear disarmament in the late 1950s. For Granatstein, Robertson had succumbed to the traditional Canadian temptation to play to the house, to be a scolding "moralist."

Historian Adam Chapnick sounds a similarly cautionary note in his chapter on Canada and the United Nations. In the immediate postwar period, Chapnick argues, the success and viability of the new international organization represented a genuine Canadian interest. Realists and functionalists, almost to a man, Canada's diplomats exerted an influence proportionate to Canada's middle-power status. Their diplomacy was professional, cautious, and moderate, and aimed at small measures designed to enhance United Nations operations or administrative efficiencies. Like Granatstein's wayward under-secretary, however, Chapnick's diplomats and politicians were seduced by global acclaim and domestic enthusiasms into betraying the conservative principles of the 1940s and early 1950s. A decade later, prime ministers John Diefenbaker and Mike Pearson embraced the United Nations for its peaceable values and the scope it provided for Canada to build East-West and North-South coalitions, forgetting that the national interest lay elsewhere.

Other assessments of the department's capacity to reconcile and balance competing national interests, a hallmark of Canada's foreign policy since 1945, are more forgiving. In chapter 6, Arctic scholars Whitney Lackenbauer and Peter Kirkett combine new archival evidence with an extensive reading of the existing literature to probe the department's role in shaping policies that reconciled Canadian claims to sovereignty across the Arctic with the country's close Cold War defence relationship with the United States. Like several contributors, Lackenbauer and Kirkett are impressed with the professional quality of the postwar department, which successfully managed this task by devising policies and tactics to handle Washington that were "civil, respectful, and mutually beneficial."

Chapters by Robin Gendron and Michael Hart explore different postwar interests, national unity and economic prosperity respectively, and endorse this sensible assessment about the capacity of the department to identify and manage these interests. Gendron echoes Metcalfe's observations on the complex connections between public opinion and definitions of the national interest. Shifting popular sentiment and expectations in Quebec thrust national unity to the top of the foreign policy agenda in the early 1960s. More important, this chapter traces the fierce debate between the department's two leading French-Canadians, Jules Léger and Marcel Cadieux, over how to respond to that new priority. Their dialogue and the policy compromises made along the way remind us that defining the national interest is rarely a zero-sum game.

Carleton University trade analyst Michael Hart, the only contributor to bridge the divide between scholar and practitioner, makes a similar point in his chapter on the department's role in shaping Canadian trade policy from 1945 to 1982. Like Granatstein and Chapnick, Hart is a frank realist; but in his economic world, there has been no great betrayal and "interests trump ideals." Admittedly, the triumph of a liberal, free trade order was not quick or smooth. In his long sweeping view of Canadian trade policy, Hart explores the competition between specific and general interests, wryly concluding that "the conjunction between good policy and good politics often proved narrow, difficult to find, and hard to implement." Staking out and defending that middle ground is the policy-maker's role, one that the department excelled in from the 1930s to the 1980s. Even the 1982 amalgamation of the Department of External Affairs with the Trade Commissioner Service and the trade policy units of the Department of Industry, Trade and Commerce to create what became the Department of Foreign Affairs and International Trade did not diminish its contribution. Foreign and trade policy, Hart concludes, were reconciled through "incremental, pragmatic, and cautious" policy adjustments.

For Liberal prime minister Pierre Trudeau, elected in the spring of 1968, pragmatism and caution were part of the problem. The prime minister doubted both the value of diplomacy and the dull, grey men at External Affairs, who seemed incapable of responding to Canada's declining international status as postwar recovery in Europe and Japan and the new post-colonial powers of Asia and Africa crowded the global stage. Sceptical of the country's recent internationalism and a foreign policy dominated by a network of U.S.-led Cold War alliances, Trudeau wanted a foreign policy that was more modest and more closely tied to the national interest. To get it, he opened up the policy-making process and erected a complex set of cabinet and interdepartmental committees that shifted the burden of defining the national interest from the foreign service bureaucracy to the politicians.¹¹ The balance of this collection explores how the altered policy-making environment has changed the department's contribution to the debate over the national interest.

Tammy Nemeth's chapter on energy policy constitutes a detailed case study of how the Trudeau government defined the national interest and pursued it in one vital sector of the Canadian economy. In Nemeth's view, Trudeau's new policy-making mechanisms shifted control over foreign policy towards domestic departments and central Canadian politicians, who favoured Ontario and Quebec. He neutered the country's foreign policy specialists, rejected their sound advice, and pursued nationalist policies that undermined the country's interests.

And the shift seems permanent. This, at least, is one of the principal conclusions reflected in Nelson Michaud's chapter on the foreign policy-making role of Canadian prime ministers since Brian Mulroney. Michaud insists that the prime minister's hold on the foreign policy agenda and notions of the national interest is increasingly absolute and irreversible.

But gaps persist. The prime-ministerial agenda is often crowded and his attention span short. Stephen Randall's chapter on Canada–United States relations offers a more nuanced view of the department's continuing relevance in shaping the national interest. Like Skelton's ministry in the 1920s and 1930s, the contemporary department, with its integrated foreign and trade policy functions, provides the institutional base for defining and pursuing the country's North American interests. Surprised by the extent to which the country's key relationship with the United States, of paramount importance to Canada on so many levels, has been mismanaged or ignored, Randall contends that influential Canadian diplomats, not presidents or prime ministers, have provided an essential bureaucratic continuity. The national interest in things American remains a departmental preoccupation.

Indeed, our final contributor might go even further in asserting the vital importance of a strong foreign and trade ministry. Political scientist Elizabeth Riddell-Dixon contends that the turn of the new millennium has seen a democratization of the foreign policy process. Canada's involvement in the Beijing Women's Conference demonstrates a broadening of the national interest, which directly involves new players of a decidedly domestic orientation. While working at a "specialist" level during much of the Beijing Conference, Foreign Affairs and International Trade also acted as a "generalist" department, managing the bargains and compromises necessary to secure "the best overall negotiating text." Riddell-Dixon's contribution underlines a fact often overlooked in the debate over the national interest in Canadian foreign policy: our condition is compromised and impure, and seeking Canada's best possible advantage is an imperfect process.

Today's Department of Foreign Affairs and International Trade has clearly come a long way from its origins, with operations in 175 countries, a personnel allotment totalling over 13,000 full-time equivalents, and an annual budget of $2.513 billion.[12] Foreign policy itself has spilled far beyond the narrow borders that defined it a century ago and embraces a vast agenda. Policy-making too has become a messier and more complex business. Amidst these enormous changes, as the papers in this collection make clear, the contemporary department still shares the concern with the national interest that excited its earlier self. Strip away the lofty idealism of Borden's imperialism or the soaring rhetoric of St. Laurent's internationalism and underneath stands revealed the enduring preoccupation with national advantage that has rightly driven Canada's diplomats and their political masters.

NOTES

1. Greg Donaghy, "All God's Children: Lloyd Axworthy, Human Security and Canadian Foreign Policy, 1996–2000," *Canadian Foreign Policy* 10, no. 2 (Winter 2003): 39–58.

2. Dean Oliver and Fen Hampson, "Pulpit Diplomacy: A Critical Assessment of the Axworthy Doctrine," *International Journal* 43, no. 3 (Summer 1997–98): 379–407; Norman Hillmer and Adam Chapnick, "The Axworthy Revolution," in *Canada among Nations, 2001: The Axworthy Legacy*, ed. F.O. Hampson, Norman Hillmer, and M.A. Molot (Toronto: Oxford University Press, 2001), 68.

3. Andrew Cohen, *While Canada Slept: How We Lost Our Place in the World* (Toronto: McClelland & Stewart, 2003).

4. See, for instance, J.L. Granatstein, "The Importance of Being Less Earnest: Promoting Canada's National Interest through Tighter Ties with the U.S." Benefactors Lecture, (Toronto: C.D. Howe Institute, 2003); Allan Gotlieb, "Romanticism and Realism in Canada's Foreign Policy," Benefactors Lecture (Toronto: C.D. Howe Institute, 2004); Norman Hillmer, "The Secret Life of Canadian Foreign Policy," *Policy Options* (February 2005): 32–33.

5. Canada, House of Commons, *Debates*, 2 February 2004, 2–3.

6. Accessed at http://www.pm.gc.ca/eng/media.asp?id=1863.

7. Cited in John Hilliker, *Canada's Department of External Affairs*, vol. 1: *The Early Years, 1909–1946* (Kingston and Montreal: McGill-Queen's University Press, 1990), 36.

8. Robert Bothwell, *Loring Christie: The Failure of Bureaucratic Imperialism* (New York: Garland, 1988).

9. L.B. Pearson, *Mike: The Memoirs of the Right Honourable Lester B. Pearson*, vol. 2: *1948–57* (Toronto: University of Toronto Press, 1972), 28–32.

10. Department of Foreign Affairs and International Trade, *Punching Above Our Weight: A History of the Department of Foreign Affairs and International Trade* (Ottawa: DFAIT, 2009).

11. Greg Donaghy, "A Sad General Decline?: The Canadian Diplomat in the 20th Century," in *Canada among Nations, 2008: 100 Years of Canadian Foreign Policy*, ed. Robert Bothwell and Jean Daudelin (Montreal and Kingston: McGill-Queen's University Press, 2008), 41–60.

12. Department of Foreign Affairs and International Trade, *Report on Plans and Priorities, 2009–2010*, available at http://www.tbs-sct.gc.ca/rpp/2009-2010/inst/ext/ext-eng.pdf.

NATIONAL INDEPENDENCE AND THE NATIONAL INTEREST: O.D. SKELTON'S DEPARTMENT OF EXTERNAL AFFAIRS IN THE 1920S

Norman Hillmer

The national interest is a slippery beast – frequently invoked, seldom defined, adjustable to shifts of circumstance and differences of perspective.[1] Yet O.D. Skelton was confident that he knew precisely what Canada's interests in foreign policy were, and just as sure that the service of those interests must underpin the state's conduct. Skelton's three-decade-long crusade for independence from Britain, first as a professor and then as a public servant, was linked to his conviction that Canada's international policies could only be right if they were based on a fully autonomous and objective stock-taking of "the real interests of one's own country."[2] When he was named the permanent head of the Department of External Affairs half way through the 1920s, Skelton embraced the opportunity, turning his efforts to the building of an institution of independence capable of projecting national interests out into the world. The results were mixed.

Oscar Skelton wrote the prologue to his service in External Affairs in January 1922, with a much-publicized address to the Canadian Club in Ottawa.[3] Six weeks earlier, a federal election had brought W. L. Mackenzie King's Liberals to power; the prime minister was in the audience, along with other members of the government.[4] As he unwrapped his argument, the Queen's University professor insisted that the country's national interests resided in Canada and nearby, not in a revived and highly centralized British Empire run by and for the British alone. Canada – liberal, flexible, constantly evolving, like the empire when it was at its best – had been inching towards the ultimate goal of unfettered self-government for decades. As a first principle, Skelton declared, Canadians must maintain the steady trajectory to freedom. It would not be easy. He warned that Britain's leaders, alive to the fragility of their empire, were intent on drawing Canada into the imperialist web. Furthermore, they had the power to do so, abetted by Anglo-Canadians whose loyalties were divided between the Mother Country and Canada, or belonged entirely to Britain. The British would have that clout as long as the Canadian condition fell short of independence.

Sovereignty was Skelton's precondition of the capacity to act in the national interest. More than that, it was an interest in itself, the supreme interest that made the successful mobilization of all other interests possible. Skelton did not often explicitly invoke the notion of national independence because that remained highly controversial in the Canada of the 1920s. "Autonomy" was the term of choice, the safe middle ground preferred by contemporaries, shuttling Canada between liberty of movement and the comfort of the British connection, as the occasion demanded. Independence, however, was what Skelton wanted and thought necessary.

Proceeding from self-determination, Skelton put the emphasis on the core responsibilities of all national governments: to ensure security and stability, and to establish the conditions for prosperity. These were interests shared by the foreign and domestic realms of government activity, rightly he thought, since they were inseparable from one another as aspects of policy. What was foreign policy, he asked his Canadian Club listeners, but "simply an extension of domestic policy,"[5] an argument that allowed him to make the case for as much control of external affairs as Canadians had painstakingly established in their internal affairs.

Next in the inventory of interests came the working out of relationships, problems, and modalities on the North American continent. The foreign affairs of every country, Skelton told the Canadian Club, took place mainly at the fence lines that separated it from its neighbours, and largely arose from everyday matters of trade and economics. This assertion served two of Skelton's purposes. First, it gave prominence to his belief that in foreign policy geography was destiny. The United States could not be ignored as a factor in Canada's future: North America was where, he had believed since he was a young man, the country's "lasting community of interest" was situated.[6] Second, Skelton's North Americanism diverted attention from Canada's deeply entrenched British connection. By stipulating that foreign policy ought to concentrate on the United States, he was divorcing Canada's prime national interests from Britain's. Unlike King and so many other Canadians of the time, Skelton thought that the strict separation of Canadian interests from British interests was possible and, if Canada was to seize control of its future, imperative.

Last, and deliberately last in the Canadian Club catalogue of interests, Canada's connection to the world beyond North America had to be accounted for and attended to, although its responsibilities in that direction had to be kept limited for the time being. Co-operation with Britain was not out of the question, but it should take place only on the basis that the two countries were distinct entities and when it could be demonstrated that interests were held in common. Nevertheless, Skelton maintained, the country was "in the world and must be of it."[7] At bottom, he was convinced that in the long run the way ahead for the national interest lay in measured engagement with the international community. For now, though, Canadians had to find their own way to maturity, coherence, and freedom.

In the folklore of Canadian foreign policy, a straight line is drawn between the Canadian Club speech and Skelton's appointment three years later as under-secretary of state for external affairs. The staying power of this account of events is understandable enough. "Skelton's address would make an excellent foundation for Canadian policy on External Affairs," King wrote in his diary after hearing the talk, "and Skelton himself would make an excellent man for that department." He "certainly has the knowledge & the right point of view."[8] Years later, Skelton's wife Isabel scribbled in her scrapbook beside an account of the speech that it was this occasion "which really brought Oscar to Ottawa."[9]

But Skelton's ambition had a much longer pedigree. He had been on the road to the Department of External Affairs since its inception in 1909, when he told a colleague that he coveted the position of under-secretary – the departmental chief, or deputy minister, in today's terminology.[10] He had been a close observer of every important political event of the last generation, and an active participant in many of them. He was a leading Liberal nationalist voice on external policy, a frequent commentator in the press, and an advocate on the public platform. He had courted King, and advised him informally, from the moment he became leader of the Liberal party in 1919. He was anything but an unknown quantity. His transition from Queen's to External Affairs was natural, and many years in the making, even though it was difficult to leave the university that he loved.

At the Canadian Club, Skelton folded the Department of External Affairs into his contention that Canadians already had the basic outlines of the machinery to deal with the world outside. The department, he said, had not progressed very far in its development, but "so far as it has gone it has been very effective in its personnel."[11] That was without doubt a reference to Loring Christie, who had for a decade been the department's legal advisor and the government's chief external affairs analyst. After Christie, however, External Affairs had only Sir Joseph Pope, the dignified undersecretary, who had held the post since 1909 and was considerably past his prime, and a tiny headquarters staff of thirty-three, more than half of whom dealt with passports.[12]

Christie was soon on his way out, he and Prime Minister King proving incompatible, personally and professionally.[13] When Skelton was enlisted as an advisor to King and the Canadian delegation for the Imperial Conference of 1923, the professor found in the Department of External Affairs (and in the public service) competence and goodwill but not initiative or breadth. Of Pope he wrote in his diary: "perfect Civil Servant, polished, … prepared to subordinate own views to those of temporary political chief, not now very vigorous & not at all in touch with intimate affairs of office which are in hands of the P.M."[14] So Skelton did all the conference preparations himself, which was his inclination anyway, a fundamental flaw in his makeup that had a considerable impact on his effectiveness as an administrator.

King still had to squeeze Pope out, gently, and to convince Skelton to leave Queen's. This took until April 1925. As soon as he was installed as under-secretary, Skelton set course for an independent (and independence) minded External Affairs that could act as the instrument and expression of Canadian interests as he interpreted them. He was aware of the meagre resources at his disposal, but he set high standards for the first recruit to his staff, requiring (the terms of reference read) "a law degree or membership in a provincial bar association, two years of post-graduate studies in international affairs, practical experience in legal work, and a good knowledge of both English and French."[15] Jean Désy, a law professor at the Université de Montréal, was the one candidate who met the requirements, and he was immediately brought into the department. Skelton then acquiesced in the hiring of three officers, without a competition, to staff the new Canadian legation in the United States. One of them was the well-connected Hume Wrong, the grandson of former Liberal national leader Edward Blake. Wrong was supremely qualified, but he had been given his position: he had not won it after being tested against his peers. For Skelton, the arrangement was acceptable as an expedient, in order to get the Washington mission running at a high level of efficiency as quickly as possible. The under-secretary was determined to have a different sort of department, a meritocracy.

Skelton modelled the department on the British Foreign Office, with young professionals recruited by a competitive process and promoted because of their achievements, not their connections. Comprehensive competitive examinations for entry into the department began in 1927. The aim, said the under-secretary, was to locate people "of all-round ability, capable of performing in widely different assignments at short notice, rather than a highly skilled specialist."[16] Candidates were required to have a university degree or the equivalent, with training in the law, history, political science, or economics particularly favoured, and to possess the sterling characteristics of "undoubted integrity; tact; astuteness; keen perception; good judgment; and good address."[17] The first hurdle, a written exam, had four sections: a general essay designed to extract the applicant's view of imperial relations, questions on Canada's role in international affairs, a segment devoted to candidates' area of academic expertise, and a précis. Skelton set the papers, marked the results, and usually chaired the board that administered an interview to those who got at least 70 per cent overall on the exam and a pass in each of the four parts. Under the law, he had to give war veterans preference, but he refused to do so until they had satisfied him in the written examination.[18]

Skelton was disappointed by the response to his first competition, which yielded few applicants and only two who met the standard: J. Scott

Macdonald and E. D'Arcy McGreer. The under-secretary redoubled his efforts the next year in 1928, advertising nation-wide, approaching universities in search of candidates, and obtaining permission to hold exams outside the country in order to entice graduate students living abroad. This time there were sixty candidates, six of whom were successful: L. B. Pearson, Norman Robertson, H. L. Keenleyside, Kenneth Kirkwood, Paul-Emile Renaud, and Keith Crowther.[19] Pearson and Robertson, future under-secretaries of the Department of External Affairs, were encouraged to apply by Skelton personally. Robertson he had known since they had sailed across the Atlantic together in 1923, when the Rhodes Scholar on his way to Oxford had taken a violent dislike to Skelton, who was ill at ease with people he did not know, but they had a more relaxed encounter during the summer of 1927.[20] Skelton discovered Pearson, a colleague of Hume Wrong's in the history department at the University of Toronto, at a dinner in Ottawa after the Imperial Conference of 1926. In subsequent correspondence, Pearson learned of the under-secretary's plans for a foreign service governed by ability, where the genial young man, nicknamed "Mike," was assured that he could reasonably look forward "to occupying the highest diplomatic posts without private income or political influence."[21]

Skelton was surrounding himself with his own kind. Five of the six 1928 recruits had graduate degrees from institutions outside Canada and had taught university courses; two, Keenleyside and Renaud, had doctorates. This pattern persisted: a substantial proportion of the staff that Skelton selected during his years as under-secretary came from teaching, and a large number of his choices had post-graduate training. He sometimes contradicted the merit principle, naming officers to positions by order-in-council if some specific or urgent need arose, but that too reinforced the strong ties with the university world that were developing out of the examination system. In 1929, he chose John E. Read, the dean of law at Dalhousie University, as departmental legal adviser, putting through the appointment without advertising the position.[22]

In his employees, the under-secretary looked to Canada's bicultural character, if imperfectly. Although he made nothing of it at his Canadian Club speech, perhaps because he was pitching his message mainly to the likeminded King, Skelton regarded French-English harmony, and the social cohesion that was meant to flow from it, as a fundamental national interest. Following from his argument that domestic interests and international interests were intertwined, and reinforced by his belief that the French fact was an indispensable part of the Canadian story, his sermons on the importance of national unity were a staple of his speeches and writings on foreign policy. Bilingualism was not a requirement for entry into External Affairs, but Skelton encouraged French representation in the department and, by 1930, 30 per cent of his officers were francophones. Even so, the Montreal intellectual newspaper *Le Devoir* (among others) questioned why there were "si peu des nôtres dans cette carrière nouvelle" and wondered about the "perspectives d'avancement" for the few there were.[23]

French might be the language of diplomacy, but English was the language of Skelton's External Affairs. He could speak a rough French, but despite his clear regard for Jean Désy and other francophones, Skelton never seems to have communicated with his francophone officers in their own language or to have taken concrete steps to promote the use of French in the department, beyond beefing up translation services as business increased. Below the level of under-secretary, there was evidence in the late 1920s of what one British official called "bitterness and jockeying" between French and English officers[24] and already the tendency on the part of both language groups to see francophones as most useful and happiest in posts abroad. Out of sight, however, was out of mind, and continual service away from headquarters was apt to marginalize young diplomats and impair opportunities for promotion.[25]

Only men could apply to become foreign service officers, and that remained the practice throughout Skelton's time at External Affairs. He valued women, however, and a triumvirate of them ruled over the deputy's central office in the East Block of the Parliament buildings. Each had an importance belied by her title. Skelton's secretary, Marjorie McKenzie, was at the heart of everything, controlling access and the flow of information to the under-secretary, watching over his confidential records and drafting materials for his signature. She was competent in French, German, and Spanish, and in 1930 demonstrated her ability and determination when she insisted on taking the foreign service officer exam, even though she was not eligible for appointment. She tied for first place in a tough competition. Accountant Agnes McCloskey, energetic and often acerbic, was in effect the department's chief administrative officer; she scrutinized the finances and enforced regulations in a manner many found autocratic and inflexible. Hugh Keenleyside recalled in his memoirs that Skelton "was alternately amused, grateful, or impressed, and he trusted her, although not necessarily her judgement, completely."[26] Grace Hart, a graduate of Queen's and McGill hired in 1928 to organize the library, completed the group of indispensable women. Although she and her little empire had a chaotic appearance, they gave the department the professional research function Skelton realized was a vital component of an independent foreign office.[27]

The powerful McKenzie and McCloskey sat in Skelton's inner office, only a few feet from the under-secretary. The junior foreign service officers were exiled to the attic of the East Block, where they walked the corridors in darkness and fought for space with the bats.[28] When Mike Pearson won the first secretary competition in 1928, at a salary of $3,450 (a modest raise over his university salary), he rushed to Ottawa in response to a message to start work immediately, only to find there was nothing much to do. His initial job was to prepare routine background for a League of Nations conference on the causes of death, followed by requests for a list of British Empire treaties affecting Canada and materials relating to lighthouses in the Red Sea, international tariffs on cement, and the protection of women artists living abroad.[29] Pearson's companion in a cramped and depressing room under the eaves was Keenleyside, assigned in the beginning to re-organizing and filing documents, a task for which he was discovered to have some flair. Their typing was done by an inefficient but kindly secretary on a crank-handled machine, which Keenleyside recalled was "even older than herself."[30]

Paradoxically, having shaping his department around highly trained minds with the capacity for independent thought and action, Skelton showed no inclination to employ them systematically. External had the unrushed, ramshackle air of a university campus, and it was growing without any clear organizational direction. Skelton was no administrator, and he was certainly no sharer of responsibility. He ran the department as a benign dictator sensitive to others but intent on having his own way. He understood his shortcomings as a manager and administrator, and the way office routine was absorbing so much of "my nights & days."[31] Yet he was too busy and preoccupied to stick to the rough parcelling out of duties that he knew was in the best interests of efficiency, and his "young men," as they were called, were given work that overlapped and went far beyond their areas of assignment. All were directly accountable to the under-secretary, who reviewed every scrap of paper written in the department and every communication that entered or went out of headquarters.[32] The prime minister might interview top candidates during the recruiting process, but he was only dimly aware of them after they were hired. Every memorandum or recommendation he saw came from Skelton.[33] The department was Skelton, and he wanted it that way, whether he would have admitted it or not.

His employees complained about Skelton's weak commitment to matters of administration and delegation. They found him tightlipped and tightfisted, retiring and even distant. Only Keenleyside of the early recruits believed that they became friends, and he was almost certainly wrong about that.[34] Most of them, with Wrong as a notable exception, revered "Dr. Skelton" for his command of language and international affairs, for his immense political influence, for his unselfishness and high principle.[35] They shared his rock-solid nationalism – the examinations and interviews were designed to show that – and his disdain for the showiness and hierarchy of high diplomacy. He gently improved their drafts, suffered their practical jokes without complaint, and tolerated a diversity of views on social, economic, and political questions.[36] Everyone was treated equally and with respect, whatever their rank.[37] When Keenleyside had been in the department for only a few days, Skelton arranged travel to Vancouver on business so that the new man could help with his family's move to Ottawa. A short time later, the under-secretary took Keenleyside to a Canadian–American smuggling conference, keeping him carefully under control but offering an early taste of raw diplomacy. It was Keenleyside's first intimate glimpse of Skelton – quiet and diffident, but also astute, easy to underestimate, and far harder on the Americans than his reputation suggested. He was "at least as strongly opposed to the neo-imperialism of Washington as he was to the remnants of colonialism in London."[38]

The growth of the department in Ottawa was paralleled by the beginnings of a foreign service abroad. In 1927 Vincent Massey took up his post as Canada's minister in the United States, the first diplomatic representative in a foreign country. There was trouble between him and Skelton from the beginning, generated in some part by their differing attitudes about what diplomacy meant and was meant to achieve. Massey wanted to purchase a luxuriously furnished Washington mansion at 1746 Massachusetts Avenue, with a price tag of $500,000, to serve both as a residence and chancery. Skelton opposed the idea as extravagant and politically risky, instead suggesting that the patrician Masseys live in and work out of a hotel until something suitable was found.[39]

Skelton acknowledged that diplomatic prestige demanded a good front, especially for a new player on the international scene. Some of the expenditure could be justified on the grounds of national advertising and, just as banks tried to do with their palatial quarters, providing assurances of stability. Long-established traditions and standards could not easily be set aside. Diplomats were dined and wined, "and must retaliate in kind." But discreetly: Canadians in Washington ought to keep in mind that their national interests in the United States were limited and specific, and so was their target audience. Their aim had to be squarely at influential politicians in Washington, not the American public at large and certainly not foreigners. As to contacts with the diplomats of other countries, Skelton sniffed: "Our jobs in Washington are our own and call for little of that daily hobnobbing with other legations which is inevitable in European capitals where everyone is playing the same game – how to tilt the balance of power a little more his own way – and is interested in every move and intrigue of every other representative."[40]

With King's help, Massey got his mansion. That did not change Skelton's view that the purchase had handed ammunition to the many domestic critics of representation in foreign capitals and seriously prejudiced the Washington experiment "in the eyes of a great part of the country."[41] Skelton and Massey then extended their battle over resources to expenses for the Washington legation staff, causing the under-secretary to apologize for a fit of temper over the telephone: "I have been brought up in a thrifty school and sky high estimates of living needs irritate me."[42] Skelton said that he was open to convincing, and he was soon proposing salary increases for Canadian diplomats. Miserly wages meant that only wealthy men could take on such work. "That unduly restricts the choice of men and involves serious political dangers. The state should foot its own bills … : it should provide as much for a rich man as for a poor man."[43] Massey, a very rich man himself, probably would have seen those words as part of the war against him, although he too believed that diplomats with fewer advantages than his own ought to get jobs at the top, even if only a few of them.⁴⁴

Skelton loathed pomp. Massey adored it. When Skelton told Massey that his American counterpart, William Phillips, was about to be welcomed to Ottawa as minister "quite informally," Massey protested to the prime minister, after tattling to the United States State Department, that it would be "distinctly unfortunate" if the reception was any less grand or dignified than the one he had been given in Washington.⁴⁵ Skelton responded angrily, reminding Massey that the suggestion had come from the governor general, not the Department of External Affairs, and that, even if the State Department was unwilling to trust Ottawa to do right by Phillips, the under-secretary might have hoped that Massey would take it for granted. As for the Americans, "personally I wish more of their time might be given to such questions of diplomatic procedure as remembering that His Majesty's Government in Canada is not a branch of His Majesty's Government in Great Britain."⁴⁶

Skelton and Massey also clashed on the giving of British honours and titles, which the King government had discontinued, and on the wearing of diplomatic uniforms. His tone laced with sarcasm, Skelton asked the minister in Washington what ought to be done about the question of formal dress for Canada's fledgling diplomatic service: "Do you think we should seek some sartorial genius to devise a new one, or vary the British with some distinctive Canadian feature? Or should we try the frock coat of the American gentleman, or the overalls of modern democracy?"⁴⁷ Massey replied that British diplomatic uniforms could be easily adapted with some maple leaves and Canadian buttons.⁴⁸ Skelton's own preference was clear. He favoured the overalls.⁴⁹ Skelton had contempt for Massey's aristocratic pretensions and condescension, and his anglophilia made it worse. The under-secretary's project was a democratic, independent, modern country, alive to its own separate interests and determined to step away from Britain's influences, the very antithesis of the Canada for which he imagined Massey stood.

The establishment of the legation at Washington was followed by an announcement early in 1928 that Paris and Tokyo would be next.⁵⁰ Action in this field was part of Skelton's grand but gradualist scheme of national independence, which he characterized as the natural outgrowth of evolving self-government. As the country grew in population, industrial development, and foreign trade, and as the progress of science increased contact with the world outside, the national interest demanded that Canadians begin to make provision for their distinct requirements abroad. Representation in three major capital cities was only a start, but it was important in both symbolic and real terms, setting the seal on Canada's international standing and allowing important work to be done on the spot. To those, notably in the Conservative party, who predicted that Canadian diplomats running amok in foreign capitals would damage the British and their empire, Skelton replied that disintegration had been prophesied at every step forward since responsible government had been achieved in the nineteenth century. The British Empire, in one of his favourite phrases, was "still doing business."[51]

For public consumption, Skelton put an elegant geographical gloss on the decision to locate legations in the United States, France, and Japan. Canada's position was "that of the centre of a sort of world amphitheatre, surrounded as we are, on three sides, by these great powers, our frontiers are completely exposed of necessity. In friendship and good-will ... lies our security." Each of those states, moreover, had a significant relationship with the United Kingdom. It was Canada's role to foster goodwill between the British Empire and the three big powers where the country would have a resident diplomat.[52]

Skelton's real motives were elsewhere. He saw the diplomacy of a new nation in more concrete and down-to-earth terms – the interests of the everyday, the commonplace. At the Canadian Club, tying North America to his conception of the national interest, he had given precise Canada–United States examples of interaction, drawn from the nitty gritty of trade, fuel, fish, and shared waterways, all to make the point that foreign policy was usually about the relatively small things, that they were concentrated in the economic sphere, and that most of them took place close to home.[53] After the Washington legation's first year of operation, Skelton noted that it had helped him deal with specific problems, including immigration, radio broadcasting, aviation, smuggling, extradition, and fisheries, as well as the more general protection of the interests of Canadian citizens in matters ranging from business enquiries to claims against the United States government. Based on the Washington experience, the $80,000 additional cost of the Paris and Tokyo legations was bound to be a good investment.[54]

Paris needed little justification in terms of the national interest. The decision to mount a legation there spoke to Canada's substantial French population and the country's economic concerns. France, Skelton said, was the other of "our Mother Countries," and there was an already existing foundation for representation in the commissioner general of Canada's office, which had been in the French capital in one form or another since 1882. The French capital could also function as a European base for trade promotion and a convenient headquarters for participation in various international conferences.[55]

In justifying the establishment of a mission in Japan, Skelton again concentrated on the practical interests of an independent diplomacy, where internal Canadian forces met external opportunities. He pointed out to the prime minister, and asked him to point out to the critics of the Tokyo choice, that the Pacific was on the rise as an area of "increasing and decisive importance" in world development and that the commercial possibilities were great. Moreover, a legation in Tokyo would help, as Skelton delicately put it, in the "constructive regulation" of the immigration question that had been dividing the two countries for years. This was a contentious political issue, particularly in British Columbia, where there was a longstanding demand for a "white Canada" policy and a complete ban on Japanese immigrants to Canada. Skelton had more liberal views than some of his colleagues in the public service, many of whom were out-and-out exclusionists, but he was a realist. As an essential part of the exchange of diplomatic representatives, he was a tough negotiator of an agreement with the Japanese government limiting immigration from that country on a mutually agreeable basis.[56]

The strengthening of the Department of External Affairs and the establishment of missions abroad fit precisely with Skelton's understanding of the national interest, beginning with state autonomy and moving through Canadian unity, security, and economic progress to North American solidarity and, when feasible and necessary, international cooperation. Each of these interests was promoted and advanced by representation in foreign capitals, in the United States particularly, and by a foreign office in Ottawa that was run by Canadians for Canadians. At the core of it all,

Skelton believed, must be people and policies that were "stoutly Canada First."[57] Where King wanted external relationships that Canadians could *feel* were their own, Skelton stipulated that they *must* be his country's own. As he told the Canadian Club in 1922, "in all matters of foreign relationship the stand that Canada is to take must be decided in Canada by Canada's elected representatives – by men responsible to the people of Canada."[58]

During the 1920s, Skelton pushed for expanded resources for the conduct of external affairs, while campaigning for the removal of every vestige of Canadian dependence on Britain. He had some success on both fronts, but Skelton's vision of national interests tied to national independence had further to go than he realized. Part of the problem was of Skelton's own making: utterly dominating his Department of External Affairs, he was unwilling to employ it to anything like its full capacity or potential. King meanwhile had no intention of creating more foreign missions and did not do so for another decade, partly on the grounds of expense but also because his diplomats might find trouble abroad, getting him into trouble at home. Nor, more fundamentally, would the prime minister take the steps that were needed to separate Canada once and for all from Britain and its interests. When Canada eased into war alongside Britain in 1939, as if there was no choice, Skelton would be left wondering if his lifelong pursuit of national independence and the national interest had been a chimera.[59]

NOTES

1. See Norman Hillmer, "Foreign Policy and the National Interest: Why Skelton Matters" (Fourteenth O.D. Skelton Memorial Lecture, 17 December 2008). I am indebted to the Social Sciences and Humanities Research Council of Canada and the Marston LaFrance Fellowship for support of my research, and to Stephen Azzi, Greg Donaghy, J. L. Granatstein, John Hilliker, Philippe Lagassé, H. Blair Neatby, and Susan B. Whitney for their comments and criticisms.

2. O.D. Skelton, *Our Generation: Its Gains and Losses* (Chicago: University of Chicago Press, 1938), 46.

3. O.D. Skelton, "Canada and Foreign Policy," in *The Canadian Club Year Book, 1921–1922* (Ottawa: Canadian Club, 1922), 58–69.

4. "Sir Robt. Borden's Washington Status," *Ottawa Citizen*, 23 January 1922, Isabel Skelton Papers, Scrapbook, Queen's University Archives (QUA).

5. Skelton, "Canada and Foreign Policy," 60.

6. Norman Hillmer, "O.D. Skelton and the North American Mind," *International Journal* 60 (2004–5): 96.

7. Skelton, "Canada and Foreign Policy," 66.

8. W.L.M. King Diary, 21 January 1922, King Papers, Library and Archives Canada (LAC).

9. Annotation to a clipping of "Sir Robt. Borden's Washington Status," *Ottawa Citizen*, 23 January 1922, Isabel Skelton Scrapbook, QUA.

10. Carl Berger, *The Writing of Canadian History: Aspects of English-Canadian Historical Writing, 1900–1970* (Toronto: Oxford University Press, 1976), 52.

11. Skelton, "Canada and Foreign Policy," 61.

12. John Hilliker, *Canada's Department of External Affairs*, I: *The Early Years, 1909–1946* (Montreal and Kingston: McGill-Queen's University Press, 1990), 88.

13. Robert Bothwell, *Loring Christie: The Failure of Bureaucratic Imperialism* (New York: Garland, 1988), 324–33.

14. O.D. Skelton Diary, 1923, folio 17, Skelton Papers, LAC.

15. Quoted in Hector Mackenzie, "Recruiting Tomorrow's Ambassadors: Examination and Selection for the Foreign Service of Canada, 1925–1997," in *Diplomatic Missions: The Ambassador in Canadian Foreign Policy*, ed. Robert Wolfe (Kingston, ON: School of Policy Studies, Queen's University, 1998), 102.

16. Quoted in Gilles Lalande, *The Department of External Affairs and Biculturalism* (Ottawa: Queen's Printer, 1969), 36.

17. Quoted in J. L. Granatstein, *A Man of Influence: Norman A. Robertson and Canadian Statecraft, 1929–1968* (Ottawa: Deneau, 1981), 25.

18. Hilliker, *Canada's Department of External Affairs*, 119–20.

19. Ibid., 120.

20. Granatstein, *A Man of Influence*, 10, 21.

21. L. B. Pearson, *Mike: The Memoirs of the Right Honourable Lester B. Pearson*, I: *1897–1948* (Toronto: University of Toronto Press, 1972), 59.

22. Lalande, *The Department of External Affairs and Biculturalism*, 77, 81; Hilliker, *Canada's Department of External Affairs*, 123.

23. *Le Devoir*, 12 April 1929.

24. Whiskard to Hadow, 30 April 1929, Records of the Foreign Office (FO) 627/11/U291, The National Archives, Kew, England.

25. Interviews with Jean Chapdelaine, 25 May 1983, and Charles Ritchie, 24 May 1990; Hilliker, *Canada's Department of External Affairs*, 121–22.

26. H. L. Keenleyside, *Memoirs of Hugh L. Keenleyside*, I: *Hammer the Golden Day* (Toronto: McClelland & Stewart, 1981), 230.

27 Hilliker, *Canada's Department of External Affairs*, 83, 103–4, 124, 142, 243–44; Keenleyside, *Memoirs*, 229–31; Margaret K. Weiers, *Envoys Extraordinary: Women of the Canadian Foreign Service* (Toronto: Dundurn, 1994), 13–34.

28 Pearson, *Mike*, 71; Keenleyside, *Memoirs*, 217.

29 Keenleyside, *Memoirs*, 233; John English, *Shadow of Heaven: The Life of Lester Pearson*, I: *1897–1948* (Toronto: Lester and Orpen Dennys, 1989), 140, 150.

30 Keenleyside, *Memoirs*, 217–18.

31 Skelton Diary, 4 March 1926, Skelton Papers, LAC.

32 Hilliker, *Canada's Department of External Affairs*, 127; compare 123.

33 Ibid., 127.

34 Keenleyside, *Memoirs*, 215.

35 Pearson, *Mike*, 70–71; Keenleyside, *Memoirs*, 215–18, 233–44.

36 Interview with J. W. Pickersgill, 20 September 1985; Keenleyside, *Memoirs*, 231–32.

37 Hilliker, *Canada's Department of External Affairs*, 119, 122–23, 127.

38 Keenleyside, *Memoirs*, 233–34, 241–44.

39 Vincent Massey, *What's Past is Prologue: The Memoirs of the Right Honourable Vincent Massey* (Toronto: Macmillan, 1963), 129–34.

40 O.D. Skelton, "Notes on the Washington Legation Appropriations," n.d. [1927], King Papers, J4, vol. 59, file 380, C45711-14.

41 Skelton to Massey, 16 April 1927, in Massey, *What's Past is Prologue*, 132–34.

42 Skelton to Massey, 8 February 1927, Massey Papers, box B-12, University of Toronto Archives.

43 Skelton, "Notes on the Washington Legation Appropriations."

44 Massey to Skelton, 1 November 1928, in Massey, *What's Past is Prologue*, 137.

45 Massey to King, 21 May 1927, in ibid., 135–36.

46 Skelton to Massey, 23 May 1927, in ibid., 136–37.

47 Skelton to Massey, 13 August 1928, in ibid., 139.

48 Massey to Skelton, 15 August 1928, in ibid.

49 See Massey, *What's Past is Prologue*, 251–52.

50 Hilliker, *Canada's Department of External Affairs*, 125–27.

51 O.D. Skelton, "Notes on Legations," n.d. King Papers, J4, vol. 114, file 815, C84216-24.

52 W.L.M. King, "Canada's Legations Abroad," *Canadian Nation* 2 (1929): 5–7, 24–26, an article that beyond any doubt was written by Skelton.

53 Skelton, "Canada and Foreign Policy," 61.

54 Skelton, "Notes on Legations."

55 Ibid.

56 Ibid.; Canada, House of Commons, *Debates*, 31 January, 11 June 1928; Patricia E. Roy, *The Oriental Question: Consolidating a White Man's Province, 1914–41* (Vancouver: UBC Press, 2003), 83–88; and, generally, Tou Chu Dou Lynhiavu, "Canada's Window on Asia: The Establishment of the Tokyo Legation in 1928–1931," *Journal of Canadian Studies* 31 (1996–97): 97–123.

57 Skelton Diary, 1923, folio 17, Skelton Papers, LAC.

58 Skelton, "Canada and Foreign Policy," 66.

59 For details, see Hillmer, "Foreign Policy and the National Interest."

"BEHAVING AS ADULTS:" EXTERNAL AFFAIRS AND NORTH AMERICAN SECURITY IN THE 1930S

Galen Roger Perras

As historians J.L. Granatstein and Norman Hillmer argue elsewhere in this volume, it was abundantly clear by the 1930s that Canada's national interest lay in increasingly closer defence relations with the United States. British political and military weakness, already apparent in the face of growing Japanese militarism and Nazi aggression in Europe, left Canada exposed and isolated on the North American continent with only the United States for company. Then, as it would in 1945 and again today, an uncertain and fearful Washington looked north towards its vulnerable border as a source of danger. While Canada itself was clearly no threat, American policy-makers fretted that its lacklustre defence efforts made it a potential launching pad for an attack on the American homeland. Already, by 1934, President Franklin Roosevelt was anxious to establish some form of bilateral continental security cooperation to address this threat.

This chapter explores the readiness of Canadian diplomats to recognize this changed reality and their capacity to deal with the consequences effectively. For O.D. Skelton, Canada's influential under-secretary of state for external affairs, continentalist connections with the United States – economic, political, or military – initially seemed to offer Canada an opportunity to extract itself from the dangerous connections to the weakened and bankrupt British Empire that had killed 60,000 Canadians during the First World War. But this continentalist view was slow to triumph. Of course, part of the problem lay south of the border, where many of Roosevelt's key foreign policy aides, worried about the president's interest in Canadian security at a time when American opinion was profoundly isolationist, sought to block security cooperation with Canada. This was compounded by more important considerations north of the border. Prime Minister W.L. Mackenzie King showed little inclination to take a North American road when it came to security. Officers in the department of national defence, too often British by training and outlook, mounted a determined opposition to closer security ties with the United States. More important, Skelton and his diplomats in External Affairs too found reasons, thanks to American clumsiness and the vast continental power disparity, to suspect Washington's motivations after 1936. As a result, Canadians were slow to acknowledge where their national security interests really lay in the 1930s, delaying genuine continental defence cooperation until German power threatened Britain's, and Canada's, very survival in 1940.

Canada had only a sporadic formal defence relationship with the United States before the 1930s. The two countries had cooperated briefly during the final years of the First World War to coordinate military plans and industrial cooperation. The United States and Pacific security loomed large again for Canadians in 1921, when Britain proposed to renew the Anglo-Japanese Alliance over strong American, and then Canadian, objections. Formal defence relations reverberated too through the halls of Parliament in 1923, when the dynamic prophet of American air power, Brigadier General William (Billy) Mitchell, unsuccessfully floated the idea of a bilateral aviation alliance.[1] Ottawa's lack of official interest in building bilateral military connections with Washington was confirmed in 1927. Concerned by the volume of traffic between military authorities in Ottawa and British military attachés in the United States, Canada's first minister at its new legation in Washington, Vincent Massey, insisted that Canadians "must stand on our own feet" and recommended posting Canadian military attachés to London and Washington. "Damn nonsense," sniffed the prime minister, quickly killing Massey's sensible proposal.[2]

The absence of Canadian military officers in the Washington legation in the early 1930s meant that the young mission was ill-prepared to anticipate and handle American security concerns in the face of Japan's growing aggressiveness in the Far East. Certainly, United States Army Air Corps (AAC) plans to conduct operations in western Canada and Alaska caught Canadian officials by surprise in 1934. Keen to restore its tattered prestige, worried about Japan's ambitions and strength, and recalling Billy Mitchell's earlier notions for a northern aviation alliance, the Air Corps proposed sending ten bombers to Alaska through Canada. The AAC told the State Department vaguely that the flight would "further" relations with Canada. However, the corps' secret orders directed the flight to assess "the practicability of dispatching an air force to Alaska" in the event of war with Japan.[3]

Canada's chief of the general staff, General A.G.L. McNaughton, was not fooled. Anxious to maintain good relations with Washington – he told Maurice Hankey, secretary of Britain's powerful Committee on Imperial Defence (CID), in December 1934 that estrangement from the United States only aided Canadians "opposed to cooperation with the Empire in time of war" – McNaughton feared that neither the United States nor Japan would respect Canada's neutrality in a conflict. Indeed, he thought that the United States might even intervene militarily in British Columbia.[4] Labelling the Alaskan flight a military reconnaissance likely to induce "similar requests from any other foreign power that could not well be refused," the general worried that acquiescence would "make it very difficult to maintain our neutrality."[5]

McNaughton, who was castigated as a "little Canadian" anti-imperialist by some of his officers,[6] enjoyed the confidence of Conservative prime minister R.B. Bennett. As historian Steve Harris has argued, the general was guided by two overarching objectives: modernizing the army so that it could fight again in Europe alongside British forces if needed; and making the military into the pre-eminent adviser on security matters to the Canadian government. McNaughton's ambitions put him up against Skelton, whom King described as the "ablest man in the public service."[7] Skelton saw himself as a Canadian nationalist and believed that calls for imperial solidarity "concealed a hard-headed attempt to exploit colonial loyalties for the benefit of Great Britain."[8] Convinced that a strong Canadian military meant involvement in more bloody imperial wars, Skelton refused to allow his department to plan jointly with the Department of National Defence and opposed forming a Canadian defence committee that would bring together key departments to ponder security issues. As for relations with the United States, Skelton felt that Canada's security lay "in her own reasonableness, the decency of her neighbour, and the steady development of friendly intercourse, common standards of conduct, and common points of view." As an American diplomat observed in 1934, Skelton "has always been a friend of the United States and an advocate of more confident relations with us."[9] Skelton doubted that allowing American planes to overfly Canada once would imply a permanent arrangement. He challenged McNaughton's claim that other countries might seek similar rights, pointing out that Washington "alone possesses territory on this continent between which a route through Canada is a natural one." Still, as a sop to McNaughton – National Defence had asked Skelton not to mention its concerns about the planned flight path to the Americans – Skelton asked that the Air Corps avoid the commercially promising Mackenzie River Valley. But when puzzled American Legation official Pierre de la Boal said that this policy was "likely to be looked upon in both countries as a measure prompted by military considerations quite unusual in the relationship between Canada and the United States and reminiscent of the inhibitions which exist in other parts of the world,"[10] Skelton told Bennett that "it would be preferable to refuse on the ground that the route is not available rather than bringing in any military defence issues." McNaughton protested that opening a route for American warplanes in a war with Japan involved broad issues associated with the maintenance of Canadian neutrality. Bennett was unconvinced. Indeed, the prime minister permitted the Air Corps fliers to employ the Mackenzie Valley path.[11]

Skelton was harder on America, as historian Norman Hillmer observes in his chapter, than his historical reputation suggests. The undersecretary soon regretted his reasonableness when the *Washington Herald* declared that the Air Corps's flight would test the route's value in a war with Japan. Skelton feared that relations with Japan would suffer if Canada was seen to help Washington prepare to confront Tokyo in the Pacific and he insisted that the *Herald*'s claim made it impossible to permit further military flights to Alaska. While Skelton declined to obstruct the approved mission, American minister Warren Robbins correctly observed that the disclosure had strengthened the position of the Department of National Defence, which was already inclined "to view our military operations with some suspicion."[12]

The Army Air Corps's flight north in July 1934 drew huge crowds at five Canadian stops from Winnipeg to Whitehorse. The American consul in Edmonton proudly reported that locally based Canadian servicemen expressed pleasure "over what they regard as a symbol of identity between the interests of Canada and the United States in the matter of Alaskan defense." Flight leader Colonel H.H. Arnold, a Mitchell acolyte and the future head of United States air forces in World War II, declared that an Alaskan flyway was feasible.[13] Yet bilateral security relations languished. Carping to the British War Office that "the gradual establishment of a practice of dispatching aircraft to Alaska over Canadian territory might give rise to a rather awkward situation on some future occasion," McNaughton did more than complain. Wanting options other than cooperation with Washington, the chief of the general staff laid plans for Defence Scheme No. 2, a plan to assert Canada's neutrality forcefully in any military confrontation between Japan and the United States not involving Britain.[14] Some in the Department of External Affairs also now viewed American plans more cynically. After the United States Navy surveyed the Aleutians in 1934 for bases against Japan and then announced large north Pacific naval exercises for 1935, an acerbic Hume Wrong – he had called the United States a "a barbarous country" in 1928 – warned that these plans to militarize the Pacific constituted "a matter of deep interest and concern to Canada."[15]

Canadian worries about American plans deepened when the House of Representatives' Committee on Military Affairs examined a proposal for an Army Air Corps base in the Great Lakes region during in-camera hearings in February 1935. Brigadier General C.E. Kilbourne fretted that it "would look as though we contemplated passing away from the century-old principle that our Canadian border needs no defense." But AAC officer Captain H.L. George countered that British warplanes could shuttle via Labrador to bomb American cities. General F.M. Andrews, commander General Headquarters Air Force, doubted that Canada would join an anti-United States coalition; but if it did, American bombers flying from the new base could strike Toronto and Montreal. Emphasizing the importance of aerial warfare's short operational lines, Lt. Colonel J.D. Reardan stressed that only Canada offered such a threat. If Canada could not stop hostile powers from attacking the United States, Reardan concluded that we "would have to do so."[16] These were not marginalized opinions. The 1933 Drum Board report, a 1934 Baker Board submission, a general headquarters report, and two U.S. Navy documents all had identified potential aerial threats coming from Canada.[17] When the Government Printing Office mistakenly released the testimony in April 1935, the *Washington Post* chastised President Franklin D. Roosevelt's "hypocrisy" for advocating a Good Neighbor policy while his military plotted Canada's doom. In response, the committee's chair, Representative J.J. McSwain, argued that the base was analogous to France's Maginot Line and was designed "not against Belgium, but against what might come over or through Belgium." He added that the limits on Great Lakes warships imposed by the Rush-Bagot Agreement of 1817 did not apply to aircraft and that American fortifications lined the Canadian frontier.[18] An incensed Under Secretary of State William Phillips assured Wrong that such "provocative references to Canada" were uncalled for. Roosevelt, in turn, repudiated the testimony and forced public apologies from McSwain and Secretary of War George Dern.[19]

The president's "well merited rebuke" mollified critics, although Canadian and British newspapers were "inclined to treat the matter with a good deal of ridicule at the expense of the Congressional Committee and of our military authorities."[20] Initially amused by the public fumblings in Washington, Skelton told Boal on 2 May that he would not have objected had the project proceeded quietly. On further reflection, however, the Canadian official concluded that Congress had camouflaged the facility's location and purpose by describing it as an intermediate flight station. Skelton, making clear that the revelations could affect Canada's attitude towards a United States–Japan conflict, now believed that the Air Corps had deliberately forced Canada's hand in 1934. To ensure that Air Corps overflights should not become a matter of course, the under-secretary demanded that American planes adopt flight paths that minimized Canadian geographic and political exposure.[21] Skelton's considered statements contrasted sharply with McNaughton's views. McNaughton urged Prime Minister Bennett on 5 April to rebuild Canada's military since an American incursion into British Columbia could end Canada's political independence.[22] The general argued that the United States "would not hesitate for one moment to occupy our country in order to deny potential bases to their enemy" and insisted that the testimony of the committee of the House of Representatives presaged "an American protectorate over Canada." Largely unmoved by this plea, Bennett offered National Defence a handful of new warplanes.[23]

McNaughton's fear was at least partly valid. In 1924 Billy Mitchell had warned that if the United States and Japan clashed, "Canada would either openly side with the United States or run the risk of occupation."[24] While he praised Norman Armour, the new United States minister to Canada, as "one of the crack men in the Foreign Service," Wrong ridiculed assertions that Roosevelt's administration did "not in any of its plans or policies envisage the possibility of any change in the friendly relationship between the United States and any foreign country." If so, he asked, why have a military?[25] Once hopeful that the president would fix the grievous economic injustices that Canada had suffered at protectionist American hands at the start of the Great Depression, Wrong found it difficult "to find one positive action taken by the Roosevelt Administration which has been beneficial to Canada." He added that "this Administration has proved itself more strongly isolationist than its two predecessors." Roosevelt was "undoubtedly" full of good will towards Canada, but so far it "has been shown in words and not in deeds." Unless something useful happened soon, his Good Neighbor Policy would stand as nothing "more than a slick and hypocritical phase."[26]

Something quite useful soon followed Wrong's complaint. Triumphant at the polls in October 1935 after five years in opposition, King quickly signed a trade deal with Roosevelt, fulfilling Robbins' claim that the Liberal Party was "a little bit" more inclined "than the other party to play the game with us."[27] Skelton told Armour that he sought the creation of a "North American mind" to stop Canada from being further drawn into a "world-wide British economic empire whose interests, as progressively developed from London, might soon diverge seriously from" American needs. Armour was also pleased that King preferred "the American road."[28] King, a master of fuzzy statements, hoped that Canada might "link" the

United States and Britain during the London Naval Conference and Italy's invasion of Ethiopia. Declaring that "we must stand together on all these questions," King saw the trade deal as the "herald of a better day and a better way" for a troubled world.[29] Even Wrong, surprisingly, agreed that Roosevelt was reaching beyond isolationism for a new foreign policy, "the definition of which is of immense importance to Canada as a North American country, as part of the British Commonwealth, and as a member of the League of Nations."[30]

Indeed, unknown to Canadians, Roosevelt had already begun to think in these broad terms. Increasingly fearful of growing German and Japanese power, he told Secretary of State Sumner Welles as early as 1933 that "we here on this Continent must work out a continental understanding of identification of interests." When Britain pondered naval concessions to Japan in 1934, the president threatened "to approach public sentiment in Canada, Australia, New Zealand and South Africa in a definite way to make these dominions understand clearly that their future security is linked with us in the United States."[31] After telling Quebecers in July 1936 that the undefended Canada–United States frontier inspired other nations to live in peace, Roosevelt informed King privately that some American senators favoured military intervention if Japan attacked British Columbia.[32] Anxious to flesh out his continental vision, the president backed proposals to build a highway through Canada to Alaska so that American forces could reach the state quickly in a crisis. When a Canadian military report claimed that U.S. Army planning was "based on the general idea of a Far Eastern country making an attack on the United States by way of Canada,"[33] King's previously parsimonious Cabinet speedily approved $200 million in new military spending with an emphasis on west coast defence. The alternative, King claimed, was relying on Washington's protection and "losing our independence."[34]

The possibility that a highway to Alaska might have its military uses was not a new subject, but it was a troubling one. In 1931, a joint Canadian–American board, anxious to build a highway to boost economic development, had said it "would have no more military significance than any other road that might extend north beyond the British Columbia boundary." Still, its American members, echoing Mitchell, had agreed it could possess "a very definite value from an aviation standpoint in cases where Canada and the United States might be allies."³⁵ Before leaving the Department of National Defence for a post with the National Research Council in 1935, McNaughton cautioned that the road "would confront us with a somewhat delicate situation." Even if the United States had no desire to use the road militarily, the new chief of the general staff, Major General E.C. Ashton, concluded in "a great international struggle military necessity would tend to overcome political scruples." Canada would be foolish to create "what would then become a military asset of a very high order if possessed or utilized by our neighbours to the south."³⁶ Skelton was more judicious. He thought the route a perfectly intelligible aspiration by west coast peoples and argued that unless Canada "incurred a 'moral' obligation by allowing the United States to assume the ... cost of building the highway in Canadian territory," Ashton's worries should not "be allowed to overcome such a project." As a result, when American diplomats met with a senior External Affairs official to inquire about the highway in October 1936, Counsellor Loring Christie, though he offered no official support, stated that Canadian military objections to the road merited no consideration.³⁷

Christie's reluctance to discuss the highway's security implications reflected his growing concern about the deteriorating global situation and American motives in seeking closer relations with Canada. When King travelled to Washington in March 1937 to encourage a re-elected Roosevelt to confront communism and fascism in an effort to prevent another war, Christie was skeptical.³⁸ Fervently opposed to Canadian participation in international collective security, Christie advised King in 1937 that relying upon America could render Canada an American protectorate.³⁹ Skelton agreed. Canada could not "escape being affected by developments elsewhere," he admitted. But, he added, Canada was "still the most secure, the least exposed of all countries," and it did not need American or British aid.⁴⁰ At the White House, Roosevelt told King that an Alaska Highway "would be of a great military advantage, in the event of trouble with Japan." When King asserted that while some Canadians believed that America's controversial Monroe Doctrine of 1823 protected them from extra-hemispheric threats, "no self-respecting [Canadian] Government could countenance any such view," the president replied soothingly that "what we would like would be for Canada to have a few patrol boats on the Pacific Coast, and to see that her coast fortifications around Vancouver were of a character to be effective there." As King later told Armour in Ottawa, Roosevelt had discussed Canada's security in such "a nice way and without in any way suggesting how Canada should handle her own affairs."[41] But if a pleased King sought in an undefined manner to bridge Anglo-American differences over the response to fascist and communist aggression, Skelton remarked caustically to a visiting American that a bridge was designed "to be walked on."[42]

Indeed, the tread of heavy boots resounded following Japan's attack upon China in July 1937. Neither London nor Washington individually had the political will or military strength to re-establish the shifting balance of power in Asia. British overtures to Washington to mediate the conflict jointly were rejected by Roosevelt, who sought "cooperation on parallel but independent lines."[43] And Roosevelt expected Canada to fall into line. As a result, when Ottawa declined to endorse Secretary of State Cordell Hull's peace plan, J. Pierrepont Moffat, assistant under-secretary of state for Western European affairs, had Armour browbeat Skelton to back the initiative.[44]

More important, the crisis strengthened American interest in closer continental security relations, and in early August, the president told Hull that he wanted an Alaska Highway "as soon as possible." When Hull reported that Canada had shown little inclination to discuss the matter, Armour suggested that a presidential visit to British Columbia would emphasize the "solidarity existing between our own northwest and the stretch of territory separating Alaska from the continental United States."[45] Confident that a visit would influence opinion in the right quarters, Armour assured Moffat that Canada's governor general, Lord Tweedsmuir, felt an Alaska Highway would have enormous strategic importance. Moffat was doubtful, fearful that the Canadians might misinterpret the stopover's rationale.[46] Hull overruled his under-secretary and Roosevelt briefly stopped in Victoria on September 30 to give a short public address.[47]

The visit, however, did not remove Canadian doubts about closer cooperation with Washington, and when Roosevelt asked for talks on an Alaskan highway in September, Ottawa was unsure how to react. Skelton was inclined to reject the request, pointing out that internal east-west communications ranked first. Christie was more diplomatic. Worried that the White House might resent a rejection and keen to keep the matter on an "economic plane," Christie suggested a joint feasibility study. If Washington insisted on paying, Christie cautioned that Canadian military objections "presumably would have to be considered."[48]

The American president had more than just Canada on his mind. In late July 1937, he had asked British Prime Minister Neville Chamberlain to come to Washington to discuss broad questions of global stability. Though the dire Asian events "justified our worst fears" and cordial relations with totalitarian states seemed unlikely, Chamberlain declined to meet any time soon.[49] Thus, in October, Roosevelt declared that "peace-loving nations must make a concerted effort" to quarantine countries seeking to foster international anarchy and instability. In response to critics, who worried that his plan could lead to a war with Japan, the president argued for a general peace treaty, not political and military sanctions[50] Historian James MacGregor Burns has argued that the speech was a trial balloon to test the public mood; when the mood proved "unheroic," Roosevelt "pulled in his horns further."[51] When the League announced a nine-power conference in November to discuss China, the president told Hull, Welles, and his personal representative to the talks, Norman Davis, that if mediation of the Sino-Japanese conflict failed, he would consider further steps. Smarting from Chamberlain's rejection, he told Davis in October that the United States would not lead against Japan as it could not "afford to be made, in popular opinion at home, a tail to the British kite."[52]

Against this uncertain background, Roosevelt saw greater security cooperation with Canada as a step towards meeting American goals in the Pacific. Buoyed by his Victoria trip, which he judged a great success, the president told Armour in September that he wanted coordinated defence plans "for that important section of territory lying between northern Washington [state] and the 'panhandle' of Alaska." Describing British Columbia as defenceless, Roosevelt dismissed Armour's rejoinder that Canada had begun to revamp its coast defences. Recalling Anglo-American naval cooperation in the North Pacific in 1917–18, he wanted a U.S. Navy officer to broach the subject in Ottawa. Armour suggested instead that King or his minister of national defence, Ian Mackenzie, meet with Roosevelt or Hull. Wisely, Armour consulted the influential under-secretary of state, Welles, who was doubtful. Like his two closest assistants, Moffat and Adolf Berle, Welles practised "Europhobic-Hemispherism" and opposed speaking to Ottawa lest the United States find itself drawn into Britain's imperial affairs.⁵³

Welles' fears that Roosevelt might be using a Canadian back door to secure an alliance with Britain against Japan seemed justified by events in late 1937. While the nine-power conference failed to resolve the Sino-Japanese conflict, neither the United States nor Britain offended "one another over the crisis: a feat of diplomatic trust, full of hope for future cooperation."⁵⁴ In late November, a hopeful Chamberlain told British Ambassador Robert Lindsay to seek Anglo-American naval conversations and an overwhelming display of naval force in the Pacific. Welles declined to cooperate since the United States would have to provide the naval display.⁵⁵ Davis, an Anglophile who counted many friends among British diplomats, championed the view "that the existence of the British Empire is essential to the national security of the United States and that while we should not follow Great Britain nevertheless we should not allow the Empire to be endangered." This was a view that Moffat ridiculed, and when Davis groused that Canada wanted to benefit from geography, imperial ties, and its friendship with the United States without assuming any responsibilities, Moffat declared "three cheers for Canada."⁵⁶ Even so, though he opposed Armour's renewed suggestions that King should use a planned vacation in Florida to meet with Roosevelt in December, Welles promised to raise the issue with the president despite his fear that Roosevelt might be seeking a dangerous British alliance through a back door.⁵⁷ While Armour agreed the matter should not be hurried, he told Welles that Canada's Colonel Harry Crerar had met United States Army Chief General Malin Craig in November. Thinking that this chat may have marked the "first move" towards the president's goal of closer defence cooperation with Canada, the American minister in Ottawa sent Welles news clippings about British Columbia's new fortifications. As Canada was finally awakening to the necessity of west coast defences, Armour thought this would be as good a time as any to initiate military conversations.⁵⁸

Japan's shocking sinking of the USS *Panay* on the Yangtze River and its attacks upon British ships in Chinese waters in early December 1937 generated a war scare. Britain, or so American diplomats reported, was anxious for a synchronized Anglo-American response. Berle believed that this request for synchronicity, so reminiscent of British manipulations during the

1915 *Lusitania* crisis, was Davis's doing, while Moffat assailed Britain for "treating us as their seventh dominion." When Lindsay broached the matter in mid-December, Welles preferred concurrent action. But Roosevelt overruled Welles and sent Captain Royal Ingersoll to London for direct naval talks with the Admiralty about possible joint action against Japan.

Meanwhile, on December 20, Welles forwarded Armour's letter of December 17, asking Roosevelt to "let me know what your desires may be." Ever cautious of the anti-British and isolationist lobby, Roosevelt insisted that "nothing ... be put in writing," but he finally invited King to visit Washington in January.[59] King declined, worried that his presence in the American capital might damage ongoing Anglo-American trade talks. A reluctance to act decisively typified the cautious King; as he told a British diplomat in 1938, "his experience of political life had taught him that any success he had attained had been due far more to avoiding action rather than taking action."[60] Armour explained Roosevelt's desires personally to King in early January 1938 but failed to change his mind. When the prime minister nervously offered a spring visit to the American capital, Armour countered that Canadian officers could begin security discussions with Craig and Admiral William Leahy immediately and "without any publicity." King agreed that such a discussion might be useful, but tempered his interest by adding that he "was merely thinking out loud."[61]

In early January, in what Armour called an extraordinary coincidence, Canadian newspapers discussed British Columbia's coastal defences, Anglo-American staff talks, and a possible Canada–United States west coast security scheme.[62] Four days later, Skelton told Armour there was "much to be said for getting our defence programme on a realistic North American basis." Still, given his history of suspicion towards military planning, Skelton did not want "such discussions to take place solely between technical defence officials."[63] Ashton, who had sent officers to Washington in 1937 to study American military industrial mobilization plans, was cautious. He told his minister, Ian Mackenzie, that he wanted definite assurances that Roosevelt "would safeguard Canada's situation and would not force her into a serious situation." Having complained in 1937 about "the frequent difficulties experienced by this Department in the pursuit of its approved objectives through obstruction or, at least, lack of sympathetic action elsewhere," Ashton condemned the "ultra-isolationist" view that Canada need not fight at Britain's side, a clear swipe at Skelton and Christie. That policy, Ashton asserted, comprised "an act of secession from the Commonwealth" while a defenceless Canada would obviously concern the United States. Crerar, whom Armour had suspected of starting this process with his November 1937 meeting with General Craig, thought that enhanced security cooperation with the United States would "knock the feet from under" subversive Canadians who opposed joint military initiatives sponsored by Britain.[64]

A few days later, Armour indicated that two Canadian officers would be welcome in Washington to meet their American counterparts. Skelton, having apparently lost the fight (if there had been one) to send External Affairs officials with the military officers, insisted that Canada's legation in Washington must host the talks to ensure no "possibility of the slightest publicity."[65] There were other last minute complications. Prompted by the anglophile Canadian minister Herbert Marler, Commodore Percy Nelles proposed inviting British military attachés in Washington to join the talks between the Canadian and American officers at the legation. Warning that he "could not receive the British Military Attaché," Craig balked and phoned Welles for guidance. Concerned that Canada was trying to bring Britain into the talks, a dangerous complication if the American press got wind of the matter, Welles ruled that only Craig and Leahy, not the Canadians, could provide American defence data to the British.[66] Lacking knowledge of potential topics, Ashton was authorized "to give and receive information, but to make no commitments." Possessing his own limited instructions, but willing to talk soldier to soldier, Craig discussed west coast defences generally before offering to defend Canada's west coast and asking if British Columbia's airfields could support American bombers. Stunned, Ashton sought to divert Craig by outlining scenarios facing Canada: an Anglo-Japanese war in Asia; British neutrality in an United States–Japan war in the north Pacific; and Canada joining an Anglo-American conflict against Japan. Craig thought only the third option was relevant and dropped his offer to focus on British Columbia airfields and coast defences.[67] The next day, while Craig feared considerable Japanese air attacks against the west coast, Leahy wished solely to meet Japan's fleet in the central Pacific. The Americans could offer no formal defence commitments, a statement the Canadians did not dispute.[68]

Had the legation discussions progressed, it is doubtful that External Affairs or King would have welcomed even an informal alliance with Washington. In early 1937, after Escott Reid of the Canadian Institute of International Affairs suggested a Canada–United States military alliance, diplomat Hugh Keenleyside accused Reid of excessive rationality. Asserting that governments and peoples could not be expected to be "intelligent enough" to see logically the necessities of their situations, Keenleyside argued that practical politics ruled out any "serious and well-thought-out defensive agreement between Canada and the United States."[69] Keenleyside had not misjudged the political situation in Ottawa. Having purchased two destroyers in January 1938 expressly to protect the vulnerable west coast, less than two months later King felt more strongly than ever "how inadequate are Canada's defence forces, and how necessary it is for us to do something to preserve this country to future generations against nations that place all their reliance upon force."[70]

But King worried too about nations, including the United States, which seemed to place their reliance upon resisting force. In August 1938, worried by German aggressiveness, Roosevelt sought to send a very public message to Adolf Hitler. Taking advantage of a speech in Canada marking the opening of a bridge linking Ontario with New York State across the St. Lawrence River, the American president admitted that his nation could no longer say that "the eddies of controversy beyond the seas could bring no interest or no harm." He promised dramatically that "the United States will not stand idly by if domination of Canadian soil is threatened by any other empire."[71] While Roosevelt claimed that what he had said "was so obvious that I cannot understand why some American President did not say it half a century ago" and Canada's media praised the Monroe Doctrine's northern extension,[72] King was concerned. The prime minister judged Roosevelt's comments most significant, and he said publicly a few days later that his government was "putting our own means of defence in order" to make Canada "as immune from attack or possible invasion as we can reasonably expect to make it." During the Munich Crisis, a shaken King advised his Cabinet that if Britain was "worsted in a world struggle, the only future for Canada would be absorption by the U.S., if we are to be saved from an enemy aggressor."[73]

Indeed, until he expressly sought military talks with the United States as France collapsed in June 1940, King showed little enthusiasm for any of Roosevelt's security-related schemes. Present in Washington in late 1938 when Roosevelt suggested producing 50,000 warplanes for the United States and western democracies, King declined to commit his nation to the president's plan to build planes in Canadian-based factories. Similarly, during the long summer of 1939, with war clearly on the horizon, King remained cagey. When Roosevelt mused that the U.S. Navy might need access to Halifax's harbour, the Canadian said that access would depend on unspecified "developments." When a deal was finally struck in late August to allow the American military vessels to use Halifax, King insisted that use must not interfere with Canadian naval activities.[74] Continental security only reigned once the August 1940 Ogdensburg Agreement created the Permanent Joint Board on Defence. King took the lead, calling in the new American minister to Canada, J. Pierrepont Moffat, in June 1940, to suggest bilateral military staff talks. The prime minister also used Christie, now Canada's minister in Washington, to inform Roosevelt of his new willingness to do more. Thus, it was unsurprising when Roosevelt asked King in August to meet him in Ogdensburg, New York, to consider "the mutual defence of our coasts on the Atlantic."[75] King happily signed on when Roosevelt presented him with a short proposal to create a Canada–United States Permanent Joint Board on Defence (PJBD) that would formulate continental defence plans for the two governments to consider. According to American Secretary of War Henry Stimson a relieved King signed the pact "almost with tears in his eyes."[76]

Conspicuously absent from the Ogdensburg meeting was Skelton. King, instead, took Moffat with him, a choice King apparently did not see fit to explain or justify even in the privacy of his diary. If Skelton's pride suffered any injury, it did not show. Indeed, he called the PJBD's creation "the best day's work for many a year" and a result of "the inevitable sequence of public policies and personal relationships, based upon the realization of the imperative necessity of close understanding between the English-speaking peoples."[77] Furthermore, both Skelton and Keenleyside, as early as June 1940, had warned King that if the strategic situation worsened – Skelton especially feared that Japan might enter the war on Germany's side – Canada would have no choice but to seek American military assistance.

According to Keenleyside, the United States might simply demand that Canada accept a bilateral continental defence arrangement.[78]

Theoretical impediments to cooperation ended when the United States entered the Second World War in December 1941. Canada's dual problem then, as Norman Robertson, Keenleyside, and Reid pointed out in 1941–42, was to prevent American domination of the Allied war effort and ensure that Canada's interests were protected. As Reid put it, there was no sense in "being indignant about what the United States was doing" for Canadians "were being treated as children because we have refused to behave as adults" in foreign affairs. Reid wanted to bolster the legation in Washington, have Canadian officials meet senior State Department officials regularly, separate the posts of prime minister and secretary of state for external affairs, and make "the construction of an effective collective system the main goal of our policy."[79] Reid was right in 1942. However, his judgment of External Affairs' stand on security cooperation with the United States in the 1930s was unnecessarily harsh. The department's hesitations carefully sought to balance its national security interests and its independent scope to manoeuvre while retaining a circumspect view of a powerful United States. Given Roosevelt's sustained interest in closer bilateral ties and the strong opposition of the Department of National Defence to closer ties with the United States, this was not an easy task.

NOTES

1. Galen Roger Perras and Katrina E. Kellner, "'A perfectly logical and sensible thing': Billy Mitchell Advocates a Canadian–American Aerial Alliance against Japan," *Journal of Military History* 72 (July 2008): 801.

2. W.L.M. King Diary, 9 May 1927, W.L.M. King Papers, Library and Archives Canada (LAC); Vincent Massey, *What's Past is Prologue: The Memoirs of the Right Honourable Vincent Massey* (Toronto: Macmillan, 1963), 138; John Hilliker, *Canada's Department of External Affairs*, vol. 1: *The Early Years, 1909–1946* (Montreal and Kingston: McGill-Queen's University Press, 1990), 117–18. King's terse rejection of Massey's idea has been described as "unusually vehement"; see C.P. Stacey, *Canada and the Age of Conflict*, vol. 2: *1921–1948: The Mackenzie King Era* (Toronto: University of Toronto Press, 1984), 226.

3. Adjutant General to Chief Air Corps, "Alaskan Flight," 15 May 1934, Records of the Army Air Corps (RAAC), box 706, file 373, National Archives and Records Administration (NARA). Japan's threat to Alaska is discussed in Galen Roger Perras, *Stepping Stones to Nowhere: The Aleutian Islands, Alaska, and American Military Strategy, 1867–1945* (Vancouver: UBC Press, 2003).

4. "Impressions of Canadian Defence Policy – December 1934 by Sir Maurice Hankey," 1 January 1935, Maurice Hankey Papers, CAB63/8, The National Archives, Kew, England [TNA]. A.G.L. McNaughton to Prime Minister R.B. Bennett, "Sino-Japanese Dispute. Possible Canadian Commitments in Respect to the Maintenance of Neutrality," 24 January 1933, in *Documents on Canadian External Relations*, vol. 5: *1931–1935*, ed. Alex I. Inglis (Ottawa: Information Canada, 1973), 343–46.

5. Deputy Minister (DND) L.R. LaFleche to Skelton, 9 June 1934, Department of External Affairs Records (DEAR), vol. 1684, file 53-AB, LAC.

6. Brigadier J. Sutherland Brown to Colonel W.W. Foster, 31 December 1932, J. Sutherland Brown Papers, Queen's University Archives (QUA).

7. Stephen J. Harris, *Canadian Brass: The Making of a Professional Army* (Toronto: University of Toronto Press, 1988), chap. 8; W.L.M King Diary, 7 August 1930, W.L.M. King Papers, LAC.

8. H. Blair Neatby, *William Lyon Mackenzie King*, vol. 3, *1932–1939: The Prism of Unity* (Toronto: University of Toronto Press, 1976), 134–35.

9. Skelton cited in Norman Hillmer, "The Anglo-Canadian Neurosis: The Case of O.D. Skelton," in *Britain and Canada: A Survey of a Changing Relationship*, ed. Peter Lyon (London: Frank Cass, 1976), 76; Pierre de la Boal to John D. Hickerson, 23 June 1934, Department of State Records (hereafter RG 59), Decimal File 1930–39, file 811.2342/460, NARA.

10. Skelton to LaFleche, 12 & 13 June 1934, DEAR, vol. 1684, file 53-AB, LAC; Skelton to Warren Robbins, no. 59, 14 June 1934, RG 59, Decimal File 1930-30, file 811.2342/425, NARA; Boal to Robbins, "Projected good will flight from the United States to Alaska," 15 June 1934, RG 59, Decimal File 1930-39, file 811.2342/460, NARA.

11. Skelton to Bennett, "United States' Request re Flight to Alaska," 15 June 1934; McNaughton to Bennett, 15 June 1934; Bennett to Robbins, 18 June 1934, DEAR, vol. 1684, file 53-AB, LAC.

12. "Army to make mass flight from the United States to Alaska," *Washington Herald*, 21 June 1934; Robbins to Hull, "Projected Washington–Alaska Flight," 22 June 1934, RG 59, Decimal File 1930-39, file 811.2342/431, NARA.

13. Harold M. Collins, "Visit of United States Army Bombing Squadron," 28 July 1934, RG 18, Entry 166, box 705, file 373, NARA; Colonel H.H. Arnold, "Report on

the Alaskan Flight," October 1934, RG 18, Entry 166, box 705, file 373, NARA.

14 McNaughton to General A.A. Montgomery-Massingberd, 31 July 1934, Ian Mackenzie Papers, vol. 30, file X-28, LAC.

15 Wrong quoted in J.L. Granatstein, "Hume Wrong's Road to the Functional Principle," in *Coalition Warfare: An Uneasy Accord*, ed. Keith Neilson and Roy A. Prete (Waterloo: Wilfrid Laurier University Press), 63; Wrong to Bennett, no. 956, 27 September 1934, R.B. Bennett Papers, reel M-1028, vol. 281, file U-110 1934, LAC.

16 Testimony by C.E Kilbourne, H.L. George, F.M. Andrews, and J.D. Reardan, 11–12 February 1935, *Hearings before the Committee on Military Affairs House of Representatives Seventy-Fourth Congress, First Session, on H.R. 6621 and H.R. 4130, 11–13 February 1935* (Washington, DC: Government Printing Office, 1935), 7–8, 16–17, 51–52, 60–61, 72.

17 Drum Board Report, 11 October 1934, War Plans Division Records, Entry 281, RG 165, file WPD888, NARA; WPD, "Suggestions for the Secret Annex" (Baker Board Report), 5 July 1934, Entry 281, RG 165, file 3828, NARA; "Preliminary Report of the Board of Officers on Airdrome Requirements of the GHQ Air Force," 5 November 1934, Entry 281, RG 165, file 3809, NARA; Rear Admiral E.J. King to Clark Howell, 13 December 1934, Ernest J. King Papers, box 5, file Correspondence 1936–38, Library of Congress (LC); Commander H.H. Frost, "Blue Strategy Against a Coalition of Great Powers," May 1932, Strategic Plans Division Records, box 39, File Blue [United States] Strategy, Naval Historical Center (NHC). George to Mitchell, 4 April 1934, Mitchell Papers, box 19, file General Correspondence 1934, LC; George added "IT IS NOT FANTASTICAL OR VISIONARY EITHER" to expect a multinational coalition attack upon America, including attacks from Canadian bases.

18 "Air Bill Provides Secret Base Near Canada to Protect Lakes," *Washington Post*, 29 April 1935; "The Good Neighbor?" *Washington Post*, 2 May 1935; J.J. McSwain to Roosevelt, 1 May 1935, J.J. McSwain Papers, box 11, file correspondence 1935: April 22–Aug., Duke University Archives (DUA).

19 Phillips was "more angry than [Wrong] had ever seen him before"; see Wrong to Bennett, no. 515, 29 April 1935, DEAR, vol. 1746, file 408, LAC; Roosevelt to McSwain, 29 April 1935, McSwain Papers, box 11, file Correspondence 1935: April 22–Aug., DUA; George Dern to Roosevelt, 30 April 1935, RG 59, Decimal File 1930-39, file 811.248/80–1/2, NARA.

20 "A Well Merited Rebuke," *New York Herald*, 2 May 1935; Boal to Hull, no. 1241, 2 May 1935, RG 59, Decimal File 1930-39, file 811.248/77, NARA; "U.S. Air Base Near Canadian Border is Aim," *Ottawa Morning Journal*, 29 April 1935; "Seizing British Islands," *Manchester Guardian*, 29 April 1935; "U.S. Air Base Plan Near Border," *London Daily Telegraph*, 30 April 1935.

21 Boal to William Phillips, 30 April 1935, RG 59, Decimal File 1930-39, file 811.248/80–1/2, NARA; Boal to Hull, no. 1246 plus Enclosure No. 1, 2 May 1935, RG 59, Decimal File 1930-39, file 811/248/80, NARA.

22 McNaughton, "The Defence of Canada (A Review of the Present Position)," 5 April 1935, DEAR, vol. 1747, file 469, LAC; McNaughton to Bennett, April 1935, file 014.014, Directorate of History and Heritage, Department of National Defence (DHH).

23 McNaughton, "Canada and the United States Security against Air Attack," 29 April 1935, DEAR, vol. 744, file 172, LAC; McNaughton, "The Defence of Canada (A Review of the Present Position)," 28 May 1935, file 74/256, DHH.

24 Mitchell, "Report on Inspection of United States Possessions in the Pacific and Java, Singapore, India, Siam, China, and Japan," 24 October 1924, Mitchell Papers, United States Air Force Archives.

25 Wrong to Skelton, 4 May 1935, DEAR, vol. 1726, file 26-u, LAC; Roosevelt and Wrong cited in Stacey, *Canada and the Age*

of Conflict, vol. 2: *1921–1948* (Toronto: University of Toronto Press, 1984), 154.

26 Wrong, "What has the Good Neighbour Policy Accomplished in the Case of Canada?" 6 July 1935, Hume Wrong Papers, vol. 1, file 2, LAC.

27 Robbins to Roosevelt, 18 December 1934, Franklin D. Roosevelt Papers, President's Secretary Files (PSF), file Diplomatic Correspondence Canada: 1933–35, Franklin D. Roosevelt Library (FDRL).

28 Armour to Phillips, 22 October 1935, and Armour memorandum, Franklin D. Roosevelt Papers, PSF, file Diplomatic Correspondence Canada: 1930–35, FDRL.

29 W.L.M. King Diary, 24 and 25 October 1935, W.L.M. King Papers, LAC; King to Roosevelt, 25 November 1935, W.L.M. King Papers, Correspondence, reel C2313, 181549-50 LAC.

30 Wrong to King, no. 1293, 14 December 1935, W.L.M. King Papers, Correspondence, reel C3685, 183253-54, LAC.

31 Sumner Welles memorandum, 14 June 1933, Welles Papers, box 149, file Roosevelt 1934, FDRL; Roosevelt to Norman Davis and Davis to Roosevelt, 9 and 27 November 1934, in Edgar B. Nixon, ed. *Franklin D. Roosevelt and Foreign Affairs*, vol. 2: *March 1934–August 1935* (Cambridge, MA: Belknap Press of Harvard University Press, 1969), 263, 291.

32 "Address on the Occasion of a Visit to Quebec, by President Roosevelt, July 31, 1936," W.L.M. King Papers, Memoranda and Notes, reel C4279, C141959-64, LAC.

33 W.L.M. King Diary, 31 July 1936, W.L.M. King Papers, LAC; "Militia and Air Force Confidential Intelligence Summary Volume XIV. Serial No. 3/36," 30 June 1936, file 112.3M1023 (D23), DHH.

34 W.L.M. King Diary, 5 August 1936, W.L.M. King Papers, LAC.

35 Alaska Road Commission, "The Proposed Pacific Yukon Highway," 1 April 1931, Herbert Hoover Presidential Papers, box 172, file Highways, Herbert Hoover Presidential Library (HHL).

36 McNaughton to Montgomery-Massingberd, 31 January 1935, Department of National Defence Records (DNDR), reel C4975, file HQS3367, LAC; Canadian General Staff, "USA–Alaska Highway, via British Columbia & Yukon," 24 August 1935, DEAR, vol. 1739, file 221, pt. 1, LAC; E.C. Ashton to Skelton, 14 September 1935, in *DCER*, vol. 5, 267.

37 Skelton to Ashton, 14 September 1935, in *DCER*, vol. 5, 267; Ely Palmer memorandum, 19 October 1936, Department of State Diplomatic Post Records (hereafter RG 84), Canada, Entry 2195A, file 815.4 Alaska Highway, NARA.

38 W.L.M. King Diary, 24 January 1937, W.L.M. King Papers, LAC.

39 Stacey, *Canada and the Age of Conflict*, vol. 2, 6–7; J.L. Granatstein, *The Ottawa Men: The Civil Service Mandarins, 1935–1957* (Toronto: Oxford University Press, 1982), 64–73.

40 Loring Christie, "Re: Monroe Doctrine," 16 February 1937, in *Documents on Canadian External Relations*, vol. 6: *1936–1939*, ed. John H. Munro (Ottawa: Department of External Affairs, 1972), 177; Skelton to King, February 1937, O.D. Skelton Papers, vol. 27, file 9, LAC.

41 W.L.M. King Diary, 5 March 1937, W.L.M. King Papers, LAC; Armour memorandum, 22 March 1937, RG 84, Entry 2195A, file 800, NARA.

42 Skelton cited in Helen Moorhead to Raymond L. Buell, 22 March 1937, Raymond L. Buell Papers, box 10, file Moorhead, Helen Howard, LC.

43 Greg Kennedy, *Anglo-American Strategic Relations and the Far East 1933–1939* (London: Frank Cass, 2002), 232; Robert Dallek, *Franklin D. Roosevelt and American Foreign Policy, 1933–1945* (New York: Oxford University Press, 1979), 147.

44 John D. Meehan, "Steering Clear of Britain: Canada's Debate over Collective Security in the Far Eastern Crisis of 1937," *International History Review* 25 (June 2003): 253–81; J. Pierrepont Moffat Diary, 12 August 1937, J. Pierrepont Moffat

Papers, vol. 39, Houghton Library, Harvard University [HL].

45 Roosevelt to Hull, 4 August 1937, Roosevelt Papers, PSF, box 73, file Hull, Cordell 1933–37, FDRL; Hull to Roosevelt, August 1937, Roosevelt Papers, PSF, box 73, file Hull, Cordell 1933–37, FDRL.

46 Armour to Moffat, 2 September 1937, RG 84, box 35, file 800.1 1937 Chief Executive, NARA; Armour to Moffat, 10 September 1937, Moffat Papers, vol. 12, HL; Moffat to Armour, 14 September 1937, RG 84, box 35, file 800.1 1937 Chief Executive, NARA.

47 Hull to Marvin McIntyre, 13 September 1937, Roosevelt OF, box 36, file OF200-ss Alaska and British Columbia, FDRL; Armour, "Telephone Conversation," 16 September 1937, RG 84, box 35, file 800.1 1937 Chief Executive, NARA.

48 Armour to Skelton, no. 564, 14 September 1937, DEAR, vol. 1739, file 221, LAC; Skelton to Christie, 16 September 1937, DEAR, vol. 1739, file 221, LAC; Christie memorandum, 12 November 1937, DEAR, vol. 1739, file 221, LAC.

49 Roosevelt to Chamberlain, 28 July 1937, Roosevelt Papers, PSF, file Great Britain 1937–38, FDRL; Chamberlain to Roosevelt, 28 September 1937, Roosevelt Papers, PSF, file Great Britain 1937–38, FDRL.

50 Roosevelt cited in Dallek, *Franklin Roosevelt*, 148; Roosevelt, "Quarantine Address," 5 October 1937, in *An American Primer*, ed. Daniel J. Boorstin (Chicago: University of Chicago Press, 1966), 847–52; John E. Wiltz, *From Isolation to War, 1931–1941* (New York: Thomas Y. Crowell, 1968), 63.

51 James MacGregor Burns, *Roosevelt: The Lion and the Fox* (New York: Harcourt Brace, 1956), 318–19.

52 Roosevelt cited in Dallek, *Franklin Roosevelt*, 149–51; Roosevelt, "Notes of Conversation with Norman H. Davis," 19 October 1937, Roosevelt Papers, PSF, file State Department Norman Davis, FDRL.

53 John Lamberton Harper, *American Visions of Europe: Franklin D. Roosevelt, George F. Kennan, and Dean G. Acheson* (Cambridge: Cambridge University Press, 1994), 60.

54 Kennedy, *Anglo-American Relations and the Far East*, 238.

55 Welles memorandum of conversation with Lindsay, 27 November 1937, Welles Papers, box 162, file Great Britain 1936-1937, FDRL.

56 Lawrence Pratt, "The Anglo-American Conversations on the Far East of January 1938," *International Affairs* 47 (October 1971): 749; J. Pierrepont Moffat Diary, 10 & 13 November 1937, Moffat Papers, vol. 39, HL.

57 Armour's idea to build upon existing west coast military arrangements came from Robert Hale, a U.S. legation clerk in Ottawa. Robert Hale memorandum, 17 November 1937, Welles Papers, box 161, file Canada, FDRL.

58 Armour to Welles, 10 December 1937, Welles Papers, box 161, file Canada, FDRL; Armour to Welles, 17 December 1937, Welles Papers, box 149, file Roosevelt 1937, FDRL.

59 U.S. Embassy London to Hull, no. 772, 13 December 1937, Roosevelt Papers, PSF, file Great Britain, FDRL; Diary, 30 November 1937, box 210, FDRL; J. Pierrepont Moffat Diary, 13 December 1937, Moffat Papers, vol. 39, HL; Welles memorandum of conversation with Lindsay, 15 December 1937, Welles Papers, box 162, file Great Britain 1936-1937, FDRL; Welles to Roosevelt, 20 December 1937, Roosevelt Papers, PSF, box 70, file State: 1937, FDRL; Roosevelt to Welles, 22 December 1937, Roosevelt Papers, PSF, box 70, file State: 1937, FDRL; Roosevelt to King, 21 December 1937, King Papers, Correspondence, reel C3729, LAC.

60 King to Roosevelt, 30 December 1937, King Papers, Correspondence, reel C3729, LAC; F.L.C. Floud to Harry Batterbee, 24 May 1938, Dominions Office Records, DO35/586, TNA.

61 Armour to Welles, 8 January 1938, RG 59, Decimal File 1930-39, file 842.20/68, NARA.

62 Armour to Welles, 6 January 1938, Welles Papers, box 44, file 13, FDRL; "Canadian Defence Weakness 'Menace' to U.S. Security," *Ottawa Citizen*, 6 January 1938; "Joint Coastal Defense Plan Envisaged," *Toronto Globe and Mail*, 6 January 1938; "Defence Co-operation between Britain, U.S. Suggested in London," *Toronto Daily Star*, 6 January 1938.

63 Skelton, "Conversations on West Coast Defence," 10 January 1938, DEAR, vol. 2959, file B-80, LAC.

64 Ashton to Mackenzie, "The Defence of Canada: A Survey of Militia Requirements," 10 January 1938, file 114.1 D11, DHH; Ashton to Mackenzie, "Observations on Canada's Defence Policy," 14 October 1937, file 112.3M2009 (D27), DHH; Ashton to Crerar, 29 November 1937, DNDR, vol. 2448, file HQC631-52-1, LAC; Crerar to Col. W.W.T. Torr, 13 January 1938, file 000.8 (D3), DHH.

65 Skelton to Herbert Marler, 14 January 1938, DEAR, vol. 2453, file Visits of General Ashton, LAC.

66 Percy W. Nelles to MacKenzie, "Conversations held in Washington DC, on the 19th and 20th January 1938," 22 January 1938, W.L.M. King Papers, Memoranda & Notes, vol. 157, file F1411, LAC; Royal Air Force Attaché C.G. Pirie, Memorandum, 22 January 1938, Foreign Office Records, FO371/22107, TNA; Gregory Allan Johnson, *North Pacific Triangle? The Impact of the Far East on Canada and Its Relations with the United States and Great Britain, 1937-1948* (PhD diss., York University, 1989), 113–14.

67 Ashton to Mackenzie, "Conversations held in Washington DC, on the 19th and 20th January 1938," 22 January 1938, file 112.3M2009 (D22), DHH.

68 Nelles to Mackenzie, "Conversations held in Washington DC, on the 19th and 20th January 1938," 22 January 1938, W.L.M. King Papers, Memoranda & Notes, vol. 157, file F1411, LAC.

69 Hugh L. Keenleyside to Escott Reid, 14 May 1937, Escott Reid Papers, vol. 34, file Keenleyside, Hugh L., LAC.

70 W.L.M. King Diary, 11 January 1938, King Papers, LAC; Armour to Hull, no. 1938, "Growing consciousness in Canada for need of defense," 13 January 1938, RG 59, Decimal File 1930-1939, file 842.20/68, NARA; W.L.M. King Diary, 12 March 1938, W.L.M. King Papers, LAC.

71 Roosevelt, "Reciprocity in Defense," 18 August 1938, Skelton Papers, vol. 5, file 5-6, LAC.

72 Roosevelt to Tweedsmuir, 31 August 1938, John Buchan Papers, box 10, file Correspondence July–August 1938, QUA; "The New 'Roosevelt Doctrine,'" *Montreal Daily Star*, 18 August 1938; "Monroe to Roosevelt," *Winnipeg Free Press*, 20 August 1938.

73 W.L.M. King Diary, 18 & 25 August and 27 September 1938, W.L.M. King Papers, LAC.

74 Galen Roger Perras, *Franklin Roosevelt and the Origins of the Canadian–American Security Alliance: Necessary But Not Necessary Enough* (Westport, CT: Praeger, 1998), 51–52.

75 Ibid., 72–76; W.L.M. King Diary, 16 August 1940, W.L.M. King Papers, LAC.

76 Henry J. Stimson Diary, 17 August 1940, Henry J. Stimson Papers, vol. 30, Yale University Library.

77 Skelton to King, 19 August 1940, King Papers, Memoranda and Notes, reel H1516, C220892-94, LAC.

78 Skelton to King, no. 274, 1 July 1940, in *Documents on Canadian External Relations: 1939–1941*, part II, vol. 8, ed. David R. Murray (Ottawa: Information Canada, 1976), 449–50; Keenleyside to King, "An Outline Synopsis for a Reconsideration of Canadian External Policy with Particular Reference to the United States," 17 June 1940, DEAR, vol. 781, file 394, LAC.

79 Escott Reid, "The United States and Canada: Domination, Co-operation, Absorption," 12 January 1942, Escott Reid Papers, vol. 13, file U.S. and Canada, LAC. See also Norman Robertson to King, 22 December 1941, in *Documents on Canadian External Relations*, vol. 9: *1942–1943*, ed. John F. Hilliker (Ottawa: Department of External Affairs, 1980), 1125–31; Hugh Keenleyside, "Recent Trends in United States-Canada Relations," 27 December 1941, DEAR, vol. 5758, file 71(s), LAC.

NATIONAL IDENTITY, PUBLIC OPINION AND THE DEPARTMENT OF EXTERNAL AFFAIRS, 1935-1939

Heather Metcalfe

The anticipation simmered just below the surface of Quebec City on a fresh May morning in 1939. Crowds of Quebecers, leavened by a sprinkling of notables from elsewhere in Canada, focused their attention on the quay on the St. Lawrence. In the distance an ocean liner, the *Empress of Australia*, was heaving into sight. This was by itself nothing special: ocean liners were not strangers to the port; but today the *Empress* was carrying special guests. Royalty was coming to town, and not just any royalty – for Quebec had hosted princes and princesses before – but the reigning monarch of the British Empire, George VI, and his consort, Queen Elizabeth. This was a first, for no reigning British king or queen had ever visited Canada.

The royal tour of 1939 had been the focus of in-depth planning on the part of the Canadian government, and of the Canadian people, since the idea of the tour had been advanced by Prime Minister W.L. Mackenzie King at the Imperial Conference of 1937. As the yacht ferrying the king and queen made its way – majestically, in the eyes of the crowd – from the *Empress* to the quay, Quebec's citizens would be the first, as the Canadian media reported, to have the honour of receiving Canada's king and queen – and the empire's too, of course. The Canadian papers could think of nothing better than to reprint the words of the London *Times*, which concluded that it "comes to them in a sense by geographical accident, but no province of the dominion can show better title than the right of seniority which belongs to the French-Canadians of Quebec."[1] Certainly the crowds that swarmed the Quebec docks seemed to justify that faith.

Support for the monarchy notwithstanding, controversies over international policy erupted regularly in Canadian politics during the period leading up to the Second World War. Liberal Prime Minister William Lyon Mackenzie King and his French-Canadian "lieutenant" Ernest Lapointe responded carefully to these debates, conscious that Canadian involvement abroad would rouse strong currents of opinion at home that represented a danger to national unity, still fragile in the wake of the divisive clash over conscription during the First World War. They recognized that in any major war involving Britain, increasingly likely after the unfortunate Munich settlements of 1938, Canadian involvement was inevitable, given the strength of imperialist sentiment across the country. But participation, they feared, would likely generate an isolationist backlash from Quebec. As international relations became more dangerous in the late 1930s, the stakes for Canadians, particularly those concerned with Canadian public opinion, increased dramatically. As a result, King's key concern in the immediate run-up to the conflict was to ensure that Canada's entrance into the war do only minimal damage to the delicate state of Canadian unity. At best, it seemed that internal conflict could be managed, but not avoided.

Canadian foreign policy during the 1930s was important therefore not only for its international implications but also for its internal consequences. The decade's repeated European crises forced Canadians to ponder the question of what it meant to be "Canadian," which differed along traditional religious, ethnic, and linguistic lines. As Canadian society split over these questions of identity, the result was an ongoing disagreement about the underlying nature of the country and its national interests. Aware that his government could not resolve these issues of policy and identity, King sought to paper over these disputes, postponing debate on international issues, and, by implication, discussions about the national identity. King instead focused on domestic issues, insisting that his government would respond to international developments on a case-by-case basis.[2]

King's policy of political compromise for the sake of national unity was not universally popular and was questioned even within his own government. This was especially true within the ranks of the Department of External Affairs. While Canada's small band of young diplomats agreed with the emphasis that the prime minister placed on national unity and applauded his efforts to recognize the strength of isolationist sentiment in Quebec, many of their number, including the department's under-secretary, O.D. Skelton, thought that the government should go further in this direction. They were convinced that courting isolationist and non-interventionist sentiment would generate a more distinct national viewpoint, one that better reflected the national interest.

These views were reflected, for instance, in a memorandum by Hugh Keenleyside, one of Skelton's early protégés in External Affairs, on his passage through the Prairies on his way home to British Columbia during the Munich crisis of 1938. Of course, Canadians of British origins, he wrote Skelton, were "prominent in Canadian business and social life, and it is natural that [they] should be over-represented in our organs of opinion. In spite of a good many shocks during the recent years – and particularly since Mr. Chamberlain took office in Great Britain – this element in the population still seems in general to approve of the idea that 'When Britain is at war we all are at war.'"[3] But Keenleyside held out hope for the future. Not only had imperialist sentiment been shaken by international developments over the last few years, but this older group had failed to fully transmit these views to the younger generation.

The development of a more "progressive" view of Canadian foreign policy, Keenleyside argued, lay with the ethnic minorities in the Prairie provinces and with the younger elements of the population. These segments of Canadian society, he wrote, had increasingly come to the conclusion that the present "mess" in Europe was largely a result of British policy, and that it was not Canada's responsibility to "sacrifice another generation of Canadians to try to straighten it out.... So if Britain and the rest of Europe want to go to Hell let them go – but let us stay out of it and try to maintain some remnants of decency on this continent."[4] Cautiously optimistic, Keenleyside argued that, given the West's "racial" and generational composition, a

Canadian political party with a policy of Canadian autonomy would gain widespread support. With the right sales-pitch, which could be developed by drawing on the growing "expertise" of the Canadian intellectual community, the young diplomat thought that an autonomous platform might sway Quebec and parts of rural Ontario. "It would, of course, precipitate a bitter fight," Keenleyside acknowledged, but hadn't "the time for such a fight arrived? Or must we go through another World War first?"[5]

Keenleyside's views found a ready echo in the East Block headquarters of the Department of External Affairs. Skelton too was concerned about the relationship between public opinion and Canadian interests. The under-secretary told his colleague Hume Wrong in March 1939 that Canadian involvement in any European war would likely be based "simply and solely on the grounds of racial sympathy with the United Kingdom."[6] Nonetheless, like Keenleyside, he remained hopeful that this imperialism might soon be the victim of its own success. "If the next year or so passes without a war," he continued, "I have little doubt that the ripening of public opinion in the assumption of more national responsibility in questions of war as well as in questions of peace will continue at a more rapid pace than in the past ten years." The implication was that this would mean a diminishing role for imperialist sentiment in the formation of Canadian policy. But, Skelton cautioned, this would not happen by itself. These changes would require Canadian intellectuals to engage public opinion and educate Canadians to "think boldly about Canada's place in the world."[7] While civil servants would not be directly involved in this exercise by virtue of their non-partisan standing, Skelton implied that External Affairs should encourage these developments. Serving the national interest for Skelton meant defining this interest, and, in particular, "educating" Canadians to think of their interests as extending beyond the imperial connection with Great Britain.

How this "education" might be accomplished was a difficult question. Public opinion and its influences are always notoriously difficult to quantify, and this was especially true of Canada in the 1930s, when there were no public opinion polls and the idea of public opinion itself was still relatively new and contested. Some of those Canadians interested in the possible role of public opinion in a democratic society embraced the ideas associated with the newest "yardstick" of public opinion, the Gallup Poll developed by the Institute of Public Opinion (IPO). Though available only in the United States in the 1930s (Gallup came to Canada in 1941), IPO rhetoric reflected progressive views of contemporary democracy. Polls, George Gallup and his colleagues argued, would provide an immediate, consistent, and accurate measure of public views and would return democracy to "'The People' in an age of increasing corporate interests."[8] Their voices could now finally be heard over those of "The Interests," who represented only the powerful few.[9]

But the rhetoric used so successfully by the IPO in the United States did not resonate as strongly in Canada. While populist ideas were present north of the border, they did not play the pivotal role they did in the American system. Canadian journalists, for instance, focused on the limitations of the new system, perhaps because they were traditionally considered, by themselves and others, as "bell-wethers" of public opinion. They showed little inclination to embrace the doctrine of *vox populi vox dei* and insisted that Canadians should embrace Britain's "cautious reserve" *vis-à-vis* public opinion. As H.T. Stanner wrote in a *Canadian Business* piece in December 1941, all "too frequently it is found that large numbers of people have little or no specific knowledge of defence problems and consequently, are in no position to form a guiding opinion."[10]

Canadian politicians argued in turn that the very philosophical foundation for the principle of polling contradicted the nature of Canadian society. Canadian democratic principles, based on the British parliamentary system, differed significantly from their American counterparts. Whereas proponents of the Gallup system heavily emphasized the role of populism, Canadian political leaders emphasized Parliament, the representatives of "the People," as the source of democratic legitimacy. Cabinet minister C.G. "Chubby" Power, for example, reminded his colleagues in the House of Commons in 1939 that their primary duty was to the nation, rather than to their constituents at home "who know nothing of the question under discussion." The same idea was also reflected in King's governing principle that "Parliament will decide."[11]

Indeed, King was especially sceptical of public opinion, which he understood in intuitive terms to represent a limit of his power. His views on public opinion are perhaps best seen in his diary recollections of a conversation he had with Conservative parliamentarian R.B. Hanson in December

1941. King, in response to Hanson's plea that he form a national government, outlined his detailed views on the nature of government:

> Hanson said, at one stage, that with my large following I could do anything I wished. I replied to him that my views of the source of power were very different to those of some other men.... I said that such successes I had had, I believed, came from the fact that I believed my power came from the people; that it was not something that arose from some 'superman' power which I myself possessed; that I felt I had held that power by being true to the people and to the promises I had given to them. That they trusted me because they knew I would not break faith with respect to their own views and wishes.
>
> Hanson then said: 'Then you feel that you should not lead?' To which I replied: That is not the case. That I believed the people had a true instinct in most matters of government when left alone. That they were not swayed, as specially favoured individuals were, by personal interest, but rather by a sense of what best served the common good. That they recognized the truth when it was put before them, and that a leader can guide so long as kept to the right lines. I did not think it was a mark of leadership to try to make the people do what one wanted them to do.[12]

Despite the hesitations of journalists and politicians, there were many in Canada during the 1930s who were determined, not only to tackle the problematic question of how to measure popular opinion, but also how to influence it. For those in the Canadian government who wanted to play a role in shaping this opinion, which included some members of the Department of External Affairs, it seemed possible to exert some influence. As historian Ernest May has shown, a "foreign policy public" can play a significant role in shaping public views on international relations. Although only a relatively small segment of the public followed international events, this group played a disproportionate role in shaping the discussion of international relations. This was largely due, he claims, to their social status, the respect given them by their community, and their access to information not readily available. Quoting sociologist Edward A. Ross, May argued that every "editor, politician, banker, capitalist, railroad president, employer, clergyman, or judge has a following with whom his opinion has weight. He, in turn, is likely to have *his* authorities. The anatomy of collective opinion ... form[s] a kind of intellectual feudal system."[13]

The formation of a consensus was aided, according to May, by the economic and political interests shared by this elite.[14] In addition, although their predominance could be challenged, their position and access to information from overseas ensured that "the establishment could determine collectively the terms on which any foreign policy debate would be conducted." This influence, however, was subject to limitation. As May argued, the foreign policy public could not radically change the terms of international involvement. Furthermore, given the fluid nature of public opinion, they "could know in advance only the extreme limits of what their constituency might approve or disapprove."[15] They could not be sure, therefore, of how to significantly shift public opinion on international relations. Those attempts were further hindered by the technical problem involved in reporting international developments during the interwar period. Information on international events took time to cross the oceans to Canada, and wire services did not provide a great deal of copy on world events to Canadian newspapers.[16]

Notwithstanding these limitations, which were only barely understood at the time, younger Canadian policy-makers and intellectuals remained convinced that public opinion could be bent to their will, provided that it was given proper leadership. As diplomat Keenleyside wrote in his memoirs almost fifty years later,

> It is perhaps true that internal stresses within Canada made an enlightened and more positive policy in foreign affairs impossible. But it is at least arguable that if the government had made any serious effort to give leadership in the interpretation of the international scene, the Canadian people, French-speaking and English-speaking alike, might have responded with the humanity and intelligence that marked many other aspects of Canadian life.[17]

While King refused to provide open leadership in shaping a debate on foreign policy, a new class of Canadian intellectuals were convinced that they had an important role to play in shaping public opinion. As historian Doug Owram has argued, English Canadian intellectuals in the 1930s, influenced by the tradition of progressive reform inherited from their predecessors and the socio-economic crisis of the depression, were increasingly tempted to play a role reforming the injustices in Canadian society. Echoing Skelton's comments to Wrong, they focused on their self-professed role of educating and shaping Canadian public opinion. They agreed with the overall sentiment that the "facts, if properly analyzed and properly interpreted, would point toward the proper policies and attitudes."[18] And they insisted that their training and expertise, in the social sciences in particular, made them uniquely qualified for this role. This assumption was reinforced by the assumptions of Canadian society, that the new challenges of the period required leadership from experts, whether self-educated or academically trained.[19] As Professor Bruce Kuklick has argued, the focus of intellectuals on public opinion reflected their belief that if politics were "rational," the appropriate course would be apparent.[20]

The efforts of intellectuals and policy-makers to mobilize public opinion in support of "rational" policy, however, were hampered by the peripheral role that they still occupied in Canadian society, the way public opinion was formed, and the rifts within the intellectual community itself. Nowhere were the divisions in Canadian society more apparent than in the country's intellectual society. This community was limited in size, in both English and French-Canada, and was often isolated, both from each other and from the larger Canadian community.

The English Canadian intellectual community was notable for its separateness, underlined by its distinctive educational achievements. In an overall population of less than 12 million, a university degree, which increasingly signalled membership in the intellectual community, was a relative rarity.[21] This was particularly the case in a society that had suffered greatly from the economic crisis of the decade. Indeed, the total number of university students formed only a tiny fraction of the community. Almost half of the Canadian population did not finish high school. In 1931, only 46 per cent of sixteen-year-old Canadians were in school.[22] In the 1935–36 academic year, Canada's universities and colleges granted 6,772 degrees. Of these, 786 were graduate degrees.[23]

This intellectual community, partially due to its small size, was extremely close-knit and insular. Members of the English Canadian intellectual community corresponded often, pursued projects in common, and socialized together. These connections started in school as many attended the same universities in Canada and were reinforced through graduate work at institutions abroad. The number of Canadians pursuing graduate degrees was so small that acquaintance was impossible to avoid.[24] Within the developing network of intellectuals, positions often overlapped in various societies such as the Canadian Clubs, the Canadian Radio League, and the Canadian Institute of International Affairs.

Individual members of this community were also very well connected with the global intellectual community. Due to their interest in international developments, the connections created by their educational experiences, and the quality of their scholarship, Canadian intellectuals connected with international streams of thought and leading global thinkers. This sense of international connection was in many ways utterly foreign to Canadians as a whole. Indeed, Owram concluded that their education and their university experiences "thus provided the elite with a sense of exclusivity and accomplishment that distinguished members from the public at large and from other groups involved in public affairs."[25]

French Canada's intellectual community occupied its own, equally fast, solitude. Though a parallel to Owram's study on the English Canadian intellectuals has not yet been published, certain themes are clear enough. Generally, the two main groups of intellectuals in Canada did not overlap, and the social and educational connections that bound each group together did not exist across them.[26] Even those intellectuals who attempted to bridge the gap were often uncomfortable with this relationship.[27] Cultural differences dividing the two groups were reinforced by the French Canadian's focus on different issues, reflecting their unique cultural and political concerns.[28]

Their main focus involved the viability of French Canadian society. Raised in an environment that stressed the values of family, church (almost all French Canadian intellectuals were Catholic), and rural life, they naturally concentrated on these themes in their own work. Those concerns focused on the contamination of Quebec society by the increasingly influential forces of industrialization, urbanization, and modernism.[29] French Canadian society was in their view an organic structure that had allowed their culture to survive for centuries in a North America dominated by Anglo-Saxon and Protestant values.[30] French Canadian nationalists, including the members of the *Action Libérale Nationale*, the *Jeune-Canada* movement, and *L'Action nationale*, argued that the spread of modern influences, including the centralization of federal power, industrialization and, most insidiously, modern, especially American, culture, was eating away at their community from the inside.[31] They pushed for policies meant to deter these influences, policies of "re-Frenchification" and colonization, of "acheter-chez-nous" and the destruction of the "Trusts."[32] These views, combined with a general sense of remoteness from international developments, encouraged a focus on domestic issues and regional views. European developments, when reported in the pages of Quebec newspapers, served to remind French Canadians that peace was precarious and implied that war threatened the establishment of a strong, autonomous French Canadian society.[33]

While Canadian intellectuals were thus inclined to hold themselves apart, Canadian society was just as inclined to hold them at arm's length. Many influential members of Canadian society, for example, continued to view academics as removed from the everyday concerns of society. As historian Michael Horn has argued, members of the Canadian business community, in particular, often contended that academics should refrain from commenting on public issues unless they had something "useful" or "constructive" to contribute.[34] This sentiment, and the fact that those who spoke out were often subject to public abuse, only encouraged the firm conviction within academia that the intellectual community ought to be removed from the cares of the world.[35] While Owram has argued that the academic community had become much more involved in public issues during the 1930s, particularly due to the social impact of the Great Depression, he, along with fellow historians Michael Horn and David Fransen, all agreed that Canadian academics had not yet achieved the prominent role in society that they would in later periods.[36]

There was one important exception; a small group of English Canadian intellectuals were able to connect in limited ways with the general public.

By the 1930s, their community increasingly included key members of the Canadian press, particularly, a group of young journalists clustered around editor John Dafoe and the Winnipeg *Free Press*. This included Grant Dexter, Max Freedman, and George Ferguson, who had long-standing connections with Vincent Massey, one of the leading power-brokers of the Liberal party.[37] These contacts were enhanced by those that Dexter and Dafoe forged with the intellectual community in Winnipeg, which included Roderick K. Finlayson, E.J. Tarr, and the Sanhedrin group. The Sanhedrin, whose name echoed the biblical description of an influential group of Jewish elders, provided a link between the intellectual community, notable journalists, and key members of the Liberal party.[38] As the intellectual community attempted to gain a greater share of influence in the shaping of policy during the Depression, it found in Dexter and Dafoe "allies who could use publicity and propaganda to encourage movement in new directions."[39]

But this was a limited and potentially dangerous liaison. Those members of External Affairs, including Lester B. "Mike" Pearson, who were interested in "educating" Canadian opinion, were at times reprimanded for any suggestion of intimacy with those outside of the government. Pearson's close association with Dexter, while both were stationed in London during the late 1930s, was of particular concern to Skelton and his political bosses.[40] Pearson eventually briefed Dexter almost daily during the Czech crisis in October of 1938, making him as informed, and certainly more up-to-date, than many officials in Canada.[41] Alarm at this kind of activity grew to the point that any publication by the *Free Press* of materials embarrassing to the government, particularly on foreign policy, led to increased scrutiny of Pearson. Thus, while the lines between the intellectual community and Canada's civil service increasingly blurred in the late 1930s, there were clear limits on how far individuals like Pearson could engage Canadian opinion.

Despite their aspirations to shape public opinion, Canadian intellectuals enjoyed only limited or inconsistent influence and were often frustrated by the lack of impact their views had in shaping political discourse or public opinion.[42] Surprisingly, they rarely considered the implications should public opinion come to a consensus with which they disagreed. The Canadian reaction to the royal tour of King George VI and Queen

Elizabeth in the summer of 1939 represented the most obvious manifestation of this problem. Canadians flocked to see their majesties in huge numbers, sincere in their enthusiasm and, at least on the surface, loudly and resoundingly loyal to the crown and to the empire. As one editorial put it "there can be no doubt that the royal visit will have created in this country a personal appreciation of the throne of nation and empire as may go so far as to make for a new era in intra-British relationships." It would also encourage a "greater sense of unity and purpose on the part of the Canadian people themselves."[43] Even in Quebec and among the ethnic communities of the Prairies, the royal tour was met with massive crowds.[44]

King's foreign policy, therefore, while far from emotionally satisfying (or even at times logically consistent), seemed to many contemporary observers to reflect the general sentiments of the majority of Canadians. In 1937, Escott Reid, not yet a member of the Department of External Affairs, had published a generally positive analysis of King's foreign policy. The Liberal prime minister's focus on national unity, relations with the United States and Britain, and the maintenance of Canadian autonomy in relations with the League of Nations and the British Empire seemed to represent the realities of Canada's position, both politically and emotionally. While there were many questions that King's foreign policy left unanswered, including international economic grievances and, more importantly, Canada's position in response to a war involving the United States or Britain, Reid concluded that this policy of ambiguity was, in fact, an appropriate one:

> If Mr. King were to give unambiguous answers to the seven questions he has left unanswered, he would raise a tremendous political storm in Canada. Parties would split. Passions would be aroused. The national unity of Canada would be subjected to severe strains. If war should break out, such a crisis will probably be inevitable.... A crisis now would settle the question, and as a result there would be no crisis of any importance when the war did break out.... In other words, a crisis today would be a 'preventive' crisis. But democracy and democratic statesmen hate both preventative wars and preventative crises.[45]

While historians today might share Reid's conclusions, those who wanted King to pursue a more proactive approach to shaping public opinion in the 1930s did not find these sentiments comforting. Certainly Skelton appeared disheartened by the trends of opinion during the lead up to Canada's declaration of war in September of 1939. His memorandum, entitled "Canada and the Polish War, A Personal Note," touched on the limitations inherent in Canada's involvement in a global empire.

> The first casualty in this war has been Canada's claim to independent control of her own destinies. In spite of a quarter century of proclamation and achievement of equality and independent status, we have thus far been relegated to the role of a Crown colony. We are drifting into a war resulting, so far as the United Kingdom's part is concerned, from political and diplomatic actions initiated months ago without our knowledge or expectation. An Ottawa paper has gloated over the fact that the foreign policy of Canada is in the hands of the Prime Minister of Great Britain; it has not yet called attention to Inskip's sideshow, 'the Dominion Office as the Foreign Office of the British Empire.'[46]

The under-secretary was ultimately frustrated with the way in which Canadian opinion remained unable to overcome its imperialism and the government's unwillingness to act in shaping it.

The 1939 royal tour demonstrated both the continuing appeal of this imperialism and the impact of public opinion on government policy. The issue became increasingly important as the likelihood of Canadian involvement in a European conflict increased after the Munich agreements of October 1938. Pearson, for example, expressed his concerns regarding the long-term consequences of the royal visit on Canadian public opinion in his correspondence with Skelton.

> I can't help feeling that all the outbursts of Royal and Imperial sentiment which the tour has evoked and which has naturally been reported here in fulsome terms will make it even more difficult for this country to understand the unsentimentally

nationalist basis of Canada's external policy. There is not much use in saying that the enthusiasm shown was to Their Majesties in their personal capacities as King and Queen of Canada. I am afraid 99 per cent of the people in this country are not so expert in constitutional subtleties as to be able to distinguish between patriotic outbursts for the King of Canada and patriotic outbursts for the Ruler of the British Empire.... In this respect, I feel personally that whereas the Royal Visit seems to have done so much good in many respects, in this respect, it does make even more complicated certain complicating features of Canada's imperial relationship.

His letter concludes wryly that from "reading the Canadian newspapers, I am sure I would be shot as a traitor on sight if I were ever rash enough to give expression to such views [on the negative aspects of Canadian imperialism] in the hearing of my intoxicated countrymen at the present time."[47]

Pearson's observations and the massive coverage of the royal tour provides a different, grimmer, perspective on the views of department officials regarding the potential of "educating" Canadians about their national interests. Canada entered the war on 10 September 1939 with overwhelming support from English Canada. There was also very little active resistance on the part of French Canadians or their representatives in the House of Commons, despite the expectations of both internal and external observers.[48] The *Globe and Mail*, although disappointed that the declaration had not immediately followed that of Britain, happily reported the unanimity of the result.[49]

Ian Rutherford, in his discussion of the public debate in the United States regarding the possibility of war with Iraq in 2003 concluded that the result "was not really dialogue, an exchange of views, but a series of clashing monologues.... The debate that occurred was mostly in the heads of the journalists and the citizens at the receiving end of all this propaganda."[50] The nature of Canadian public debate during the 1930s, as much as anything, brings this formulation clearly to mind. Canadians during the decade were largely uninterested in understanding divergent views, let alone their context. The historiography of public opinion, especially when contrasted to the views of contemporaries, encourages the conclusion that public opinion shifted slowly in response to international developments that Canadians saw as challenging their longstanding, if underlying, interests. The fact that the conclusions they reached regarding this role represented their continuing embrace of a connection with both Britain and the United States *and* the maintenance of Canadian autonomy, did not reflect a failure to "think boldly." Rather, it reflected their realization, whether they thought in those terms or not, that a continuation of these policies would best reflect their national self-interest.[51]

NOTES

1. The *Times* article concluded that the "Canadians will see in George VI the very incarnation of those ideals which have made it possible for two nationalities to dwell … within the confines of a harmonious state." See "French-Canadian Honour Stressed," *Winnipeg Free Press*, 17 May 1939, 7, and "Le 'Times' de Londres et les Canadiens français," *Le Devoir*, 17 May 1939, 3.

2. C.P. Stacey, *Canada and the Age of Conflict: A History of Canadian External Relations*, vol. 2: *The Mackenzie King Era, 1921–1948* (Toronto: University of Toronto Press, 1981), 195. The fact that Parliament's decision was a foregone decision, given the Liberal majority, does not limit the importance of the policy in limiting controversy.

3. H.L. Keenleyside, Memorandum to Skelton, 6 October 1938, Department of External Affairs Records (DEAR), vol. 715, Library and Archives Canada (LAC).

4. Ibid.

5. Ibid.

6. Skelton to Wrong, 2 March 1939, Hume Wrong Papers, vol. 3, LAC.

7. Ibid.

8. George Gallup and Saul Rae, *The Pulse of Democracy: The Public Opinion Poll and How it Works* (New York: Simon and Schuster, 1940), 125.

9. Ibid., 11.

10. Daniel J. Robinson, *The Measure of Democracy* (Toronto: University of Toronto Press, 1999), 90.

11. Ibid., 70.

12. W.L.M. King Diary, 9 December 1941, W.L.M. King Papers, LAC.

13. Ernest R. May, *American Imperialism: A Speculative Essay*, new ed. (Chicago: Imprint, 1991), 29.

14. Ibid., 29.

15. Ibid., 83.

16. May, *American Imperialism*, 37.

17. Hugh L. Keenleyside, *Memoirs of Hugh L. Keenleyside*, vol. 1: *Hammer the Golden Day* (Toronto: McClelland & Stewart, 1982), 505.

18. Ibid., 154.

19. Ibid., 122, 137.

20. Bruce Kuklick, *Blind Oracles: Intellectuals and War from Kennan to Kissinger* (Princeton, NJ: Princeton University Press, 2006), 4.

21. The *Canada Year Book* of 1938 estimates the population for 1937 at 11,720,000. Canada, Ministry of Trade and Commerce, *Canada Year Book*, 1938 (Ottawa: King's Printer, 1938), 155.

22. John Herd Thompson and Allen Seager, *Canada 1922–1939: Decades of Discord* (Toronto: McClelland & Stewart, 1985), 159.

23. *Canada Year Book*, 1938, 996–97.

24. The *Canada Year Book* for 1937 lists 1,645 students enrolled in Graduate Studies. Canada, Ministry of Trade and Commerce, *Canada Year Book*, 1937 (Ottawa: King's Printer, 1937), 977.

25. Doug Owram, *The Government Generation: Canadian Intellectuals and the State, 1900–1945* (Toronto: University of Toronto Press, 1986), 147.

26. For a discussion of the educational experiences of French Canadian intellectuals, see John English's biography of Trudeau, *Citizen of the World: The Life of Pierre Elliott Trudeau*, vol. 1: 1919–1968 (Toronto: A.A. Knopf Canada, 2006).

27. Owram, *Government Generation*, 147. They were also anxious concerning the political implications of too close of a connection, although it seems apparent that the connection was uncomfortable more for cultural rather than political reasons. David Lenarcic, *Where Angels Feared to Tread* (Ph.D diss., York University, 1990), 96.

28 An example of this is seen in the response of French Canadian society to the new political forces represented in the Cooperative Commonwealth Federation and its intellectual core, the League for Social Reconstruction. As Horn has argued, the LSR simply failed to gain many proponents among the French Canadian community, due not only to organizational failures and lacklustre effort, but also due to divergent cultural influences. Michael Horn, *The League for Social Reconstruction: Intellectual Origins of the Democratic Left in Canada, 1930–1942* (Toronto: University of Toronto Press, 1980), 58. The same is true of the French Canadian response to isolationist groups within English Canada. Unfortunately, there has been little work done in the area.

29 Esther Delisle, *The Traitor and the Jew: Anti-Semitism and Extremist Nationalism in Quebec from 1929 to 1939* (Montreal: R. Davies, 1993), 38. See also Ramsay Cook, *Quebec and the Uses of Nationalism*, 2nd ed. (Toronto: McClelland & Stewart, 1995), 91; and Conrad Black, *Duplessis* (Toronto: McClelland & Stewart, 1977), 106.

30 Delisle, *The Traitor and the Jew*, 41. See also Cook, *Quebec and the Uses of Nationalism*, 107.

31 Delisle, *The Traitor and the Jew*, 61. See also Everett Hughes, *French Canada in Transition* (Chicago: University of Chicago Press, 1943), 127.

32 Delisle, *The Traitor and the Jew*, 95. See also Bernard Vigod, *Quebec before Duplessis: The Political Career of Louis-Alexandre Taschereau* (Montreal: McGill-Queen's University Press, 1986), 173; English, *Trudeau*, 42; and Patricia Dirks, *The Failure of l'action liberale nationale* (Montreal: McGill-Queen's University Press, 1991), 37.

33 Dominique Marquis, Un quotidian pour L'Eglise: *L'Action catholique, 1910–1940* (Montreal: Lemeac, 2004), 125. Marquis' discussion of the transformation of the French Canadian religious press, particularly *L'Action catholique*, allows her a means of discussing the role that the Catholic Church continued to play in Quebec society. She argued that *L'Action catholique* became much more of a mainstream journal by the 1930s, one that could compete with the major secular journals.

34 Horn, *The League for Social Reconstruction*, 196.

35 Ibid.

36 Owram, *Government Generation*, 169; and David Fransen, "Unscrewing the unscrutable: The Rowell-Sirois Commission, the Ottawa bureaucracy and public finance reform, 1935–1941," PhD diss., University of Toronto, 1984, 462.

37 Grant Dexter, for example, shared similar generational experiences with many of the intellectuals on whom Owram focuses, including participation in the Great War and a growing attachment to Canadian nationalism. He also shared a number of views with this group, as well as a shared sense of purpose. See Owram, *Government Generation*, 185.

38 Ibid.

39 Ibid.

40 Patrick H. Brennan, *Reporting the Nation's Business: Press-Governmental Relations during the Liberal Years, 1935–1957* (Toronto: University of Toronto Press, 1994), 22.

41 Brennan, *Reporting the Nation's Business*, 25.

42 Arthur Lower, *My First Seventy-Five Years* (Toronto: Macmillan of Canada, 1967), 177, 179, 189, 195.

43 "Saskatchewan's Goodbye," Regina *Leader-Post*, 6 June 1939, 4.

44 For two examples among many, see "Apothéose Royale," *La Presse*, 19 May 1939, 6, for an overview of the arrival in Quebec, and "Crowds Jam Melville for Visit," *Winnipeg Free Press*, 5 June 1939, 20, for the stop at the small town of Melville, Saskatchewan, one of the highlights of the tour where tens of thousands of Canadians from the Prairies gathered to get their chance to see the royal couple.

45 Escott Reid, *Radical Mandarin: The Memoirs of Escott Reid*. (Toronto: University of Toronto Press, 1989), 109.

46 "Canada and the Polish War, A Personal Note," Skelton Papers, vol. 5, LAC.

47 Lester B. Pearson to O.D. Skelton, 9 June 1939, Pearson Papers, vol. 14, LAC.

48 H.B. Neatby, *William Lyon Mackenzie King*, vol. 3: *The Prism of Unity, 1932–1939* (Toronto: University of Toronto Press, 1976), 290. This included a large number of British officials. See Ritchie Ovendale, *'Appeasement' and the English-Speaking World. Britain, the United States, the Dominions and the Policy of 'Appeasement,' 1937–1939* (Cardiff: University of Wales Press, 1975), 328.

49 *Globe and Mail*, 11 September 1939, 6.

50 Paul Rutherford, *Weapons of Mass Persuasion: Marketing the War against Iraq* (Toronto: University of Toronto Press, 2004), 24.

51 As C.P. Stacey points out, Canadians were acting in their own interests when they decided to go to war in 1939, even if they were not entirely aware of the ways in which they did so. See Stacey, *Canada and the Age of Conflict*, vol. 2, 268–69.

WHEN THE DEPARTMENT OF EXTERNAL AFFAIRS MATTERED – AND WHEN IT SHOULDN'T HAVE

J.L. Granatstein

"Relations with the United States are at the centre of Canada's foreign and domestic policy interests at every level," wrote Michael Hart in his new book, *From Pride to Influence: Towards a New Canadian Foreign Policy*. "The principal foreign policy challenge for Canada is to manage the pervasiveness of this U.S. reality."[1] There can be no question that Hart is right, and his judgment stands as correct at least since the end of the Second World War and arguably from 1938 when American President Franklin Roosevelt and Prime Minister Mackenzie King exchanged defence pledges at Kingston and Woodbridge, Ontario. But our foreign policy-makers have not always recognized reality, sometimes putting other concerns, global or domestic, ahead of the reality of Canadian national interests.

And what are those national interests? Here is my list with which, I suspect, few would quarrel seriously:

1. Canada must protect its territory and the security of its people;
2. Canada must strive to maintain its unity;
3. Canada must protect and enhance its independence;
4. Canada must promote the economic growth of the nation to support the prosperity and welfare of its people;
5. Canada should work with like-minded states for the protection and enhancement of democracy and freedom.

There is nothing remotely contentious here. Of course, these interests are simple enough to state but not always easy to achieve because they sometimes conflict. It is the task of national leaders to sort out the conflicts and determine the best strategy to protect and advance Canada's interests. What is surely clear is that the presence of the United States is omnipresent in most, if not all, of them.

***

Oscar Douglas Skelton was the senior official in the Department of External Affairs who built and shaped the department. He was the man who did the recruiting in the 1920s and 1930s, and he was the thinker who determined the policy direction, subject to political control. What made Skelton unique is that he thought in terms of the national interest from the time he became under-secretary of state for external affairs in 1925 and indeed before. Other Canadians then accepted that Britain's interests were almost automatically indistinguishable from Canada's,[2] and it was such attitudes that took Canada into the war in 1939 just as they had in 1914. Skelton wrote innumerable memoranda excoriating British policy in Europe in the 1930s and denouncing Britain's Prime Minister Neville Chamberlain's government for the way it treated the Dominions, for assuming (correctly) that they would do what they were told. The under-secretary, who, it is fair to say, missed the necessity of stopping Hitler, did not want Canada to behave as a lapdog and go to war simply because Britain did. But his prime minister, who almost always agreed with Skelton – except on the most important matters – certainly understood English-speaking Canadian opinion better than the under-secretary did and knew that Canada had to go to war in 1939. Prime Minister Mackenzie King, in other words, was a strong minister unafraid to rein in his chief foreign policy adviser when necessary.

Nothing that happened in the first nine months of the Second World War changed Skelton's mind that the war did not serve Canadian interests well. But soon even he could not be blind to the military-political realities. The Anglo-French defeat in the Low Countries and in France in May and June 1940 changed everything. Suddenly, and realistically, Britain's key national interest of survival was critical to Canada. Canada's own national interests demanded that it should work with like-minded states for the protection and enhancement of democracy and freedom, and Skelton saw this at once. "It amuses me a little," King noted in his diary on May 24, "how completely some men swing to opposite extremes. No one could have been more strongly for everything being done for Canada, as against Britain, than Skelton was up to a very short time ago. Yesterday ... he naturally did not want me to suggest any help for Canada, but rather the need for Britain. He now sees that the real place to defend our land is from across the seas."[3]

There was, of course, less contradiction than King perceived. As a national interest thinker, Skelton understood that a Nazi victory, unlikely in September 1939 but very probable in late May 1940, posed a grave threat to North America and to freedom and democracy everywhere. Everything Canada could do to defeat Hitler was necessary – and very much in the national interest. Still, the change in Skelton was marked, and he was quick to realize that Canada could not be protected unless an arrangement with the United States was reached.

The trick now was for Canada to do the maximum possible for the war effort overseas and to guarantee Canada's own security *if* – and it seemed more like *when*, that summer of 1940 – Britain fell to Hitler. This meant getting closer to the still-neutral United States and as quickly as possible. Skelton wrote at the end of April 1940 that "the United States is already giving in many respects as much help as if it were in the war, but its further diplomatic and financial and naval and perhaps air support are powerful potentialities. Our task is two fold: to make effective our own share and to speed in every practical and discreet way the cooperation of the United States."[4]

On May 19, Hugh Keenleyside from Skelton's staff went to Washington to see Roosevelt and to deliver the prime minister's appeal for aircraft to replace those Britain now could not supply for the British Commonwealth Air Training Plan. The president offered limited help, but more important, however, was Roosevelt's return message to King of two phrases: "certain possible eventualities which could not be mentioned aloud" and "British fleet."[5] If Hitler forced Britain to sue for peace, what would happen to the Royal Navy? Would it escape to Canada to carry on the fight or would it be turned over to the victors? Questions that had seemed unthinkable on 9 May 1940 were ten days later urgently seizing the attention of the American president and the Canadian prime minister.

Skelton was not the only one who had altered his thinking under the press of events. Informed public opinion, watching the evacuation of allied troops from Dunkirk and the surrender of France, understood that Canada had now been forced to re-think its political and defence relationship with the United States. In mid-July, "A Group of Twenty Canadians," largely associated with the Canadian Institute of International Affairs but including some public servants (Keenleyside, J.W. Pickersgill, and Robert Bryce) and Liberal Members of Parliament (Paul Martin and Brooke Claxton) produced "a programme of Immediate Canadian Action" that called for this reappraisal. "Co-operation with Washington," the programme said bluntly and correctly, "is going to be either voluntary on Canada's part, or else compulsory; in any event it is inevitable." Skelton "took a positive attitude towards the talks," and received the statement "with interest and appreciation."[6] Suggestions for a closer relationship were heard in Washington too, and in mid-August, Roosevelt invited King to meet him at Ogdensburg, in upstate New York.[7]

The result was the Permanent Joint Board on Defence (PJBD), the first Canada–United States defence alliance. As someone who had long believed that "the North American mind"[8] was markedly distinct from that of the Old World and its age-old conflicts, Skelton was overjoyed. It was "the best day's work done for many a year. It did not come by chance," he wrote to King, "but as the inevitable sequence of public policies and personal relationships, based upon the realization of the imperative necessity of close understanding between the English-speaking peoples."[9]

Exactly so. Canada had guaranteed its safety no matter the result of the war in Europe, thanks to the new American alliance. Moreover, with this guarantee, Canada could now offer maximum military support to Britain, sure that its own defence was secure. Even better, public opinion, aside from a few Tory stalwarts who feared Canada being swallowed by the United States,[10] was overwhelmingly supportive.

British Prime Minister Winston Churchill, however, was less pleased, telegraphing King that if Hitler could not invade Britain, all such transactions "will be judged in a mood different to that prevailing while the issue still hangs in the balance."[11] The British leader obviously believed that Canada was scuttling to safety. Skelton prepared a draft response to Churchill's imperial rant – "we can perhaps safely leave the verdict of history for the future to determine" – which was not sent, but it took a propitiatory telegram from Churchill on September 12 before King – and Skelton – were mollified.[12]

The creation of the PJBD was arguably the high point of Skelton's career. Skelton had always insisted that North America was where Canada's "lasting community of interest" and its "current of destiny" resided.[13] But he had never before managed to have the national interest determine the government's actions on questions of war and peace. But now in the midst of a terrible military debacle, he had seen his prime minister take a historic step. In August 1940, the national interest demanded a defence alliance with the United States. For the first time, Canada had put its interests ahead of all others, and Churchill's intemperate, foolish response made this very clear. The British leader saw only the new alliance and a weakening of the old, and failed to note that the PJBD brought the United States closer to Britain's ranking ally and, simultaneously, let that ally do more for Britain. His imperial blinkers on, Churchill missed the point, and Skelton, never having worn those particular blinkers, got it.

Then ten months later and just a few weeks after Skelton's death at the wheel of his car, the Hyde Park Declaration, again reached by Roosevelt and King, secured Canada's wartime economic interests.[14] This again was brilliant prime ministerial negotiation, driven by immediate necessity but also by a clear understanding of future reality. The national interest demanded that Canada promote the economic growth of the nation to support the prosperity and welfare of its people, something that could only be achieved by the closest economic cooperation with the United States. Canada was fighting Canada's war and Britain's, and the Hyde Park Declaration let it keep its factories going, employment and production high, and to do the maximum possible for a financially strapped Britain. Canada was also recognizing at last that it was a North American nation and that its national interests, first and foremost, had to be Canadian.

The turn to the south, the move toward a national interest policy, was Skelton's great achievement, accomplished because he had helped his prime minister prepare the ground. The two men did not always see eye to eye, but in the summer of 1940 they did, and they achieved a historic realignment that protected Canadian interests and advanced the Allied cause.

***

A very different sequence of events would occur some two decades later, one that changed Canadian politics and came close to jeopardizing the defence relationship with the United States that Skelton and King had created.

One of Skelton's ablest recruits to External Affairs was Norman Robertson, a British Columbia Rhodes Scholar, who joined in 1929 at the age of twenty-five. Robertson had worked mainly on trade questions through the 1930s, but he had greatly impressed King who appointed him, rather than the more senior Lester B. "Mike" Pearson, to succeed Skelton as undersecretary in 1941. He ran the Department of External Affairs throughout the war and held a variety of critical appointments in Ottawa, London, and Washington until his death in 1968. He was a Canadian nationalist but also very much an internationalist, someone who understood that Canada had to work with its friends to advance its interests.

In late 1958, Robertson left his post as ambassador to Washington to become under-secretary for a second time, first for Sidney Smith, a university president turned hapless politician and foreign minister, and then from early June 1959 for his fellow British Columbian Howard Green in the Progressive Conservative government led by Prime Minister John Diefenbaker.

A key national interest for any country is that it must strive to protect and enhance its independence. This was something that concerned the Diefenbaker government, fearful as it was that Washington's sometimes bullying ways might stampede Canada into decisions, whatever the consequences might be. Diefenbaker believed that this had occurred, aided and abetted by the Canadian military, when the North American Air Defence Command (NORAD) was created just after the Tories took power. He may have been right; certainly he suffered attacks from the Liberals who had negotiated the agreement before their defeat in the 1957 election and knew its details better perhaps than the incoming government. Nonetheless, it was Diefenbaker in February 1959 who agreed to install nuclear-armed Bomarc surface-to-air missiles at two bases in Canada and soon after to arm Canada's troops in Europe with nuclear weaponry. The difficulty was that a myriad of details remained to be settled before the weapons were in place, and it was here that Robertson and Green exercised their influence.

Or perhaps it was the under-secretary who exercised his influence on the minister. Howard Green was a fine gentleman without much experience of foreign affairs. He was from birth an Empire-first Tory, and he remained innately suspicious of the United States and fearful of its influence, but he could learn and he quickly came to admire the officers in his department. Still, he was a naif, and disarmament, a subject of interest to Robertson as well, captivated him despite its hopelessness in the darkest period of the Cold War.[15] That led inevitably to the primacy of the nuclear question.

In his various postings, Robertson had dealt with nuclear issues and generally accepted the necessity of the weapons. He understood the need to protect the American deterrent, and he recognized that intimate cooperation in air defence between the two North American nations was necessary. But by 1959, he had begun to worry about the effects of radioactive fallout on humankind's ability to survive, and the mutuality of assured destruction that underlay deterrence theory had begun to trouble him. The nationalist internationalist that he had always been was about to be replaced by the traditional Canadian moralist.

The catalyst that turned Robertson from tacit supporter to opponent of nuclear weapons was an article in the British magazine *The Spectator* that argued that hydrogen bombs had changed the nature of war. There could be no victor and no chance that civilized life could survive. The answer, author Christopher Hollis said, was unilateral nuclear disarmament and a build-up of conventional forces. The Soviets had no interest in destroying the West for did not Marxist theory postulate that victory over capitalism was certain? Why then destroy what you would eventually take? Robertson sent the article to the prime minister with a note declaring that his "personal views" coincided with Hollis'.[16] Two days later Green became secretary of state for external affairs and the anti-nuclear forces had their champions.

For the next three-and-a-half years, Robertson's fertile mind produced delaying tactic after dilatory response. American policy required United States control of warheads? Then Canada should be for dual control or, even better, no warheads at all on Canadian soil. Should the cabinet discuss the nuclear question, as defence minister Douglas Harkness wanted? No, if word leaked out, this might jeopardize Canadian disarmament efforts at the United Nations. Time and again, the wily diplomat in External Affairs fought off the Department of National Defence's cack-handed efforts to move the nuclear issue along so that Canada could negotiate the arming of the weapons the Diefenbaker government had secured from the United States. Canada's ambassador in Washington, Arnold Heeney, noted that Green's "own attitudes and prejudices, in a curious way, combine with [Robertson]'s cosmic anxieties, particularly in our defence relationships, external and domestic, to produce a negative force of great importance."[17] The issue that was to destroy the Diefenbaker government had been delineated, and the tumbrils of Tory collapse had begun to roll.

The difficulty with the Robertson-Green position was that it flew directly in the face of Canada's national interests. These required Canada to get along with the United States in the interests of its security and its economic well-being, not to mention Canada's reliance on alliances to advance democracy and freedom. The Americans had large burdens to bear in Europe and Asia, but the defence of their homeland was properly their highest priority, and Canada needed to recognize that. Robertson's delaying tactics put his judgment, his values, and his high sense of morality ahead of Washington's – all fine except when the superpower neighbour's security was involved. A refusal or a delay in arming the Canadian component of

NORAD with nuclear weapons may not have jeopardized United States security outright – Canadian Bomarcs and interceptors, nuclear-armed or not, did not rule the skies over Canada – but it was a harbinger of even more troubling Canadian attitudes to come during the Cuban missile crisis of October 1962. And these were troubling enough that President John F. Kennedy's frustrated, angry administration moved successfully to topple the dry husk of Diefenbaker's government in January 1963.

Nonetheless the responsibility for the government's collapse should not be placed on the delaying tactics of Robertson and Green. It was John Diefenbaker's alone. His inability to make up his mind on the nuclear question had pitted External Affairs against National Defence, divided his cabinet, caucus, party, and country, and reduced Canadian–American relations to their lowest point in the twentieth century.[18] Still, Robertson, fighting for the moralistic and unrealistic position he believed in and unchecked, indeed encouraged, by his weak minister, seemed to have forgotten the national interest.[19] That was not a mistake Skelton would have made, and there was some irony in the fact that Mike Pearson, the friendly rival Robertson had beaten out (without trying) for the under-secretary's job in 1941, would accept nuclear weapons as soon as he came to power as prime minister in early 1963. Getting on with the Yanks was essential and necessary, and Pearson was nothing if not a practical man.[20]

***

Skelton had been heard in 1940, and should have been. Robertson was listened to from 1959 to 1963, and ought not to have been. The Canada of 1940 was still psychologically a colony; the nation of the early 1960s was in an age of confidence and wealth, and after the Suez Crisis of 1956 in particular, it had begun to believe that it was a player in foreign policy. It wasn't, not really, and in fact its influence was in the midst of a slow decline after the flush of power and influence created by the Second World War faded.

What Diefenbaker had done was to make the pulling of tail feathers from the American eagle the national sport, and his successors, Brian Mulroney aside, successfully emulated him. The highpoints of this approach came under Prime Ministers Pierre Trudeau, Jean Chrétien, and

Paul Martin, with Lloyd Axworthy, Chrétien's foreign minister, as the prime exponent of this tactic. With its security, trade, and economy dependent on the United States, this was never wise policy. Canada was not a great power, not a self-sufficient island, and tail-feather pulling, while one of few sports other than hockey at which Canadians had long excelled, was foolish and appealed to the lowest common denominator of shrill anti-Americanism.

All Canadians want Canada to be independent; certainly Skelton and Robertson did. But wise counsellors understand the limitations within which they must operate, and the most realistic Canadians have understood that their nation's aim should be to be as independent as possible in the circumstances, as one correspondent once told the late Peter Gzowski on the Canadian Broadcast Corporation's radio program, "This Country in the Morning." That is precisely it. Seize an opportunity if it comes, as Skelton did in 1940. But don't, as Robertson did, pretend to be a major player by inventing obstacles to throw in the way of the great power on whom we depend, and especially not on issues, like disarmament, that we can only influence at the margins. Don't shout out that Canada is a moral superpower, in other words, forever telling the Yanks that we know best. Robertson – and Trudeau, Chrétien, Martin, and Axworthy – did that, and they were wrong.

NOTES

1. Michael Hart, *From Pride to Influence* (Vancouver: UBC Press, 2008), 334.

2. This point is made in Norman Hillmer's 2008 Skelton Lecture, "Foreign Policy and the National Interest: Why Skelton Matters," Department of Foreign Affairs and International Trade, Ottawa, 17 December 2008.

3. W.L.M. King Diary, King Papers, 24 May 1940, Library and Archives Canada (LAC).

4. O.D. Skelton, "The Present Outlook," 30 April 1940, Department of External Affairs Records (DEAR), vol. 774, file 353, microfilm reel T-1791, LAC.

5. J.L. Granatstein, *Canada's War: The Politics of the Mackenzie King Government 1939–1945* (Toronto: University of Toronto Press, 1975), 119ff.

6. Copy in Alan Plaunt Papers, box 9, file 1, University of British Columbia Archives [UBCA] and in King Papers, attached to Brooke Claxton to W.L.M. King, 23 August 1940, 241683ff, LAC.

7. For a full account, see J.L. Granatstein, "Mackenzie King and Canada at Ogdensburg, August 1940," in *Fifty Years of Canada–U.S. Defence Cooperation: The Road from Ogdensburg*, ed. J. Jockel and J. Sokolsky (Lewiston, NY: Edwin Mellon Press, 1992), 9–29.

8. Norman Hillmer, "O.D. Skelton and the North American Mind," *International Journal* 60 (Winter 2004–5): 93–110.

9. Skelton to King, 19 August 1940, King Papers, LAC. King used almost the same phrase: "finest day's work in his career," or so Skelton recorded in his memorandum, 18 August 1940, file 5-14, LAC.

10. J.L. Granatstein, "The Conservative Party and the Ogdensburg Agreement," *International Journal* 22 (Winter 1966–67): 73ff.

11. Churchill to King, 22 August 1940, Cabinet War Committee Records, LAC.

12. Skelton to King, 28 August 1940, King Papers, C282306ff, LAC; Granatstein, *Canada's War*, 131; Skelton, Memorandum for Prime Minister, 9 September 1940, King Papers, C282360ff, LAC.

13. Hillmer, Skelton Lecture.

14. See J.L. Granatstein and R. D. Cuff, "The Hyde Park Declaration 1941: Origins and Significance," *Canadian Historical Review* 55 (March 1974): 59–80.

15. J.L. Granatstein, *A Man of Influence: Norman A. Robertson and Canadian Statecraft, 1929–1968* (Ottawa: Deneau, 1981), 333.

16. Ibid., 336ff.; Christopher Hollis in *The Spectator*, 1 May 1959.

17. Heeney Diary, 4 February 1962, Arnold Heeney Papers, vol. 2, LAC.

18. The fullest account is Denis Smith, *Rogue Tory: The Life and Legend of John G. Diefenbaker* (Toronto: Macfarlane Walter & Ross, 1995), chap. XII.

19. I have written on the conflict between interests and values, most especially in *The Importance of Being Less Earnest: Promoting Canada's National Interests through Tighter Ties with the U.S.* (Toronto: C.D. Howe Institute, 2003).

20. See Robert Bothwell, *Alliance and Illusion* (Vancouver: UBC Press, 2007), 172ff., for the most recent analysis of Pearson and nuclear weapons.

THE DEPARTMENT OF EXTERNAL AFFAIRS AND THE UNITED NATIONS IDEA, 1943-1965

Adam Chapnick

In 1965, while the United Nations was celebrating its twentieth anniversary, Canada's Department of External Affairs drafted a short book, *We the Peoples: Canada and the United Nations, 1945–1965*. According to its authors, the text presented "in compact form, an accurate and balanced survey of Canada's participation in United Nations activities." It explained "something of the philosophical basis of Canadian policy, or in other words, the Canadian 'approach' to issues coming before the United Nations."[1] More realistically, the tone of the publication was faithful to the department's understood duty to reflect the sentiment of the time: Confident and optimistic, *We the Peoples* celebrated Canada's early United Nations experience.

Neither the tone nor the sentiment lasted. In 1967, Egypt brashly dismissed the United Nations Emergency Force (UNEF) in Sinai, shocking and disillusioning Canadians who saw the peacekeeping force and their participation as a symbol of their county's worldly effectiveness. The following year, Canada's new prime minister, Pierre Elliott Trudeau, promised to recalibrate Canada's approach to world affairs. As historian Robert

Bothwell has explained, to Trudeau, and others, Canadian foreign policy "had become the handmaiden of a misguided devotion to international institutions. Along the way, Canada's national interest had been lost, or at least submerged, and Canada had earned itself the reputation of an international busybody."[2] When Trudeau's secretary of state for external affairs revised *We the Peoples* ten years later, he went so far as to take explicit aim at its predecessor, noting that *his* text was "written from a more critical point of view; failures as well as successes [were] recorded, and disquietude [was] expressed as well as satisfaction."[3]

What caused Canadians to become so distressed about the United Nations? And how did their understanding of the venerable international institution become so detached from their interpretation of the national interest? While some of the answer lies in objective developments in New York and further abroad, part of it lies in the way that External Affairs and its political masters explained their conduct on the world stage during the organization's opening decades. This explanation was regularly given in annual reports, which permit historians to see how the Canadian public's understanding of Canada's place and role within the United Nations became increasingly removed from the national interest.

During the negotiations to create the United Nations and through the term of Secretary-General Trygve Lie (1945–52), the Department of External Affairs pursued a United Nations policy of advocacy without insistence: a measured approach that acknowledged the country's strengths and weaknesses and was indeed informed by the government's interpretation of the national interest. The ultimate goal during this period was to ensure the institution's long-term viability. As the United Nations adjusted to the leadership of Secretary-General Dag Hammarskjöld (1953–61), the death of Soviet dictator Joseph Stalin, and the beginnings of decolonization, the department experienced its own transition. Having established a reputation in New York for diplomatic excellence, it often found itself in the spotlight. What resulted was an approach to the organization that was at times less pragmatic but also more outwardly and politically rewarding. In the words of the former official turned commentator, John Holmes, Canada's United Nations diplomacy "was not yet self-conscious,"[4] but it was heading that way. Departmental reports during the early U Thant years (1961–65), a time largely characterized by global optimism and idealism, were more boldly positive. Although still conscious of the national interest, two successive secretaries of state for external affairs, Conservative Howard Green and Liberal Paul Martin (Sr.), reshaped the Canadian commitment to the United Nations, framing it as a self-serving means of asserting a national presence on the world stage more than a necessary strategic duty. Canadian rhetoric came to emphasize what Ottawa was doing for the world rather than what an effective United Nations meant to the national interest. In summary, then, the language of the External Affairs' reports throughout the organization's first two decades reflected an evolving Canadian attitude towards the United Nations that was consistent with the changing national and international mood of the time. Nevertheless, by developing and articulating policy that was consistent with the aims of its political masters, the Department of External Affairs was complicit in diplomatic efforts that increasingly lost sight of Canadian national interests.

Demands for Canada to commit itself to the "construction of an effective collective system" could be heard within the Department of External Affairs as early as January 1942, but the mandarins who worked in the East Block on Parliament Hill were not genuinely involved in discussions of the United Nations organization until more than eighteen months later.[5] Before that, a plebiscite to release the government from its promise not to impose conscription and a much slower evolution of public attitudes in favour of greater internationalism allowed the reluctant Canadian prime minister, William Lyon Mackenzie King, to limit any opportunities for comprehensive planning. King did not receive a serious update on the state of British and American thinking about a new world organization until the end of March 1943, and it was only in July that the prime minister, who served as his own secretary of state for external affairs, publicly declared his support for what became the United Nations.[6] Later that month, King's under-secretary of state for external affairs, Norman Robertson, finally set in motion a process that resulted in the department's first postwar planning groups, the advisory and working committees on post-hostilities problems.[7]

Over the next year and a half, the occupants of the East Block strove to determine how Canada might best contribute to the creation of a world organization that promoted the interests of the United Nations allies.[8] Ensuring that the small powers were not taken for granted – while Britain, the United States, and eventually the Soviet Union devised the basic framework of the world body – was a priority.⁹ The chair of the working committee on post-hostilities problems, Hume Wrong, explained Canadian thinking in February 1944: "as a secondary country we have not a great enough influence to make our views prevail. We should, however, be in a position at least to decide what is not acceptable and to advocate greater changes or additions to fit our particular interests."¹⁰ Those interests included multilateral cooperation to promote national security, freedom to diverge from the United States on foreign policy, and fair representation of the smaller and medium-sized powers on the most significant UN bodies.

Not much later, Wrong described a Canadian dilemma. His government, he wrote, "had two points of view to consider. We did not want to throw a monkey-wrench into the harmony among the Great Powers, but, on the other hand, we wanted to protect the Canadian position as well as that of the small countries."¹¹ It was vital to Canada's interests that the new world organization be created. Once its establishment had been confirmed, Ottawa had to do its utmost to ensure that the perspective of smaller states was considered before significant decisions affecting Canadians were made. What became known as the functional principle – the idea that non-great powers should be granted influence in world affairs on a case by case basis commensurate with their capacity and willingness to contribute – formed the basis of the department's philosophy going forward.¹²

The functional principle was based on the premise that there were two types of states in the global order: great powers, who participated in all international decisions; and everyone else, whose impact varied by issue. A corollary to this principle, albeit one that was never explicitly articulated, was that lesser states could exert more significant influence on those issues that concerned the great powers the least. Led by Wrong, the Department of External Affairs therefore focused its postwar planning exercises on those elements of the United Nations Charter that played a lesser role in the US–UK–USSR negotiations. This meant thinking seriously about the economic and social aspects of the new organization, as well as making a significant contribution to the development of international law.¹³ At the founding conference of the United Nations in San Francisco in April 1945, the department ultimately disappointed many of its smaller allies by supporting a relatively broad interpretation of the great power veto. Its middle power-like leadership came through its exemplary diplomatic behaviour during the drafting of the more innocuous articles of the United Nations Charter, which established the Economic and Social Council as well as in the discussions to create a world court.[14]

Diplomatic professionalism became the defining feature of the department's approach to the United Nations during the Trygve Lie era. Described generously by political scientist Anthony Gaglione as "turbulent years" for the organization, the period between 1945 and 1953 largely disappointed. Cold War politics dominated UN meetings and caused the great powers to lose faith in the organization as a legitimate stage for diplomatic negotiations.[15] External Affairs therefore channelled its efforts into low-key initiatives designed to ensure the long-term viability and credibility of the United Nations as a whole. As Prime Minister King had explained at San Francisco, the ultimate goal was to build a structure "which over the years and decades to come will be strong enough to stand any strains to which it may be subjected."[16]

The department sent many of its best officials to the early UN meetings.[17] They were drawn from the First Political Division – the ultimate domestic destination for talented diplomats – which was aptly renamed the United Nations Division in 1948. The group was assigned a broad mandate, including the provision of all advice on the government's United Nations policy as well as public relations and communication with the organization's secretariat. As historians John Hilliker and Don Barry have explained, Canada's permanent delegation in New York shouldered greater responsibilities than many of its international equivalents. It liaised with other states' UN offices and took the lead on virtually every foreign policy issue that related even indirectly to United Nations activities.[18]

From the beginning, Canadian diplomats were concerned with the composition of the United Nations Secretariat. At the international meetings that followed San Francisco (which focused on the technical challenges of turning a blueprint for a new world body into a functioning political structure), the Canadians emphasized, in their own words, "the necessity of securing the highest standards of efficiency, competence and integrity ... in the selection of the staff."[19] The call for competent representatives extended to individuals chosen to serve on UN committees and chairpersons selected to run their meetings. Members of the East Block also advocated a new committee on procedures and organization to maximize the efficiency of General Assembly sessions and to guarantee that, when the political and diplomatic elite did travel to New York, their time would not be wasted by faulty organization and rhetorical excess.[20]

This rather conservative approach – emphasizing the little things and staying clear of the spotlight – was in evidence at the second part of the first session of the General Assembly in 1946. When the Soviet Union introduced an unhelpful resolution on disarmament, the Canadian delegation declined to respond publicly. As the official report on the session made clear, Ottawa did not "consider it appropriate that a nation with a comparatively small population which had never had armed forces which might constitute a threat to the peace of the world should take the lead in putting forward the necessary amendments." Rather, the Canadians argued, it was the United States – the only state then capable of launching an atomic weapon – that was best positioned to lead the effort.[21]

In spite of its disappointment with the world organization during its initial sessions, the Department of External Affairs orchestrated a successful campaign to obtain a seat on the Security Council for 1948–49. Although some states viewed accession to the ineffective council as an ill-advised misuse of diplomatic resources, and others looked upon membership on the elite body merely as an opportunity to bolster international prestige, the Canadians considered service on the council to be a duty and indeed a responsibility that self-proclaimed middle powers were obligated to accept. Just as Canada contributed more than its per capita share to the United Nations' budget, it also allocated the human resources necessary to maintain the organization's viability. Moreover, while other middle-sized states seemed to aspire for greatness, Canada's diplomats remained focused on the basic practicalities that made international order possible.[22]

Ottawa's term on the Security Council began just as the Cold War increased in intensity. Even as the great power conflict brought much of the work of the United Nations to a stand-still, however, Canada's representatives remained calm. The difficulties were not grounds to dissolve the organization, they argued; rather, increasing use of the great power veto at the Security Council meant that expectations would have to be lowered, and member states would have to become more creative in their efforts to maintain peace and order. One of the most effective ways forward was to minimize grounds for great power conflict. Canadian representatives therefore spoke in favour of a rigorous and transparent budget-setting process. Their campaign to minimize duplication and promote fiscal restraint among a proliferation of United Nations agencies continued as well.[23] Members of the Canadian delegation also did not hesitate to criticize their international peers for idealistic overreach, with Secretary of State for External Affairs Lester Pearson going so far as to proclaim: "We must not dissipate the moral and other resources of a world which desperately needs peace on too many secondary objectives, however desirable they may be in themselves." In 1948, the delegation publicly identified the United Nations' Educational, Scientific, and Cultural Organization as one of the worst offenders.[24]

As Canada's term on the Security Council came to an end in 1949, members of the Department of External Affairs remained guarded in their hopes for the organization as a whole. In reflecting on the international response to a Soviet blockade of Berlin, they noted,

> The United Nations did what it could ... to provide the machinery through which an agreement could be reached if and when both parties wanted to agree. Although the importance of this function ought not be exaggerated, it should not be underestimated. At a time of crisis, negotiations such as those which took place through the non-permanent members of the Council may well serve to reduce tension and to find ways out of a dilemma which might otherwise lead to war.[25]

The department continued to lobby for greater efficiency in the conduct of United Nations meetings and remained outspoken in its criticism of speeches that were clearly intended to serve a domestic political agenda rather than to advance the global dialogue. It persisted in linking economic and social development to peace and security – lending credence to the value of the proliferation of UN agencies – but at the same time it urged the secretariat to manage the organization's budget prudently.

The department's plea for caution and moderation hardly abated as the United Nations entered its second decade. In his preface to the report on Canada's involvement with the United Nations in 1950, Pearson wrote:

> The United Nations should not be judged as if it were a court to try offenders, with a police force always ready and able to punish those found guilty. The United Nations is not an entity in itself. It is the sum total of the wills of its members and of the combined contributions which they are willing to make. It is not now able to apply overwhelming pressure at all times on all offenders, major or minor. Its members must therefore conserve their limited resources in order to be able to apply them collectively where they are most needed.[26]

Focusing on the unspectacular, setting realistic expectations, and managing efficiencies: this was the Department of External Affairs' approach to UN engagement as the 1950s began.

There is scholarly debate over the extent of Canada's loyalty to the United Nations during the Korean War, which dominated the organization's agenda toward the end of the Trygve Lie era. Although it is clear that Canadian policy-makers disagreed over whether their country should support the United Nations at the expense of Western solidarity, most analysts have concluded that Canada remained a moderate actor throughout the conflict, perpetually concerned with the long-term viability of the United Nations as a global institution.[27] The East Block continued to measure the United Nations' successes and failures realistically and recognized the limited impact of the General Assembly on any particular crisis.[28] Nonetheless, argued Pearson, in spite of this lack of influence, Canada could not forsake its international commitments. "The basic principles of our national life," he argued in the report for 1951–52, "our need for unity and security, our belief in political liberty, the protection of our heritage of Christian civilization – affect every aspect of our external affairs. Canadian policies – though they should be national policies – will always be influenced by international factors."[29] Such thinking did not imply that Canada would be everywhere every time; Ottawa's acceptance of global responsibilities remained contingent on the state of its and its allies' resources and a strategic assessment of where Canada could maximize its impact.

The measured, conservative approach of Canada's Department of External Affairs was similarly evident in United Nations discussions of North-South issues. As countries in the rapidly decolonizing developing world demanded greater freedoms, if not outright independence, the Canadian response favoured deliberate evolution over radical, and potentially violent, change. Moreover, in spite of the broad political failures of the United Nations as a whole, and of the international campaign for disarmament more specifically, it was incumbent upon member states to remain diligent and committed to promoting peaceful means of conflict resolution. This was not to say that alternatives to the United Nations could not and should not be explored – the department noted repeatedly that its membership in NATO in no way contradicted its commitment to the UN – but that abandoning the world organization was not consistent with Canadian interests.[30]

The end of Lie's term as secretary-general in November 1952 coincided almost exactly with Lester Pearson's accession to the presidency of the United Nations General Assembly. (Pearson was elected less than a month before.) Both occurrences were critical to the Department of External Affairs' subsequent United Nations experience. Lie's successor, Dag Hammarskjöld, was a pragmatist, but he was also an activist, determined to use his position as secretary-general to rehabilitate the reputation of the world organization and increase both its influence and its effectiveness.[31] Joseph Stalin's death in March 1953 and the subsequent thaw in Cold War tensions empowered the secretary-general to act more boldly than his predecessor could have ever thought possible. Over the next eight years, the United Nations played a more aggressive role on the world stage, one that included Canada to a greater extent than historical precedent might have supported.

The increase in Canadian activism began symbolically with Pearson's election. The foreign minister, already popular with the international media and within diplomatic circles, emerged as a recognized UN leader, and Canadians grew proud of his significance in New York. The combination of global acclaim and domestic enthusiasm for Canadian internationalism gradually shifted the focus of the Department of External Affairs. Over time, the United Nations became less of an organization to be nourished, and more of a platform to celebrate and perpetuate Canadian international achievements.

At first, changes in the behaviour in New York were hardly noticeable. Members of External Affairs continued to focus on the importance of sound economic management: the reach of the organization as a whole was not to exceed its grasp.[32] The 1953 department's general report recalled the significance of the great powers to UN affairs, noting that their disagreements limited the ability of the smaller states to advance their own initiatives.[33] Nonetheless, there were signs of political adjustments. The report on Canada and the United Nations from 1953 to 1954 expressed hope that the organization would become "the principal forum for the *settlement* of contentious international issues."[34] Such an ambitious statement was a departure from previous depictions of the United Nations as "a meeting place of rival political and economic philosophies,"[35] one that had "not yet achieved sufficient strength to resolve the major political problems of the contemporary world," nor had "yet been able to provide to its Members the degree of security which would enable them to put it to full use for the peaceful settlement of international disputes."[36]

In 1954, Canada accepted a seat on an exclusive subcommittee of the UN's disarmament commission, a position which placed it on a relatively equal level with four of the five great powers. (Only China was excluded.) Again, recalling the prior unwillingness of Canadian delegates to assume a public leadership role on this issue, one might infer at least a modification of Canadian policy. The decision to co-sponsor a resolution praising the establishment of an International Atomic Energy Agency in 1955 is consistent with such a conclusion.[37] Perhaps in part reflective of an improved international mood – made possible by an increasingly moderate and conciliatory Soviet Union – there was also a new optimism in the tone of the official departmental reports. Writing in early 1956, Pearson remarked,

> There is now, it seems to me, a much greater comprehension of how closely the nations of the world are bound together, and the more fortunate peoples of the earth have assumed increasing responsibility for the progress of less technically advanced countries. All this, and more, constitutes a considerable body of achievement. If we have the wisdom and courage to avoid the ultimate catastrophe of war, the United Nations can grow and develop as an effective and well-equipped organization for man's progress toward an incomparably better life.[38]

Pearson's idealism built on his colleague Paul Martin's success in facilitating the admission of sixteen new members to the United Nations General Assembly in 1955. Martin, the federal cabinet minister who had been asked to lead the Canadian delegation while the secretary of state for external affairs was away in Moscow, lobbied tirelessly to secure an agreement among the great powers who had previously vetoed the application of any state whom they viewed as an opponent in the Cold War.[39]

Whether Martin's efforts should be considered an achievement in line with Canadian interests is debatable. Certainly, the Department of External Affairs thought so. In the words of its 1954–55 UN report: "The United Nations could have been formed with a membership 'exclusive to those who see alike on most things,' but Canada never had any doubt as to the infinitely greater value of an organization embodying all the major traditions and contemporary philosophies of government."[40] The official history of External Affairs is similarly positive, noting the impact of Martin's initiative on Canada's international reputation.[41]

Political scientist Tom Keating's analysis, however, is more measured. Although Martin's achievement demonstrated Canada's ability to negotiate multilaterally, expanding the United Nations membership changed the organization fundamentally, and not necessarily in a way that benefited Canadian national interests. Certainly, the United Nations better reflected the contemporary geopolitical environment but, in doing so, it became less of a servant of the West in the Cold War.[42] John Holmes, who spent close to a decade as the department's primary conduit on United Nations affairs, concurs, adding that because Minister Martin forced the United States to compromise on the world stage, the influence of Canada's greatest ally over the rest of the world body declined.[43]

Regrettably, none of these analyses link the department's United Nations experience in 1955 to Canadian conduct during the Suez crisis the following year. In 1956, Lester Pearson played a leading role in brokering a compromise between the warring factions of Britain, France, and Israel on one side and Egypt on the other. The result was the imposition of what is known today as the first modern United Nations peacekeeping force. For his efforts, Pearson received the Nobel Peace Prize in 1957. His success, following so closely after Martin's, signified to many what one analyst called "a kind of break-through to new levels of responsibility for Canada in the world." To the respected commentator Maxwell Cohen, Ottawa had assumed the obligations of a great power, setting a precedent that could lead to significant changes in Canada's international role and responsibilities.[44]

The Department of External Affairs was initially less optimistic than the general public. Pearson's achievement had been a source of significant national division at home (the Conservatives had accused him of selling out the British), and it coincided with the UN's failure to respond to a brutal Soviet invasion of Hungary.[45] On the peacekeeping force itself, the department wrote cautiously: "we have been able to introduce a new element into the conduct of international relations which may be important if – and it is well to emphasize the 'if' – it works effectively on this occasion."[46]

Indeed, the theme of the United Nations report for 1956–57 was the familiar one of restraint. "The fact to remember," wrote the foreign minister, Pearson, "is that the United Nations is none other than the nations of this earth with all their weaknesses and conflicts. It is not some heavenly body beyond our world's problems. It cannot accommodate what we its members are unprepared to do."[47] He went on to accentuate the limits of the organization and praised Canadians for their consistently moderate expectations of the United Nations as a global actor. Rather than advocating complete nuclear disarmament, the report suggested a more realistic short-term goal of limiting any further arms build-up. It cautioned against devising international development strategies based on any perceived moral necessity while encouraging greater focus on the possibility of success. It noted the potential benefits of the creation of an international civil service, but then conceded the perhaps insurmountable challenge of convincing United Nations member states to contribute their most effective diplomats to a cause that obligated them to put global interests ahead of national concerns. On the development of a covenant on economic, social, and cultural rights, the department sided with a minority in opposing the explicit enumeration of the steps necessary to make global commitments. "By their nature they were not rights which could be guaranteed unequivocally by legislation," Ottawa explained, "and might more appropriately be considered as objectives to which governments and peoples should strive, by legislative or other means, as appropriate to the conditions and systems of individual countries."[48]

In summary, the final report on the United Nations published under the leadership of Prime Minister Louis St. Laurent and Secretary of State for External Affairs Pearson downplayed recent national accomplishments and lowered expectations of what Canada might achieve in the future. That the new Conservative prime minister, John Diefenbaker, allowed it to be published after winning the 1957 election, however, did not mean that his government planned to follow its implicit advice. Diefenbaker's early public statements as prime minister and acting secretary of state for external affairs suggest that he was much more enamoured with Maxwell Cohen's thinking than with the message that his department was sending him. At the meeting of the General Assembly in September 1957, Diefenbaker announced to the world that, "so far as Canada is concerned, support of the United Nations is the cornerstone of its foreign policy."[49]

Departmental publications under Diefenbaker's first secretary of state for external affairs, the sincere, yet inexperienced Sidney Smith, reflect the conflict between the two approaches. The 1957 report was measured, yet optimistic. Smith conceded that the United Nations had often struggled because of the great powers' inability to compromise, noting that accepting its limitations was "merely to face the facts of international life." But he also called the organization "a unique and indispensable instrument of international diplomacy which has achieved important results in all of the various spheres of activity for which it was created." The latter statement was an exaggeration that even the rest of the report itself could not sustain. The department in fact admitted that there were significant limits to what the organization had achieved in the security realm, emphasizing instead the importance of the UN's social and economic accomplishments.[50]

Smith passed away before the 1958 report had been completed, and its relatively modest assessment of the United Nations and Canada's contribution to its conduct that year is consistent with a department whose leadership was in flux.[51] The 1959 version was similarly restrained, prompting one analyst to observe that under the foreign policy novice, Howard Green, Canada appeared to have withdrawn from the international spotlight.[52]

There were signs, however, that the pressures – domestic and international – that were pushing a more idealistic approach to the fore were becoming greater. In September 1959, the department published an unusually comprehensive and retrospective summary of Canada's UN contribution in its magazine, *External Affairs*. "Canada and the United Nations: The Record after Fourteen Years" was the first comprehensive (official) analysis of the history of Canadian participation in the organization and marked a departure in the overall approach to reporting the East Block's activities. The tone was different from the yearly summaries. Whereas the annual publications had concentrated on the progress of the institution as a whole, this article put Ottawa front and centre, emphasizing Canada's impact on United Nations policies and practices. On the first page, the department boasted of "the frequency with which Canada and Canadians have appeared in the record of the United Nations." The essay also concluded with an optimism that was hardly consistent with the more guarded general tenor of the previous thirteen years: "the accomplishments of the United Nations during its lifetime are indeed impressive, and the successes far outweigh the failures, not only in the more serious and spectacular crises, but also in the lesser disagreements which have been settled before they could develop into something serious."[53]

The accounts of the following year confirmed that Green's era would be different. The decision to focus on Canada was proclaimed immediately: "The Annual Report of 1960 differs from previous Annual Reports. Instead of methodically recounting events in various countries and organizations during the year, it concentrates on a few main themes in which Canada has a special interest or concern and expands the Canadian Government's position on them." The document captured the zeal and passion of its minister as well as Green's personal opposition to nuclear proliferation. It emphasized Ottawa's efforts to pass a resolution at the Disarmament Commission, which admittedly had little real impact, as well as its commitment to working with like-minded countries, a statement that constituted a rejection of the unspoken tradition of ensuring that Canada's great power allies were on side for any major United Nations initiative.[54] More cynically, the report reflected what analyst Peyton Lyon later described as a Conservative obsession with Canadian prestige that was measured by the popularity of the delegation in New York.[55]

The shift in focus coincided with the UN's greatest crisis to date. At a time when Soviet intransigence, under the now firmly in power Nikita Khrushchev, was once again threatening the future of the organization, and members of the developing world were plotting to reshape the political and economic agenda, Secretary-General Hammarskjöld was killed in a plane crash. The choice of his replacement, the former Burmese diplomat, U Thant, was telling. Decolonization and its implications soon dominated the United Nations dialogue.[56] Ironically, the emphasis on the global south enabled a more rigorous pursuit of the Conservatives' agenda. As advocates of the functional principle might have predicted, once the United Nations began to tackle challenges that were of less direct concern to the great powers, Ottawa could make its public presence felt more easily.

In the departmental report on Canada and the United Nations for 1961, Green and his officials took credit for improving the atmosphere in New York in the wake of Hammarskjöld's tragic death. Canada, the account maintained, urged the organization to strive for consensus on the most pressing international issues, such as global disarmament and the impact of science and technology on national and international outer space strategies.[57] The following year, in spite of the nearly catastrophic Cuban Missile Crisis, the Department of External Affairs proclaimed that the United Nations "found itself in a position of enhanced prestige and authority increasing the confidence of members states about the future of the organization."[58] Having now fully abandoned the conservative perspective of the past, the report celebrated the organization's "remarkable resilience" and expressed hope over the future of the recently revived disarmament negotiations. Even though U Thant was precluded from playing his prescribed role in Cuba, his general assistance enhanced the UN's prestige. The specialized agencies continued to demonstrate their critical contributions to international economic and social development. And the organization in New York remained the only quasi-universal body designed to promote and support improved global understanding.[59]

The defeat of the Diefenbaker government had no impact on the increase in the announcements of Canadian leadership in New York. Rather, the period of détente (and increasing Western influence in the developing world) which followed the Cuban Missile Crisis seemed to inspire even greater internationalist optimism throughout Ottawa. When Paul Martin took over as secretary of state for external affairs under Prime Minister Lester Pearson, the Department of External Affairs became more aggressive. At the meeting of the General Assembly in September 1963, Pearson called for an expansion of both the Security Council and the Economic and Social Council as well as a new team of military experts to advise the United Nations Secretary-General on the future of peacekeeping.[60] These dramatic pronouncements betrayed the caution of the 1940s and 1950s as well as the idea that major constitutional changes should be great power initiatives.

Martin's summary of the Canadian experience at the United Nations predictably echoed Pearson's confidence in Canada's diplomatic abilities. More interesting, however, was the conflicted nature of the report as it related to the progress of the UN as an organization. The first pages presented an overly optimistic view of the state of United Nations affairs. Martin celebrated the hope, calmness, and moderation that seemed to typify the post-Cuban strategic environment and praised the work of the specialized bodies in promoting economic and social stability. Later on, however, the tone became sombre. Rejecting Pearson's call for dramatic structural changes, Martin argued that real progress was most likely to result from "a painstaking process of accommodation." The key, he alleged, was for the United Nations to "keep its house in order and all its instruments – of conciliation, co-operation and collective response – ready for instant service in the cause of peace and understanding."[61]

The next year, the general departmental report used pragmatic language but stressed idealistic thinking. "In a constantly contracting world," wrote Martin, "the national interest can be defined only in part by reference to what preoccupies us within our national boundaries. In many respects, the national interest can best be advanced by cooperative international action designed to further the interests of the world community at large." Later on, he added, "We are concerned that the United Nations should continue to have an effective capacity to keep the peace because this is something in which we believe." Peacekeeping, he wrote, "is one of the practical ways in which a middle power like Canada can meet its responsibilities as a member of the world community."[62]

These comments mark a shift in Ottawa's conception of the United Nations as an organization. With Canadians feeling more secure about their place in the world, and their government intent on transforming its minority position into a majority, the United Nations became valued for its role in promoting the ideals of peace and disarmament, not because it advanced Canada's national interest in order and stability. Ottawa became an ambitious coalition builder as opposed to a secondary actor whose greatest role played out behind the scenes. In 1957, in recalling the creation of the United Nations Emergency Force that established a temporary peace in Suez, the department had written, "The United Nations has been able to establish an Emergency Police Force in the Middle East."[63] In 1965, it celebrated Canadian leadership "not only in establishing UNEF but in securing a basis for its financing which reflected the belief that the peacekeeping endeavours of the United Nations were in every sense the collective responsibility of its members."[64] It was this optimism that explains the language and tone of *We the Peoples*, an internationalist spirit that did not survive the 'Canada First' mentality of the early Trudeau era.

In conclusion, the change in tone within the UN reports of the Department of External Affairs between 1943 and 1965 reflects the ministry's loyalty to its political masters and the circumstances of the time. Regrettably, the department's effectiveness enabled Canadian leaders to gradually set aside the national interest in favour of more parochial concerns. And although the drift was eventually arrested, elements of the misguided optimism remain in much of the historical literature.[65] More realistically, as two analysts reflected as early as 1956, "membership in the United Nations, insofar as it means an increase in responsibilities without an appreciable advance in influence, exacts a price that is far from negligible in return for its contribution to the creation of the kind of world that Canada's national interests demand."[66] Functionalism was critical: Canada's Department of External Affairs could indeed play a significant role at the United Nations, but only on particular issues based on its capabilities and the relative interest of the great powers.

NOTES

1. Canada, Department of External Affairs (DEA), *We the Peoples: Canada and the United Nations, 1945–1965* (Ottawa: Queen's Printer, 1966), 3.
2. Robert Bothwell, *Alliance and Illusion: Canada and the World, 1945–1984* (Vancouver: UBC Press, 2007), 278.
3. Canada, DEA, *Canada and the United Nations, 1945–1975* (Ottawa: Minster of Supply and Services Canada, 1977), xiv.
4. John W. Holmes, *The Shaping of Peace: Canada and the Search for World Order, 1943–1957*, vol. 2 (Toronto: University of Toronto Press, 1982), 41.
5. Escott Reid, "The United States and Canada: Domination, Co-operation, Absorption," 12 January 1942, Escott Reid Papers, vol. 30, United States and Canada 1945, Library and Archives Canada (LAC).
6. William Lyon Mackenzie King, 9 July 1943, in Canada, House of Commons, *Debates*, 4558. See also Minutes of the Cabinet War Committee, 31 March 1943, Privy Council Office Papers, vol. 12, Minutes of Cabinet War Committee, 6 January – 14 May 1943, LAC.
7. The best summary of this work can be found in Don Munton and Don Page, "Planning in the East Block: The Post-Hostilities Problems Committees in Canada, 1943–5," *International Journal* 32, no. 4 (1977): 677–726.
8. On the British connection, see Tuthill, Memorandum of Conversation with Saul Rae, 14 October 1943, Records of the Foreign Service Posts of the Department of State, Box 95, Canada, Ottawa Embassy, Security, Segregated General Records 1939–1949, 1943, 710, Relations with Great Britain, National Archives and Records Administration.
9. Adam Chapnick, *The Middle Power Project: Canada and the Founding of the United Nations* (Vancouver: UBC Press, 2005), 65–125.
10. Hume Wrong, memorandum, 23 February 1944, in John F. Hillker, ed., *Documents on Canadian External Relations*, vol. 11: *1944–1945*, part 2 (Ottawa: Minister of Supply and Services Canada, 1990), 1.
11. Minutes of the Twenty-Ninth Meeting of the Working Committee on Post-Hostilities Problems, 25 August 1944, Department of External Affairs Records (DEAR), vol. 5711, file 7-AD(s), pt. 2, LAC.
12. Chapnick, *The Middle Power Project*, 36.
13. Wrong to Heeney, 17 January 1945 and again 18 January 1945, both in DEAR, vol. 5709, file 7-V(s) pt. 5.1, LAC.
14. "San Francisco," *Canadian Forum* 25 (July 1945), 81. See also Cox to Stettinius, 9 May 1945, Oscar Cox Papers, box 151, Diary: March–April–May 1945, Franklin Delano Roosevelt Library.
15. Anthony Gaglione, *The United Nations under Trygve Lie, 1945–1953* (Lanham, MD: Scarecrow Press, 2001), ix.
16. King, 27 April 1945, quoted in Canada, DEA, *Report of the United Nations Conference on International Organization Held at San Francisco, 25th April – 26th June 1945* (Ottawa: King's Printer, 1945), 11.
17. According to a 1949 report, a typical Canadian delegation to the UN General Assembly was comprised of approximately five representatives, five alternates, ten advisors, two information officers, and a number of additional administrative staff. Unless otherwise occupied, the secretary of state for external affairs chaired the delegation. The representatives included politicians drawn from across party lines, along with senior members of the Department of External Affairs. Most of the rest of the delegation came from the East Block. See Canada, DEA, *Canada and the United Nations, 1949* (Ottawa: King's Printer, 1950), 14.

18. John Hilliker and Donald Barry, *Canada's Department of External Affairs*, vol. 2, *Coming of Age, 1946–1968* (Montreal: McGill-Queen's University Press, 1995), 33.

19. Canada, DEA, *Report of the First Part of the First Session of the General Assembly of the United Nations* (Ottawa: King's Printer, 1946), 28.

20. Canada, DEA, *The United Nations, 1946: Report of the Second Part of the First Session of the General Assembly of the United Nations* (Ottawa: King's Printer, 1947), 157, 160.

21. Ibid., 37.

22. Canada, DEA, *Canada and the United Nations, 1947* (Ottawa: King's Printer, 1948), 17, 137. See also Canada, DEA, *Report of the Secretary of State for External Affairs for the Year Ended December 31, 1947* (Ottawa: King's Printer, 1948), 13.

23. Canada, DEA, *Canada and the United Nations, 1948* (Ottawa: King's Printer, 1949), 23.

24. Ibid., 200, 142.

25. Canada, DEA, *Canada and the United Nations, 1949* (Ottawa: King's Printer, 1950), 39, 85, 173–75. For a brief summary of Canada and the Berlin Blockade, see Bothwell, *Alliance and Illusion*, 67–68.

26. Canada, DEA, *Canada and the United Nations, 1950* (Ottawa: King's Printer, 1951), viii, 56, 79, 143.

27. Those who emphasize the UN commitment include Denis Stairs, "The Diplomacy of Constraint," in *Partners Nevertheless: Canadian–American Relations in the Twentieth Century*, ed. Norman Hillmer (Toronto: Copp Clark, 1989), 214–26; Timothy Andrews Sayle, "A Pattern of Constraint: Canadian–American Relations in the Early Cold War," *International Journal* 62, no. 3 (2007): 689–705; and Greg Donaghy, "Pacific Diplomacy: Canadian Statecraft and the Korean War, 1950–53," in *Canada and Korea: Perspectives 2000*, ed. R.W.L. Guisso and Young-sik Yoo (Toronto: Centre for Korean Studies, University of Toronto, 2002), 81–100. Those who are less convinced include John Price, "The 'Cat's Paw': Canada and the United Nations Temporary Commission on Korea," *Canadian Historical Review* 85, no. 2 (June 2004): 297–324; and Robert Prince, "The Limits of Constraint," *Journal of Canadian Studies* 27, no. 4 (1992–93): 129–52.

28. Canada, DEA, *Report of the Department of External Affairs, 1951* (Ottawa: Queen's Printer, 1952), iii.

29. Canada, DEA, *Canada and the United Nations, 1951–52* (Ottawa: Queen's Printer, 1952), vi, viii.

30. Ibid., viii, x, 15, 18. See also Greg Donaghy, "Coming off the Gold Standard: Re-assessing the Golden Age of Canadian Diplomacy," http://www.suezcrisis.ca/pdfs/Coming%20off%20the%20Gold%20Standard.pdf [cited 20 May 2009], 5–6.

31. On Hammarskjöld see, among others, Peter B. Heller, *The United Nations under Dag Hammarskjöld, 1953–1961* (Lanham, MD: Scarecrow Press, 2001).

32. Canada, DEA, *Canada and the United Nations, 1952–53* (Ottawa: Queen's Printer, 1953), 101, 45.

33. Canada, DEA, *Report of the Department of External Affairs, 1953* (Ottawa: Queen's Printer, 1954), 1.

34. Emphasis added. Canada, DEA, *Canada and the United Nations, 1953–54* (Ottawa: Queen's Printer, 1954), 2.

35. Canada, DEA, *Canada and the United Nations, 1949*, 23.

36. Canada, DEA, *Canada and the United Nations, 1948*, 23.

37. Canada, DEA, *Report of the Department of External Affairs, 1955* (Ottawa: Queen's Printer, 1956), 8.

38. Canada, DEA, *Canada and the United Nations, 1954–55* (Ottawa: Queen's Printer, 1956), iv.

39. On Martin's experience, see Greg Donaghy and Don Barry, "Our Man from Windsor: Paul Martin and the New Members Question, 1955," in *Paul Martin and Canadian Diplomacy*, ed. Ryan Touhey (Waterloo: Centre for Foreign Policy and Federalism, 2001), 3–20.

40 Canada, DEA, *Canada and the United Nations, 1954–55*, 30.

41 John Hilliker and Donald Barry, *Canada's Department of External Affairs*, vol. 2, *Coming of Age, 1946–1968* (Montreal: McGill-Queen's University Press, 1995), 122.

42 Tom Keating, *Canada and World Order: The Multilateralist Tradition in Canadian Foreign Policy*, 2nd ed. (Don Mills, ON: Oxford University Press, 2002), 103.

43 Holmes, *The Shaping of Peace*, vol. 2, 346.

44 Maxwell Cohen, "A New Responsibility in Foreign Policy," *Saturday Night*, 19 January 1957, 5, 28.

45 See Pearson's cautious summary in which he noted "some practical disadvantages to be faced in swelling numbers," in Canada, DEA, *Canada and the United Nations, 1956–57* (Ottawa: Queen's Printer, 1957), 1.

46 Canada, DEA, *Report of the Department of External Affairs, 1956* (Ottawa: Queen's Printer, 1957), iv.

47 Canada, DEA, *Canada and the United Nations, 1956–57*, iii.

48 Canada, DEA, *Canada and the United Nations, 1956–57*, 67. See also 3, 52, 62.

49 John Diefenbaker, 23 September 1957, quoted in Canada, DEA, *Report of the Department of External Affairs, 1957* (Ottawa: Queen's Printer, 1958), 2.

50 Canada, DEA, *Canada and the United Nations, 1957* (Ottawa: Queen's Printer, 1958), iii, 4.

51 Canada, DEA, *Canada and the United Nations, 1958* (Ottawa: Queen's Printer, 1959).

52 Richard A. Preston, *Canada in World Affairs, 1959–1961* (Toronto: Oxford University Press, 1965), 253. See also Canada, DEA, *Canada and the United Nations, 1959* (Ottawa: Queen's Printer, 1960).

53 "Canada and the United Nations: The Record after Fourteen Years," *External Affairs* 11, no. 9 (1959): 253, 260.

54 Canada, DEA, *Report of the Department of External Affairs, 1960* (Ottawa: Queen's Printer, 1961), v, 11, 14.

55 Peyton V. Lyon, *Canada in World Affairs, 1961–1963* (Toronto: Oxford University Press, 1968), 280.

56 On the emergence of U Thant, see Bernard J. Firestone, *The United Nations under U Thant* (Lanham, MD: Scarecrow Press, 2001), vii–xxiv.

57 Canada, DEA, *Canada and the United Nations, 1961* (Ottawa: Queen's Printer, 1962), 4, 12, 14.

58 Canada, DEA, *Canada and the United Nations, 1962* (Ottawa: Queen's Printer, 1963), 9. It is worth noting that the exact same words were used in Canada, DEA, *Report of the Department of External Affairs, 1962* (Ottawa: Queen's Printer, 1963), 10.

59 Canada, DEA, *Canada and the United Nations, 1962*, 1. See also 3–9. Canada even claimed responsibility for the establishment of the World Food Programme, see 46.

60 Canada, DEA, *Report of the Department of External Affairs, 1963* (Ottawa: Queen's Printer, 1964), 11.

61 Canada, DEA, *Canada and the United Nations, 1963* (Ottawa: Queen's Printer, 1964), 8–9. See also 1–6.

62 Canada, DEA, *Report of the Department of External Affairs, 1964* (Ottawa: Queen's Printer, 1965), v, vi, vii.

63 Canada, DEA, *Report of the Department of External Affairs, 1956*, iv.

64 Canada, DEA, *Canada and the United Nations, 1964* (Ottawa: Queen's Printer, 1965), 21.

65 Adam Chapnick, "Popular Attitudes towards the United Nations in Canada and the United States: A Study in National Images," *Association for Canadian Studies in the United States Occasional Papers on Public Policy Series* 2, no. 1 (2008).

66 F.H. Soward and Edgar McInnis, *Canada and the United Nations* (New York: Manhattan Publishing, 1956), 219.

SOVEREIGNTY AND SECURITY: CANADIAN DIPLOMACY, THE UNITED STATES, AND THE ARCTIC, 1943-1968

P. Whitney Lackenbauer
and Peter Kikkert

By the spring of 1946 the spectre of a Soviet threat to North America loomed large in the minds of American officials, who warily cast their eyes over polar projection maps and saw an undefended attic to the continent. Ambitious defence plans for the Arctic began to flow onto the desks of Canadian officials, evoking grave concerns in the Department of External Affairs about Canada's sovereignty in the region. Lester B. Pearson, then ambassador to the United States, believed that these defence projects offered Canada an opportunity "to secure from the United States Government public recognition of our sovereignty of the total area of our northern coasts, based on the sector principle."[1] Canada's longstanding but officially unstated sector claim to all of the lands (and eventually waters) between 60° and 141° west longitude up to the North Pole offered the simplest solution to consolidating its opaque Arctic claims.[2] Although Pearson was confident that he could attain from his American counterparts formal recognition on this basis, he was overly optimistic.

Unwilling to push the United States into a position where they had to disagree with Canada's claims, Hume Wrong, the acting under-secretary of state for external affairs, advised Pearson to avoid any formal attempt to secure American recognition. Not only would its Antarctic interests keep the United States from accepting the sector theory, Wrong astutely noted, but any such attempt might prompt Washington to challenge Canada's claims.[3] "For a good many years now we have proceeded without difficulty on the assumption that our sovereignty was not challenged," Wrong observed. "A declaration of this sort would revive discussion of an issue which may in practice turn out to have been closed."[4] While Pearson had been willing to lay all of Canada's cards on the table in the hopes of attaining the optimum desired outcome, Wrong embraced a modest diplomacy that sought to shape a more sustainable, if less dramatic, solution to Canada's sovereignty worries.

The historical literature is divided along similar lines. One recent commentator has asserted that Canada should have embraced Pearson's approach in the postwar years and pressed for formal United States recognition of Canadian sovereignty in return for Canada's cooperation in the northern defence projects.[5] Historian Shelagh Grant has suggested that Canada actually sacrificed its sovereignty to ensure American security.[6] Such conclusions distort the context of decision-making and the nature of bilateral negotiations regarding the Arctic. Scholars David Bercuson and Elizabeth Elliot-Meisel have emphasized the cooperation, respect, and open dialogue that characterized the defence relationship after 1946 and argue that Ottawa successfully safeguarded Canada's sovereignty and effectively contributed to continental security.[7] This paper concurs with their assessment based upon a fresh appraisal of the archival record, much of it recently declassified.

Canadian policy-makers, particularly in the Department of External Affairs, did an admirable job of balancing Canadian sovereignty interests with the security needs of the United States from the early Cold War to the eve of the *Manhattan* voyage in 1969. Although Canada did not get its way on every issue, an underlying spirit of mutual respect allowed Canada to preserve – and indeed strengthen – its sovereignty while accommodating its American ally insofar as its national interests allowed. This approach secured United States acquiescence to Canadian territorial sovereignty claims, despite America's rejection of the sector principle. When the emphasis shifted to maritime issues in the 1950s, the legal issues proved more intractable, but a functional approach, predicated on "agreeing to disagree" over the status of the waters of the Arctic archipelago, maintained a cooperative bilateral relationship. Rather than seeing Canadian decision-making in the 1940s and 1950s as failing to secure American acquiescence to Canada's future claim to the Northwest Passage, a more positive appraisal might recognize how careful diplomacy helped to position Canada so that it could implement a functional approach under Prime Minister Pierre Trudeau in the early 1970s and declare straight baselines under Prime Minister Brian Mulroney in 1985. While postwar diplomatic actions appear *ad hoc*, reactionary, and tentative, they were appropriately suited to a complex situation. Officials at External Affairs acknowledged Canada's limitations but managed in steering a prudent and practical course to lay the groundwork for future assertions of Canadian jurisdiction and sovereignty in the Arctic.

The modern Canadian sovereignty debate began during the Second World War. After the Japanese attack on Pearl Harbor on 7 December 1941, the Canadian Northwest became an important strategic link to Alaska. The United States undertook a number of massive defence projects in northern Canada, including a system of airfields called the Northwest Staging Route, an oil pipeline, and the Alaska Highway. As Washington's stake in the northwest steadily grew, the Canadian government, including the Department of External Affairs, remained as uninterested in protecting the sovereignty of the region as it had been prior to the war.

Although Liberal Prime Minister William Lyon Mackenzie King allowed the Americans onto Canadian soil with few constraints, he was always suspicious of their intentions. Worrisome reports from Malcolm MacDonald, the British high commissioner who visited the defence projects in 1943 and was alarmed at the scale of American activities, spurred the prime minister to reassert control in the Canadian North.[8] To ensure greater control over American activities and protect Canadian sovereignty, the government appointed a special commissioner, Brigadier-General W.W. Foster, to oversee the various American defence projects in the Northwest.[9] As the war drew to a close, Canada increased its control over the North by securing full ownership of all permanent facilities on its territory by purchasing them from the United States. The Americans also agreed that, before they began any project on or over Canadian territory, it had to be approved by the Canadian government.[10] By 1945 most Americans had left Canadian territory and the Northwest was more secure than ever.

While it is easy to condemn the government for its reactive approach to protecting Canadian sovereignty in the North during the war, it is also understandable. In the midst of a global war and suffering from a lack of experienced personnel, External Affairs had to prioritize its areas of focus. In the early years of the war, with the European theatre the overriding national preoccupation, officials did not look to the Canadian North for obvious reasons. Neither did the department plan for the difficult sovereignty issues that arose during the war, which compelled it to deal with these problems in a reactive manner. As the war progressed, however, External Affairs grew in size and sophistication and began to handle complex problems effectively, including the situation in the North.[11] The steep wartime learning curve paid off, and the defence negotiations of the early Cold War proved that Canadian diplomats were both attentive and responsive to potential sovereignty encroachments.

Shortly after the defeat of the Axis powers, the wartime relationship between the Western allies and the Soviet Union began to dissolve. Canada's undesirable strategic position, sandwiched between two opposing superpowers, meant that "Canada could not stay out of a third World War if 11,999,999 of her 12,000,000 citizens wanted to remain neutral," to quote Louis St. Laurent's memorable phrase.[12] Canada had become the potential frontline of the next global conflict. "The dilemma," military historian David Bercuson has argued, was simple: "how could Canada help protect the continent against the Soviet Union – a job Ottawa agreed needed doing – while, at the same time, it protected the Canadian north against the United States?"[13]

In early May 1946, the United States proposed the establishment of a chain of weather stations in the Canadian Arctic. Despite American assurances that Canada's sovereignty would not be threatened, Canadian officials believed that American acceptance of the sector principle was the ideal way to protect Canada's interests.[14] Global interests, however, made it impossible for the Americans to formally accept Canadian sovereignty in the region by sanctioning the sector principle, which was also used by the Soviet Union to claim a large section of the Arctic and by several nations to claim vast portions of the Antarctic.[15] Accepting Canada's claims would have strengthened the positions of these nations to the detriment of Washington's strategic interests.[16] Had Canada insisted on a formal recognition of its sovereignty, its position would have been dramatically weakened by the inevitable American rejection.

Officials in the Department of External Affairs advised against asking Washington for a formal assurance that Canada's sovereignty would not be threatened lest this indicate "that we entertain some doubts as to our claims in the Arctic."[17] Instead, they set to work creating guidelines for the weather station program that would best enforce Canada's claims to the Arctic. Acknowledging American assurances that Canadian sovereignty would not be threatened, the department suggested that the venture be approved as a joint project so long as all permanent rights to any installations were retained by Canada, the majority of personnel would be Canadian, and the projects would be under Canadian command.[18] This approach was consistent with the steps taken during the final years of the war to gain control of the defence projects in the Northwest. Using these proven methods, Canadian officials hoped to consolidate their country's sovereignty in the Arctic.

Although the same guidelines were laid out in a report by Chief of the General Staff Major General D.C. Spry and accepted by the Cabinet Defence Committee, King decided to deny the American request for 1946. Acknowledging the American tendency to act swiftly and with little concern for Canada's needs when threatened, the prime minister hoped the United States would pause to evaluate Canada's difficult position. On 2 July, Ottawa informed Washington that the program had not been rejected – only deferred for the purposes of further study.[19] This prime ministerial-directed policy of delaying decisions on continental defence, slowing the whole process until the complex situation could be sorted out beneficially for Canada, was a cautious but prudent one. Bold, aggressive moves (particularly ones that would have entailed significant Canadian defence expenditures) would have been out of step with the cooperative defence relationship then taking shape.[20]

In early 1947, after careful negotiations, the two countries accepted a set of formal guidelines regulating continental defence, effectively assuring Ottawa that the United States had no desire to violate Canadian sovereignty claims in the North.[21] In mid-February, the prime minister announced the general principles governing Canada–United States defence cooperation in the House of Commons. "As an underlying principle," King explained, "all cooperative arrangements will be without impairment of the control of either country over all activities in its territory."[22] There was no mention of the sector principle; the wording of the agreement avoided such controversial language. This omission, however, did not concern the Canadians. Canada had explicit assurance that its terrestrial sovereignty in the Arctic would not be threatened.

Despite gaining solid assurances protecting Canadian sovereignty over the Arctic, External Affairs maintained a level of persistent concern about American activities in the region. The government carefully monitored all American activities in the region to ensure that nothing was done that could be perceived as a lack of Canadian control. When American aircraft attached to Operation Polaris, a project originally established to study the challenges related to Arctic flying, began carrying out regular reconnaissance flights and engaging in aerial photography in the Arctic in 1947, the Canadian member of the Permanent Joint Board on Defence (PJBD) argued that the Americans had strayed from the initial aims of the project and forced an apology.[23] The following year, when United States ships used the Fury and Hecla Straits without first notifying Ottawa and securing the necessary approvals,[24] External Affairs immediately complained to the State Department to set the matter right.[25] In the most effective assertion of Canada's *de facto* control of the region, savvy diplomats at External Affairs forced the Americans to adhere to the Game Laws of the Arctic Preserve, the Scientists and Explorers Ordinance, and the Archaeological Sites Ordinance. Before Americans could hunt in the Arctic, for example, they had to seek the approval of External Affairs or the Department of Mines and Resources.[26] Interestingly, the original creators of the Arctic Game Preserve, especially the former under-secretary of state for external affairs, O.D. Skelton, had hoped it would prove of distinct value as an assertion of Canadian sovereignty in the North.[27] During the early Cold War, the Arctic Preserve fulfilled this purpose.

The Distant Early Warning (DEW) Line

The decision to build a Distant Early Warning (DEW) Line across Canada's Arctic in the 1950s posed a series of more serious sovereignty questions. As early as 1946, Canadian and American authorities had begun to consider the possibility of building a radar chain in the Arctic to give warning of any Soviet attack. In June 1954 the Canada–United States Military Studies Group urged that a radar network be built stretching more than eight thousand kilometres from Alaska to Baffin Island, to provide warning of an incoming Soviet attack. By extending military outposts northward, defence planners sought to achieve strategic defence in depth.[28]

Prime Minister Louis St. Laurent's government, already stretched thin honouring its NATO commitments in Europe and the UN police action in Korea, could not afford the kind of defence installations required to satisfy its superpower ally. The Americans would have to pay for and build the high Arctic radar network, even if three-quarters of the installation stretched across Canadian territory. But Canada did not write a blank cheque, despite the claims of some critics. Ralph Campney, the minister of national defence, explained the government's logic to the Cabinet Defence Committee on 20 January 1955: "If a substantial contribution to the operation and maintenance of the line were to be made once it had been completed and was in operation, it would not, in my view, be necessary to participate in the construction and installation phase, other than to ensure that Canadian interests were protected in the ways outlined in the proposed agreement."[29] Cabinet endorsed the decision on 26 January 1955 and sought a formal agreement with the United States.

Canadian negotiators reached an advantageous agreement with the Americans. Washington bore the full cost of construction but subcontracted to Canadian companies and hired Canadian civilian technicians and support staff. Canada retained title to all sites in its northland and insisted upon the right to inspect work and to approve any change of plans. Royal Canadian Mounted Police Constables and Northern Service Officers were stationed at several sites to regulate relations with the Inuit and to oversee game laws. Moreover, the United States agreed to share geological, hydrographical, and other scientific data obtained during the construction and operation phases and agreed that Canadian government ships and aircraft could use landing facilities at beaches and airstrips. Concurrently, the United States was prohibited from using the airstrips for any activity other than DEW Line support without Canadian consent. "The list of conditions read like a litany of Canadian sovereignty sensitivities and desire for control," historian Alexander Herd notes.[30] All told, it was a small coup for Canadian sovereignty: the Americans officially acknowledged that all of the islands in the Far North explicitly belonged to Canada. "As a result of the DEW Line Agreements," strategist R.J. Sutherland explained, "Canada secured what the United States had up to that time assiduously endeavoured to avoid, namely, an explicit recognition of Canadian claims to the exercise of sovereignty in the Far North."[31]

Although journalists and politicians on the opposition benches continued to voice concerns about sovereignty after the radar network was completed in 1957, federal officials reached mutually satisfactory solutions in Washington showing that the Americans respected Canada's insecurities about sovereignty.[32] Indeed, the DEW Line contributed more to Canadian sovereignty in the North than it detracted from it. It was run in the spirit of partnership, the Royal Canadian Air Force took over the management of Canadian sections of the line in 1959, and it did not drive Canada into bankruptcy. "The capital costs of those DEW-Line stations in Canada was approximately $350 million," Clive Baxter of the *Financial Post* noted on 23 February 1963. "This was paid for entirely by the U.S. but in almost every case, construction and transportation contracts went to Canadian firms giving northern development the biggest shot in the arm it ever had." The benefits did not end there. He reported that the Americans paid $25–28 million annually to operate the DEW Line, with most of the money flowing into Canada. "Some 96% of the civilians employed on the line (there are only a handful of military men) are Canadians. Food supplies and airlift are bought from Canadian suppliers." During the construction phase, the DEW Line agreement required contractors to "give preference to qualified Canadian labour" and this continued during the operation phase. The employment of both Inuit and southern Canadian men, who represented 97 per cent of the personnel along the Canadian section of the line by 1963, may have helped to entrench Canada's claims to "effective occupation" of its arctic.[33] In short, historian Michael Evans aptly concluded, the agreement "allowed the United States to build and operate the DEW

Line ... [and] protected the sovereignty of the Canadian government while offering financial subsidies to the Canadian economy and contributing to the development of the Canadian frontier."[34]

Sober assessment of the operational phase of the DEW Line should have allayed any continuing concerns about American intentions or threats to Canada's Arctic sovereignty. International lawyer Eric Wang, a legal adviser at National Defence, visited the line in May 1969 and concluded that Canadian sovereignty had been strengthened rather than weakened as a result of the DEW Line's existence. Touring the Canadian section of the radar network, he came away convinced that reports about the insensitivities of the Americans on the DEW Line "and the inferences they carry about Canadian sovereignty in the North, are very misleading."[35] American behaviour was both accommodating and appropriate, and Wang concluded that both countries' interests in the radar network were compatible and mutually beneficial. In his assessment, anecdotal evidence of sovereignty encroachments and bilateral friction had been overblown:

> American policy towards the DEW Line appears to be based on a desire to accommodate themselves as harmoniously and as constructively as possible into the Canadian setting which they have to operate.... Perhaps it may be possible to detect some sour notes by diligent searching. I wonder, however, whether any such problems would weigh very heavily against the important benefits which accrue to Canada from this project in the development of the North, not to speak of its essential contribution to our security. Indeed we might be tempted to congratulate ourselves (with a nod to *Professor [James] Eayrs*) for enjoying a "free ride" at least in this area of our defense activities on our own soil, without any unpleasant side effects.[36]

Scholars should turn to environmental and socio-cultural legacies of the DEW Line, not alleged sovereignty erosion, if they wish to challenge Wang's claim that the effects of this continental defence megaproject were overwhelmingly benign. Canadian diplomats and defence officials did not sell out vital national interests – they secured them through quiet diplomacy, a functional approach, and a process that was "cordial, respectful, and mutually beneficial."[37]

The Arctic Archipelago and Maritime Claims

After the conclusion of the DEW Line agreement in 1955, the federal government's primary *de jure* sovereignty concerns shifted from the mainland and archipelagic islands to the water (ice) between and around the islands. The unique geography of the Canadian Arctic made it an interesting and complicated case. Its symmetrical, unitary appearance – "practically a solid land mass intersected by a number of relatively narrow channels of water" – distinguished it from other archipelagos around the world, a British diplomatic document stated in 1958.[38] That same year, External Affairs' legal expert Gilles Sicotte wrote that the properties of Canada's Arctic waters made them even more unique. They were not open to navigation without extensive Canadian assistance, their ice cover was completely indistinguishable from land for most of the year, and the sea ice was lived on and moved over. The Arctic archipelago was physically, geographically, and economically tied to the mainland.[39] But as late as the 1950s senior Canadian officials admitted that Canada had not clearly formulated its position with regard to sovereignty over the waters of the Arctic basin and the channels between its Arctic islands, both from "narrow national" and "international" points of view.[40] This clarification would take decades to realize.

While postwar military activities bolstered Canada's legal claims to the mainland and islands of the archipelago, the Arctic waters were an entirely different story. By agreement, American vessels that supplied the DEW Line applied for and received Canadian waivers under the *Canada Shipping Act* before they proceeded.[41] Captain T.C. Pullen, serving as the commanding officer of HMCS *Labrador* at the time, was appointed a U.S. Navy task group commander and reported to a U.S. Navy admiral during the 1957 sealift. One of his jobs was to ensure that three United States coast guard ships got safely through the Northwest Passage. "In those days, Canadians did not react as they would now to foreign encroachment in their Arctic waters," he reminisced thirty years later; "but they had no cause. Great care was taken by the United States to respect Canadian interests. The joint security interest in the DEW line provided a shared incentive to devise arrangements that would avoid injury to either national position."[42] Indeed, journalists heralded Canada's supply efforts as a "big gain for sovereignty" in that it "immeasurably strengthens our claim to the waters between the islands."[43] The simple fact that these vessels would have to pass through Canadian coastal waters to supply DEW Line stations on Canadian land made this a relatively uncontroversial arrangement that did not call into question the extent of Canada's maritime claims.

How far did Canada's territorial waters extend? The question reached the House of Commons on 5 April 1957, and External Affairs lawyer Jim Nutt explained that the seaward boundary of the internal and contiguous water boundaries of the Archipelago remained unclear. "Lancaster and Viscount Melville Sounds constitute the main waterway through the Arctic Archipelago and are approximately 70 miles wide at the eastern entrance and 100 at the western entrance," he noted. "The establishment and recognition of the territoriality of these waters would seem to be tantamount, at least by implication, to the establishment and recognition of a claim to all the internal waters of the Archipelago."[44] So what waters did Canada actually claim? Senior government officials in Ottawa scrambled to find out. In the mid-1950s, the government requested copies of the original British title documents to the Arctic Islands and began to study its rights to the waters in the archipelago.[45]

Before Canada formulated an official position, it had to ponder national goals and the international implications of claiming the waters and ice, as well as the underlying seabed and air space above. "In addition to any advantages," observed Gordon Robertson, deputy minister of northern affairs and natural resources and chairman of the Advisory Committee on Northern Development, "sovereignty would imply certain obligations including the provision of such services as aids to sea and air navigation, the provision of any necessary local administration, and the enforcement of law" – in other words, the expenditure of public money. In response, the Soviet Union might either reject the claim or use it as a pretext to assert sovereignty over an even larger sector north of its mainland, and other countries would likely refuse to recognize a Canadian claim.[46] Indeed, reporters recognized that "the Russians would like nothing better than to stir up a row between Uncle Sam and Canada over who owns the Arctic ice and sea on our side of the North Pole."[47]

Canadian diplomats recognized that pushing for clarity and trying to secure American and other countries' acquiescence to Canadian claims was not a straightforward matter. As the Legal Division reported to the acting under-secretary on 23 February 1954, a formal solicitation carried "an implication that we may have some doubts regarding our sovereignty in the absence of formal recognition by foreign states."[48] Another departmental memorandum noted that it was almost a "certainty that the United States would not concede such a claim and that the world at large would not acquiesce in it. It would therefore seem preferable not to raise the problem now and to implicitly reserve our position in granting permission for the U.S. to carry out work in Canadian territorial waters." It made more sense for Canada to reach agreements with Washington on "the unstated assumption that 'territorial waters' in that area means whatever we may consider to be Canadian territorial waters, whereas the U.S. does likewise."[49] Provoking protests from foreign countries would hardly serve Canada's national interests, and the longer Canada exercised authority the stronger its claims would become.

Canada could not pretend to exist in a vacuum, its sovereignty issues divorced from broader geostrategic considerations. Claiming a twelve-mile territorial sea, for example, would place Canada in conflict with British challenges to the Soviet Union regarding fishing rights up to a three-mile limit.[50] As a member of the Commonwealth and fellow North Atlantic Treaty Organization (NATO) ally, Canada was not anxious to undermine Britain's position. In addition, transits of the Northwest Passage by U.S. Navy submarines demonstrated the great strategic importance of the Arctic to Canada's closest defence partner. The Arctic Ocean, covered by a dense and noisy ice pack, sheltered submarines from aerial surveillance and sonar detection – important considerations with the introduction of submarine-launched ballistic missiles (SLBMs). Commander James F. Calvert of the submarine, USS *Skate*, told public audiences that the United States could "best hold its world leadership by gaining superiority in the Arctic," and that the Arctic waters would soon become an "entirely nuclear sub-ocean." While this was not official policy, it indicated to Canadian officials that the American government would take "ever increasing interest" in the region.[51]

What imperative was there for Canada to act unilaterally and adopt straight baselines to close off its Arctic waters, in advance of international law, and with little regard for its allies' interests? In 1958, the International Conference on the Law of the Sea adopted Article 4 of the Convention on Territorial Waters which provided for a straight baseline system to delimit its territorial sea. This, in conjunction with the International Court of Justice (ICJ) decision in the *Anglo-Norwegian Fisheries Case* (1951), might apply to the waters of the channels between the islands of the Canadian Arctic Archipelago – but not to the Polar Basin lying north of Canadian land territories. Canada had insisted during the deliberations that the baselines not be limited to twenty-four miles, given that bridging the straits between the Arctic islands would require "much longer baselines than that – the longest across Viscount Melville Sound would be about 200 miles." Such legal ambiguity meant that boldness would not necessarily serve in Canada's best interests.[52] In 1959 Gordon Robertson presciently speculated that in the future the discovery of resources in the archipelago, the closing of the Panama Canal or the development of an open polar sea, might raise the stakes and incline Canada to act unilaterally.[53] Robertson's analysis was sound and remains as pertinent today as it was in 1959. It was, of course, inherently speculative, and to cajole allies on the basis of hypothetical threats to national sovereignty rooted in questionable legal claims to water (rather than physical security threats) would be unrealistic and difficult.

By the late 1950s, External Affairs saw "little advantage and numerous disadvantages to the assertion by Canada of the claim to the waters of the [Polar Basin lying north of the Canadian mainland], at least at the present time" because "it would undoubtedly stir up international controversy." International law did not justify it, and the conditions in the region made such a claim "next to impossible to enforce." By contrast, it saw a strong case for asserting Canadian sovereignty over the waters between the Arctic islands. The "main stumbling block" would be the United States, which would presumably insist upon "free navigation" through the Northwest Passage. "However, it is not impossible perhaps that quiet negotiations with the United States leading to the granting of special privileges in … these waters might achieve reluctant acquiescence from them." In conclusion, Under-Secretary of State for External Affairs Norman Robertson, who had recently returned to Ottawa after a stint as ambassador in Washington, "thought that it would be in no nation's interest to invite an international wrangle, comparable perhaps to the one now going on concerning the Antarctic, by laying controversial claims to the waters and ice of the Arctic Basin."[54]

In the 1960s, Lester Pearson's Liberal government continued to officially endorse a three-mile territorial sea, but it also announced its intention to expand its control beyond those limits by unilaterally creating a nine-mile fishing zone adjacent to its three-mile territorial sea. Although the government introduced legislation to this effect and instituted an exclusive fishing zone based upon straight baselines along the east and west costs, it retreated from making any moves to do the same in the Arctic. The government knew that the United States would object if Canada made any internal waters claim or declared straight baselines, but it hoped that the Americans might support an extension of Canada's claim to Arctic waters for reasons of defence and national security. The United States, however, reacted sharply, fearing any move in the Arctic could set a dangerous precedent. The Canadian government thus retreated from its plans, and Canada did not officially issue any geographical co-ordinates to delineate its claim to baselines in the Arctic for another twenty-three years.[55]

Conclusions

Was this policy of caution, predicated on the uncertain status of Canada's possible internal waters claims in international law and the views of its allies, a failure? Commentators who suggest that Canada *should* have secured its claims more effectively, given that Canada *could* have acted differently, and that this *would* have yielded a stronger Canadian claim today, are practising "what if" history.[56] We must weigh our judgments on the basis of the relationships that existed at the time, prevailing norms of international law, and cost-benefit analyses of possible courses of action.

Our reading of the evidence suggests that Canada's cautious and gradualist strategy, avoiding internecine battles with our American allies over controversial legal issues like the sector principle, allowed the country to perfect its terrestrial sovereignty in the postwar period. External Affairs officials were well aware of the implications of their decisions, kept American indiscretions in perspective without succumbing to popular alarmism, and devised a modest strategy for expanding and entrenching Canada's claims. There is no indication that Washington was prepared to accept the sector principle in the postwar period, which undergirded much of Canada's confused stance on its possible maritime claims until the 1950s. Indeed, historian Gordon W. Smith, writing in the mid-1960s, found it "difficult to understand why Canadian authorities have continued to trifle with the sector principle, and it is even more difficult to understand why attempts have been made, as indicated by various official decrees, pronouncements, and maps, to try to apply it to regions other than land."[57]

While international law evolved to include the possibility of straight baselines, any Canadian case would have been precarious in the 1950s and 1960s. "Under general international law and particularly the decision of the International Court of Justice in the Anglo-Norwegian Fisheries Judgment, a case could be made for treating the Arctic Archipelago as a whole with the mainland and measuring the territorial sea from straight base lines drawn about the coastline of the outer circumference of the Archipelago," a March 1959 legal appraisal concluded. Yet "the insufficiency of evidence of a longstanding and unequivocal [Canadian] intention to assert sovereignty over these waters," particularly vis-à-vis foreign states, would bring close scrutiny.[58] Instead, quiet diplomacy allowed Canada to avoid alienating its allies and circumpolar neighbours, to contribute to continental defence, and to lay the groundwork for the functional approach initiated under Trudeau in the wake of the *Manhattan* voyages and the straight baselines invoked by Mulroney's Conservatives in the wake of the *Polar Sea*.

Franklyn Griffiths and other commentators continue to suggest that a functional Canadian approach to managing and controlling its internal waters, based on "agreeing to disagree" with the Americans on the legal status of the Northwest Passage, remains a feasible and realistic option. They usually turn to the 1988 Cooperation Agreement on icebreaker transits as evidence of bilateral willingness to forge a working compromise by avoiding core legal entanglements.[59] They might also look earlier, to the first two decades of the Cold War when Canada and the United States found space to coexist in the name of continental defence without prejudice to their respective legal positions. The United States acknowledged that the Arctic Archipelago belonged to Canada without validating the Canadian sector principle. Canada was more vague on its claims to the Arctic waters, but based upon the available evidence (which is avowedly partial) it avoided placing the United States in a position where it had to formally challenge Canada's sovereignty claims. Slowly establishing rights to Arctic waters without provoking foreign legal protests, *The Financial Post* explained in October 1958, was a prudent course. If all went well, "About 1980 we can say: 'Of course this is a Canadian territorial sea. Everyone has acknowledged this for 20 years.'"[60] Rather than seeing Canadian decision-making as a failure to secure its claim to the Northwest Passage in the 1960s, a more positive appraisal might recognize how careful diplomacy helped to position Canada so that it could implement a functional approach under Trudeau and declare straight baselines under Mulroney.

NOTES

1. Ambassador in the United States to Acting Under-Secretary of State for External Affairs (USSEA), 5 June 1946, in *Documents on Canadian External Relations (DCER)*, vol. 13: *1946*, ed. Norman Hillmer and Donald Page (Ottawa: Minister of Supply and Services, 1993), 1565–66.

2. On the sector principle, see Donat Pharand, *Canada's Arctic Waters in International Law* (Cambridge: Cambridge University Press, 1988), 3–87.

3. H.H. Wrong to A.D.P Heeney, 8 June 1946, Department of External Affairs Records (DEAR), vol. 3347, file 9061-A-40, part 1, Library and Archives Canada (LAC).

4. H.H. Wrong to D.C Abbot, 13 June 1946, DEAR, vol. 3347, file 9061-A-40, part 1, LAC.

5. Adam Lajeunesse, "Lock, Stock, and Icebergs? Defining Canadian Sovereignty from Mackenzie King to Stephen Harper," CMSS Occasional Paper No. 1 (Calgary: Centre for Military and Strategic Studies, 2007), 6–7; Adam Lajeunesse, "The True North as Long as It's Free: The Canadian Policy Deficit 1945–1985" (MA thesis, University of Calgary, 2007), 42, 59–60.

6. Shelagh Grant, *Sovereignty or Security? Government Policy in the Canadian North, 1936–1950* (Vancouver: UBC Press, 1988).

7. Elizabeth Elliot-Meisel, *Arctic Diplomacy: Canada and the United States in the Northwest Passage* (New York: Peter Lang, 1998); David Bercuson, "Continental Defence and Arctic Sovereignty, 1945–1950: Solving the Canadian Dilemma," in *The Cold War and Defence*, ed. Keith Neilson and Ronald Haycock (New York: Praeger, 1990), 153–70.

8. Elliot-Meisel, *Arctic Diplomacy*, 43.

9. Stanley Dziuban, *Military Relations Between the United States and Canada 1939–1945* (Washington: Office of the Chief of Military History, 1959), 138. Several scholars have speculated that the United States Government had a diabolical agenda for the Canadian North. See Grant, *Sovereignty or Security*, 185; Donald Creighton, *The Forked Road: Canada, 1939–1957* (Toronto: McClelland & Stewart, 1976), 74. The American response to these Canadian initiatives, if one avoids the lure of the "conspiratorial view" of history, was not a cause for concern but cautious optimism. They were actually encouraged by the involvement of Brigadier-General Foster in defence planning.

10. Whitney Lackenbauer, "Right and Honourable: Mackenzie King, Canadian–American Bilateral Relations, and Canadian Sovereignty in the Northwest, 1943–1948," in *Mackenzie King: Citizenship and Community*, ed. J. English, K. McLaughlin, and W. Lackenbauer (Toronto: Robin Brass Studio, 2002), 154.

11. Elliot-Meisel, *Arctic Diplomacy*, 56.

12. Lt. Colonel Bernd Horn, "Gateway to Invasion or the Curse of Geography? The Canadian Arctic and the Question of Security, 1939–1999," in *Forging a Nation: Perspectives on the Canadian Military Experience*, ed. Bernd Horn (St. Catharines: Vanwell Publishing, 2002), 318.

13. Bercuson, "Continental Defence and Arctic Sovereignty," 155.

14. Memorandum from Head, Third Political Division Legal Division, 1 January 1946, in Donald Page, ed., *DCER*, vol. 12, 1946 (Ottawa: Minster of Supply and Services, 1977); L.B Pearson to H.H. Wrong, 18 June 1946, DEAR, 86-87/159, box 41, file 9057-C-40, pt. 4, LAC.

15. Gordon Smith defined the sector principle as: "Each state with a continental Arctic coastline automatically falls heir to all islands lying between this coastline and the North Pole, which are enclosed by longitudinal lines drawn from the eastern and western extremities of the same coastline to the Pole." The Canadians used the Sector Principle to support their claims in the Arctic, despite its dubious veracity in

international law. See Gordon W. Smith, "Sovereignty in the North: The Canadian Aspect of an International Problem," in *The Arctic Frontier*, ed. R.St.J. Macdonald (Toronto: University of Toronto Press, 1966).

16 A close contemporary parallel to this is the position of the United States on the Northwest Passage. If the Americans accept Canada's position on the passage and allow it to be treated as Canadian internal waters, a precedent would be set for more strategically important straits throughout the world. Strategic and political implications make it unlikely that the United States will accept the Northwest Passage as Canadian internal waters, just as similar considerations kept the United States from accepting the sector principle in 1946. See Ken Coates, Whitney Lackenbauer, William Morrison, and Greg Poelzer, *Arctic Front: Defending Canada in the Far North* (Toronto: Thomas Allen, 2008), 83.

17 Note for Mr. Wrong: Proposed Arctic Weather Station Programme, 27 May 1946, DEAR, vol. 3346, file 9061-A-40C, pt. 1, LAC.

18 Memorandum for Cabinet Defence Committee, "United States Proposals for an Arctic Weather Station Programme," from External Affairs, 30 May 1946, DEAR, vol. 3346, file 9061-A-40C, pt. 1, LAC.

19 "Memorandum – United States Proposals for Weather Stations in the Arctic," 4 July 1946, DEAR, vol. 3346, file 9061-A-40C, pt. 1, LAC.

20 On this era, see Joseph T. Jockel, "The Canada–United States Military Co-operation Committee and Continental Air Defence, 1946," *Canadian Historical Review* 64, no. 3 (1983): 352–77; and David Bercuson, *True Patriot: The Life of Brooke Claxton, 1898–1960* (Toronto: University of Toronto Press, 1993), 153–74.

21 Bercuson, "Continental Defence and Arctic Sovereignty," 161. By March 1947 the Cabinet approved the construction of Arctic weather stations and three Long Range Aid to Navigation (LORAN) posts, adopting the parameters suggested by External Affairs. Although External Affairs has been praised for its use of the functional principle in international politics, it also applied the principle to the new defence projects in the North, insisting that as soon as qualified Canadian personnel could be trained they would replace the Americans. L.B. Pearson to Ray Atherton, 22 December 1947; D.M Johnson to Mr Rae, 25 April 1947, DEAR, vol. 3841, file 9061-A-40, pt. 2, LAC. Eventually functionalism would also be applied to Arctic re-supply missions, with the Canadians gradually assuming more responsibility for northern air lifts and building an icebreaker to assist in naval expeditions.

22 House of Commons, *Debates*, 12 February 1947.

23 Secretary of the American Section, PJBD, to Secretary of the Canadian Section, PJBD, 23 December 1947, in *DCER*, vol. 14: 1947, ed. Norman Hillmer and Donald Page (Ottawa: Minister of Supply and Services, 1994), 1523.

24 D.M Johnson to Mr. Magaan, 13 October 1948, DEAR, vol. 3841, file 9061-G-40, LAC.

25 Maagan to William P. Snow, 11 October 1948, DEAR, vol. 3841, file 9061-G-40, LAC.

26 See, for example, John P. Kelsall to Lewis, 31 August 1948, RG 85, vol. 302, file 1009-5, vol. 1, LAC.

27 O.D. Skelton, USSEA, to O.S. Finnie, Director Northwest Territories and Yukon Branch, Department of the Interior, 2 September 1926, DEAR, vol. 4252, file 9057-40, pt. 2, LAC.

28 The concept and diplomatic negotiations that led to the postwar radar networks are well covered in Joseph Jockel, *No Boundaries Upstairs: Canada, the United States, and the Origins of North American Air Defence, 1945–1958* (Vancouver: UBC Press, 1987).

29 Minister of National Defence, Memorandum to the Cabient Defence Committee in *DCER*, vol. 21: 1955, ed. Greg Donaghy (Ottawa: Canada Communication Group, 1999), 756–57.

30   Alexander W.G. Herd, "As Practicable: Canada–United States Continental Air Defense Cooperation 1953–1954" (MA thesis, Kansas State University, 2005), 86.

31   R.J. Sutherland, "The Strategic Significance of the Canadian Arctic," in *The Arctic Frontier*, 271.

32   James Eayrs, "Problems of Canadian-American Relations," in *Canada in World Affairs October 1955 to June 1957*, ed. James Eayrs (Toronto: Oxford University Press, 1959), 151.

33   John Nicholas Harris, "National Defence and Northern Development: The Establishment of the DEW Line in the Canadian North" (MA thesis, Simon Fraser University, 1980), 160.

34   Michael William Evans, "The Establishment of the Distant Early Warning Line, 1952–1957: A Study of Continental Defense Policymaking" (MA thesis, Bowling Green University, 1995), 72.

35   E.B. Wang, "The Dew Line and Canadian Sovereignty," 26 May 1969, DEAR, file 27-10-2-2, pt. 1, LAC.

36   Italics in the original. E.B. Wang, "The Dew Line and Canadian Sovereignty," 26 May 1969, DEAR, file 27-10-2-2, pt. 1, LAC.

37   Evans, "Establishment of the DEW Line," 76.

38   W.G. Lamarque to G. Sicotte, 5 March 1958, DEAR, vol. 7118, file 9057-40, pt. 9.2, LAC. Donat Pharand calculates that, in Canada's case, the close link between land and sea necessary to draw straight baselines is very strong. The sea to land ratio is 0.822 to 1, much better than the 3.5 to 1 ratio for the Norwegian Archipelago upon which the original legal decision was based. Furthermore, he notes that "the quasi-permanency of the ice over the enclosed waters bolsters the physical unity between land and sea." Pharand, "The Arctic Waters and the Northwest Passage," 18.

39   G. Sicotte to W.G. Lamarque, 14 April 1958, DEAR, vol. 7118, file 9057-40, pt. 9.2, LAC.

40   G.W. Rowley, Memorandum for the Advisory Committee on Northern Development, "Canadian Sovereignty in the Arctic Basin and the Channels Lying Between the Islands of the Arctic Archipelago," 16 September 1958, DEAR, vol. 7118, file 9057-40, pt. 9.2, LAC.

41   J.M. Leeming, "HMCS Labrador and the Canadian Arctic," in *RCN in Retrospect*, ed. James A. Boutilier (Vancouver: UBC Press, 1982), 286–307; Louis St. Laurent, House of Commons *Debates*, 6 April 1957, excerpted in "Public Statements regarding Arctic Sovereignty," c. June 1960, copy on DEAR, vol. 7118, file 9057-40, LAC.

42   T.C. Pullen, "What Price Canadian Sovereignty?" *U.S. Naval Institute Proceedings* 113 (September 1987): 68.

43   Leslie Wilson, "Canada Supplying Arctic: Big Gain for Sovereignty," *Financial Post*, 27 September 1958.

44   J.S. Nutt, Memorandum for File: Arctic Territorial Waters, 9 April 1957, DEAR, vol. 6510, file 9057-40, pt. 6.2, LAC.

45   R.G. Robertson to Jules Leger, 8 March 1955; M.H. Wershof to R.G. Robertson, 3 March 1955, DEAR, vol. 6510, file 9057-40, pt. 5.1, LAC.

46   R.G. Robertson, draft letter, c. fall 1958, DEAR, vol. 6510, file 9057-40, pt. 7, LAC.

47   "Arctic Sovereignty: Canada Ownership of Polar Islands Tacitly Recognized," *Montreal Star*, 8 August 1958.

48   Legal Division to Acting Under-Secretary of State for External Affairs (USSEA), 23 February 1954, DEAR, vol. 6297, file 9057-40, pt. 4.2, LAC.

49   Memorandum for file 50,0370-40, "U.S. Request for Permission to Make Submarine Installations off Cape Dyer, Baffin Island in connection with the BMEWS Cable to Thule," 29 July 1958, DEAR, vol. 6510, file 9057-40, pt. 7.1, LAC. Since no study on the status of the Arctic waters (particularly those in the archipelago) had been completed, G. Sicotte noted on 30 April 1956 that "no formal action should be taken regarding possible

Canadian claims to waters in the Arctic at the present time." He recommended that no department, however, take any action which could compromise an eventual Canadian internal waters claim. "For present purposes," he noted, "these waters might be taken as those lying within a line commencing at Resolution Island, south east of Baffin Island and running from headland to headland in a rough triangle north to the top of Ellesmere Island and thence south west to Banks Island and the Arctic coast of Canada." G. Sicotte for the USSEA to Canadian Embassy, Copenhagen, Denmark, 30 April 1956, DEAR, vol. 6510, file 9057-40, pt. 6.2, LAC.

50 Soviet Section, Arthur Ford, noted in an April 1955 memo (NS.1521/15, USSR. 178/55), DEAR, vol. 6510, file 9057-40, pt. 6.1, LAC.

51 Washington to External Affairs, 10 October 1958, DEAR, vol. 6510, file 9057-40, pt. 7.1, LAC.

52 R.G. Robertson to USSEA, 30 October 1958, DEAR, vol. 7118, file 9057-40, pt. 8, LAC.

53 R.G. Robertson to USSEA, "Arctic Sovereignty," 3 July 1959, DEAR, vol. 6510, file 9057-40, pt. 6.2, LAC.

54 USSEA to R.G. Robertson, 17 December 1958, DEAR, vol. 7118, file 9057-40, pt. 8, LAC. General Charles Foulkes, the Chairman, Chiefs of Staff, also raised concerns about foreign "sector" claims that could deny Canada "freedom of passage by sea to parts of our northland and Arctic reconnaissance would be very limited." Draft, Foulkes to Chairman, Advisory Committee on Northern Development, 12 December 1958, DEAR, vol. 7118, file 9057-40, pt. 8, LAC.

55 Territorial Sea and Fishing Zones Act, 22, 1964-65 S.C. 153 (1964); Margaret W. Morris, "Boundary Problems Relating to the Sovereignty of the Canadian Arctic," in *Canada's Changing North*, ed. William C. Wonders (Toronto: McClelland & Stewart, 1971), 322; Smith, "Sovereignty in the North," 236–37; and Elliot-Meisel, *Arctic Diplomacy*, 140.

56 See, for example, Lajeunesse, "The True North as Long as It's Free," 60.

57 Smith, "Sovereignty in the North," 226.

58 J.S. Nutt, "Status of the Waters of the Canadian Arctic Archipelago," 9 March 1959, DEAR, vol. 7118, file 9057-40, pt. 8, LAC.

59 On 11 January 1988, External Affairs Minister Joe Clark and United States Secretary of State George Shultz announced an agreement on Arctic Co-operation that was carefully framed to avoid prejudicing the legal claims of both sides. The United States agreed to seek Canadian consent before its icebreakers navigated in what Canada considered to be its internal waters, based on the principle that these were scientific missions of mutual benefit to both countries. See Christopher Kirkey, "Smoothing Troubled Waters: The 1988 Canada–United States Arctic Co-operation Agreement," *International Journal* 50 (1995): 408–26, and David L. Larson, "United States Interests in the Arctic Region," *Ocean Development and International Law* 20 (1989): 183–84.

60 "Do We Own Water and Ice around Arctic Islands?," *Financial Post*, 10 October 1959.

ADVANCING THE NATIONAL INTEREST: MARCEL CADIEUX, JULES LÉGER, AND CANADIAN PARTICIPATION IN THE FRANCOPHONE COMMUNITY, 1964-1972

Robin S. Gendron

When, in late 1965, Presidents Habib Bourguiba of Tunisia and Léopold Senghor of Senegal proposed the creation of an international organization for French-speaking states, they unwittingly created a problem for the Canadian government and the Department of External Affairs. In their initial conception of this organization, neither Bourguiba nor Senghor anticipated, nor wanted, Canada's participation. What they envisaged instead was a modest organization that would enhance the ability of French-speaking countries in Africa to preserve their shared linguistic and cultural heritage.[1] Over succeeding months, however, their proposal attracted supporters who not only embraced the idea but also broadened it. In Canada, this development compelled the government and the Department of External Affairs to consider what role Canada should play in the emerging community of French-speaking states; a question complicated by Canada's difficult relations with France in this period, as well as the challenges faced from the government of Quebec, which asserted the right to its own international personality and to conduct its own international relations.

From the mid-1960s to the early 1970s, the Department of External Affairs and its officials devoted a great deal of their time and energy to advancing Canada's interests in the international community of French-speaking states. For two of the department's officials in particular, however, this issue took on an added importance. Both Marcel Cadieux and Jules Léger played key roles in the debate over Canada's involvement in the community of French-speaking states by virtue of their official positions as under-secretary of state for external affairs and Canada's ambassador in France, respectively. Beyond that, they were also the senior francophone officials in a department struggling, like the government as a whole, to become more inclusive of, and responsive to, the francophone dimension of Canada's biculturalism. For them, Canada's involvement with the international community of French-speaking states served Canadian national interests by reinforcing traditional conceptions of French Canadian identity at a time when this identity was being threatened by the emergence of a much narrower form of Québécois nationalism. By the 1960s, French Canadian nationalists in Quebec – those who had formerly identified with a pan-Canadian community of francophones with a vibrant role to play in a bicultural Canada – were increasingly focusing their sense of identity on the territory of Quebec alone and the government of Quebec as defender of French culture in North America. For Cadieux and Léger, this development posed a significant threat to their conception of Canada and the place of French Canadians in it, though they differed widely on how best to respond to it.

From the moment that it was first proposed in 1965, there were mixed feelings in the Department of External Affairs about what the establishment of an international community of French-speaking states meant for Canada. Some officials, like Thomas Carter, the head of the department's European Division, were decidedly sceptical about the benefits for Canada of becoming involved in a community which, because of the resentment that many of its potential members still bore towards France, they felt would never be as widely embraced as the British Commonwealth. Indeed, countries like Algeria, Guinea, and Morocco were more concerned about eradicating the remnants of French colonialism in their societies than with preserving their French heritage and links with France. An international organization of French-speaking states would not, consequently, help Canada build ties with such countries. Moreover, involvement could impose extensive financial and political commitments on Canada. Because economically advanced French-speaking countries like Belgium and Switzerland had no intention of joining, Canada would be the only political and economic counterweight to France in the francophone organization. As such, French African countries would expect much greater financial assistance from Canada than it could hope to meet, in contrast to the Commonwealth where wealthy countries like Australia and New Zealand shared the burden with Britain and Canada.[2]

Based on the initial conception of the proposed community, Carter added an additional note of concern. Since no one in French Africa or France seemed to want to replicate the British Commonwealth's political focus and formal structure, the French-speaking community was likely to confine itself exclusively to issues of culture and language, precisely the sort of emphasis that would engage the ambitions of the government of Quebec. The Canadian government, therefore, could expect a long and bitter fight with Quebec over the latter's desire to participate in the community on its own behalf, especially since "the advocates of a more independent attitude for Quebec would consider it as a natural forum in which to promote their cause."[3] Given the damage to Canada's domestic harmony and national unity that would inevitably result from such a fight, would it not be better, Carter wondered, for the Canadian government to focus on bilateral rather than multilateral efforts to improve its relations with French-speaking countries?

Carter's reasoning struck Marcel Cadieux as fundamentally unsound. Cadieux believed that for Canada to eschew involvement in a multilateral association of French-speaking states would send precisely the wrong message to French Canadians, many of whom, especially in Quebec, already believed that the federal government was not interested in the French-speaking world. It was this belief, in fact, that underlay some of the arguments that individuals like André Patry, the former professor of international relations turned senior advisor to Quebec Premier Jean Lesage, and Claude Morin, Quebec's deputy minister of intergovernmental affairs, used in the early to mid-1960s to demand greater international responsibilities for the government of Quebec. If the Canadian government could not, or would not, satisfy French Canadian interests in establishing stronger relations with the French-speaking world, then according to Patry and Morin the responsibility fell to the government of Quebec to do so for itself. For Canada to ignore an association of francophone countries, even if it worked tirelessly to strengthen bilateral relations with these nations, risked letting "the feeling develop that federal policies do not take sufficient account of the aspirations of French Canada in the international sphere."[4] From Cadieux's perspective, there could be no question of the need for Canada to participate actively and enthusiastically in the community of French-speaking states, however it developed.

Secretary of State for External Affairs Paul Martin and the Liberal government as a whole shared Cadieux's view about the need for Canada to be more responsive to French Canadian interests in the realm of foreign policy. Since their election in 1963, Martin and Prime Minister Lester Pearson had devoted significant energy and resources to improving Canada's relations with French-speaking countries. New embassies were opened in Senegal and Tunisia in 1966; Canadian developmental assistance for French-speaking countries in Africa expanded rapidly from $300,000 in 1963 to $7 million just a few years later; and contacts, exchanges, and discussions with French African governments increased significantly over the same period. All of this was part of a deliberate strategy to incorporate French Canadian interests more explicitly into Canada's foreign policies and thereby help minimize the adverse effects of the growth of Québécois nationalism on Canadian unity. Long overdue, from the point of view of Cadieux and Léger, this strategy nonetheless represented an important step towards the fulfillment of long-standing French Canadian aspirations for a full and vibrant role in Canadian national and international affairs.[5]

Jules Léger and Marcel Cadieux joined the Department of External Affairs in 1940 and 1941, respectively. At that time, and for a long time thereafter, the department, its officials, and its culture were overwhelmingly anglophone, a situation against which both Cadieux and Léger struggled. Even Léger's appointment to the department's top post, under-secretary of state for external affairs, in 1954 did not fundamentally alter the relative marginalization of French Canadians in the Department of External Affairs and, more generally, in the formulation of Canada's foreign relations.[6] Throughout the late 1950s and early 1960s, Cadieux in particular fought extremely hard to change that state of affairs: he pushed to make the department bilingual in the 1950s by advocating French language training for Canada's anglophone diplomats;[7] his book, *Le Diplomate canadien*, was intended, at least in part, to attract more young French Canadians into Canada's foreign service[8] and he pleaded with his political superiors to allocate more aid to the French-speaking countries in Africa as a demonstration of the Canadian government's responsiveness to French Canadian international interests. Unfortunately, these pleas fell on deaf ears in the Conservative government of John Diefenbaker.[9]

The election of the Liberal government in 1963, however, changed the dynamic in Ottawa and the new government's broad pursuit of bilingualism and biculturalism promised to bring French Canadians and their interests more fully and equitably into the fold of the Canadian government and Canadian national affairs. For Marcel Cadieux and Jules Léger, this was a very welcome development. Both of them were French Canadian nationalists in the tradition of Henri Bourassa, the early twentieth century advocate of a bilingual and bicultural Canada.[10] Like Bourassa, Cadieux and Léger sought the widest possible participation of French Canadians in the development of Canada on the basis of equality and mutual respect between Canada's French and English-speaking peoples. After 1963, the realization of this vision of a truly bicultural Canada seemed closer than ever.

French Canadian conceptions of nationalism had not remained static since the days of Henri Bourassa, however. By the 1920s, some French Canadian nationalists had begun to reject the non-territorial, pan-Canadian definition of French-Canadian nationalism that was intrinsic to Bourassa. Instead, nationalist leaders like Abbé Lionel Groulx focused their attention much more narrowly on Quebec as the spiritual home of the French presence in Canada and the only political jurisdiction where French Canadians – being the majority of the population – could protect their culture from the threat of assimilation. Over several decades, culminating in the 1960s, this process transformed many, if not most, French Canadian nationalists in Quebec into Québécois nationalists.[11] Insofar as this development encouraged the concomitant emergence of a separatist movement in Quebec, it posed a significant challenge to Canada's national unity.[12] Even moderate expressions of Québécois nationalism, however, raised fundamental questions about the ongoing place of French Canadians in Canada and Canadian national life.

As French Canadian nationalists focused more attention on the province of Quebec, they magnified the importance of the government of Quebec as defender of the French culture in Canada. Indeed, by the early 1960s, Premier Jean Lesage was calling the government of Quebec "the political expression of French Canada." Building on the arguments contained in the Tremblay Report, the report of the Quebec Royal Commission that criticized the centralization of power in the federal government's hands at the expense of provincial jurisdictions after 1945, Lesage's government sought special powers to go along with its special responsibilities as the voice of French Canadians in Canada.[13]

Daniel Johnson, who succeeded Lesage as premier in 1966, stated Quebec's claim even more explicitly: to protect and promote French Canadian interests and culture the government of Quebec needed full constitutional equality with the rest of Canada and complete responsibility for French Canada's political, economic, social, and cultural affairs.[14] In practice, this argument inspired such initiatives as the Quebec government's attempt to gain control over the federal program of educational assistance for French-speaking countries in Africa between 1964 and 1966.[15] The move was ultimately unsuccessful but the logic of even moderate forms of Québécois nationalism nonetheless reinforced the idea that Quebec City, rather than Ottawa, was the only appropriate locus for any and all initiatives connected to the *épanouissement* of French Canada in the mid- to late 1960s.

Like the Canadian government as a whole, Cadieux and Léger rejected the premise that the government of Quebec was the sole political voice of French Canada. They understood the frustrations that had helped feed such claims, and they even sympathized with them.[16] Yet they shared the belief that French Canadian interests were best served, not by focusing solely on Quebec, but rather by maximizing the broader opportunities available through the Canadian government as a whole. Cadieux and Léger's own careers demonstrated that it was possible for French Canadians to succeed in Ottawa and, at the very moment when the Canadian government was becoming more receptive to French Canadian interests, the demands of Québécois nationalists threatened to derail what they and others had struggled so hard to achieve.[17] In essence, despite the emergence of Québécois nationalism, Cadieux and Léger remained French Canadian nationalists who felt that no good would come from abandoning Canada. Instead, they believed that the Canadian government needed to remain an outlet for the energy, skills, and aspirations of all of Canada's French-speaking peoples.[18] It was for this reason that Cadieux and Léger considered Canada's involvement in the community of French-speaking countries after 1965 not only desirable but necessary. Fundamentally, this community offered the Canadian government the opportunity to demonstrate that it was still capable of addressing French Canadian, and even Québécois, needs. Failing to demonstrate that capability, however, would only reinforce Québécois nationalists' criticisms of the Canadian government and buttress the already growing ambitions of the government of Quebec.

Cadieux and Léger had very little trouble persuading Paul Martin and Lester Pearson that the Canadian government needed to pursue involvement in the emerging community of French-speaking states aggressively after 1965. They even prevailed upon the government to try to take a leadership role in establishing the community, part of a strategy to ensure that it developed in a way amenable to Canadian interests. In particular, they hoped to nudge the community towards a more formal, politically oriented organization similar to the Commonwealth or, alternatively, a very loose, informal organization of private agencies and associations, either of which would have maximized the role for Canada while minimizing the scope for Quebec's involvement.[19] Unfortunately for the Canadian government, the initiative in determining the nature of the francophone community lay largely in French African capitals like Dakar and Tunis or in Paris rather than in Ottawa. And in Paris, at least, the French government very much wanted Quebec to play an important role in the francophone community.

From the opening of Quebec's *Délégation générale* in Paris in 1961 through the negotiation of a cultural accord in 1965, relations between the governments of Quebec and France became remarkably close during the 1960s. More to the point, the government of Quebec needed France to support its international ambitions. Without that support, Quebec's claim that it exercised the same competence over fields like education and culture at the international level that it did within Canada, articulated by the Gérin-Lajoie Doctrine of 1965,[20] would have carried much less weight. However, with French President Charles de Gaulle increasingly convinced that a bicultural Canada was ultimately unworkable and anxious to strengthen the *rayonnement* of French culture in Quebec, the French government was more than willing to recognize Quebec's claims to international competence and deal directly with it in international affairs.[21] Naturally, the Canadian government resented the special relationship that developed between the governments of France and Quebec in the 1960s, yet it could do little to impede it or to stem the deterioration of its own relations with France in the same period.[22] Nor could the Canadian government prevent France from trying to ensure that Quebec was able to participate fully and autonomously in the emerging international community of French-speaking states.

Despite leaving the initiative on the development of this community in the hands of other governments, the French government worked hard to keep its focus strictly on language and culture. It had its own reasons for doing so – it wanted to avoid the impression that it was seeking to impose some form of neo-imperialism on its former colonies in Africa[23] – yet this focus also strengthened Quebec's claim to its own membership in the community on the grounds that it involved areas of its constitutional competence. Because of its responsibility for fields like culture and education, the French government was convinced that Quebec had an important role to play in the francophone community that Canada, which de Gaulle and many others in Paris considered essentially an anglophone country, did not.[24] It was this conviction, and the French government's willingness to use its influence in French Africa, that ultimately helped Quebec secure an invitation to the Libreville meeting of ministers of education from France and French Africa in early 1968 and, subsequently, to participate in the conferences in 1970 and 1971 that established the *Agence de coopération culturelle et technique*, forerunner of the organization that would become known as *la Francophonie*.[25] In the meantime, however, the Canadian government needed to determine its own response to efforts to gain for Quebec autonomous membership in this francophone community.

Between 1964 and 1968, Cadieux and Léger were the central figures in the debate within the Department of External Affairs about how to respond to Quebec's interest in the international community of French-speaking states and in international affairs more broadly. Friends as well as colleagues, they generally shared a common view about Canada and its international interests, but on this particular issue they diverged noticeably. For Cadieux there could be no question of Quebec's being able to act on its own behalf internationally since, under both international law and the Canadian constitution, the Canadian government enjoyed exclusive jurisdiction over all aspects of international affairs. Consequently, the federal government was the only body entitled to represent Canadians, all Canadians, internationally.[26] Quebec therefore had no authority to act internationally and any pretentions otherwise had to be opposed vigorously as a threat to federal authority and, more importantly, Canada's national unity. Any concessions to Quebec's international ambitions, even in the fields of education or culture, would only encourage Québécois nationalists to make further demands at the expense of the federal government. Moreover, if France continued to encourage Quebec's ambitions, Cadieux felt that the Canadian government had to be prepared to respond forcefully, even if it meant rupturing Franco-Canadian relations.[27]

While Léger agreed with Cadieux about the need to defend the Canadian government's constitutional position aggressively, including its claim of pre-eminence in international affairs, he did not share his colleague's absolute conviction that Quebec had to be prevented from exercising any international role whatsoever. Instead, Léger advocated a more conciliatory attitude towards Quebec's international ambitions. After all, he argued, any international activities undertaken by Quebec were really only a threat to Canada if they took place in defiance of the Canadian government. Ultimately, he believed that the solution to the crisis over Quebec's intention to participate in the international community of French-speaking states lay in negotiating a settlement that allowed Quebec to join the community under the overall umbrella of Canada's own involvement. Léger consistently advocated such a settlement from 1966 to 1968.[28] Even on the eve of Quebec's participation in the Libreville Conference, when Cadieux himself was pushing Lester Pearson and Paul Martin to punish France and Quebec, Léger counselled caution and a negotiated agreement to resolve the constitutional dispute.[29]

At first, these differences did not unduly affect the relationship between Cadieux and Léger. As the Canada-Quebec-France crisis over the francophone community deepened in 1967, however, Cadieux became ever more concerned about Léger's apparent willingness to concede that Quebec did in fact have some capacity to act on its own behalf internationally. In March 1967, Léger wrote an article for the Canadian Institute for International Affairs' *International Journal* that, to Cadieux, seemed to favour allowing Quebec a role to play in Canada's relations with French-speaking countries. The article also neglected to stress to Cadieux's satisfaction that "the Canadian government [was] the instrument for the expression of Canadian foreign policy in terms of the bicultural and bilingual character of the country." Fearful of the consequences of this argument being made in such a public way by a prominent member of the department, Cadieux denied Léger permission to publish this article.[30] Fundamentally, Cadieux was concerned that Léger failed to understand the full political and constitutional implications of allowing Quebec to develop its own foreign relations, with France or any other French-speaking countries. For his part, Léger believed that Cadieux's instinctive response towards the dispute with Quebec and France was too confrontational and that this too carried long-term risks for Canada and its domestic and foreign interests.

Some of their differences with regard to dealing with Quebec and its international ambitions can be attributed to their respective positions in the Department of External Affairs and the view of events they gained from them. As under-secretary of state for external affairs from 1964 to 1970, Cadieux was at the centre of events in Ottawa, where he was much more familiar with, and sensitive to, developments in Quebec and Ottawa, including the extent of the threat that Quebec's ambitions posed to federal interests. From Paris, in contrast, Ambassador Léger's concern for the preservation of Canada's long-term relations with France led him to favour a pragmatic, conciliatory response to the crisis in Canada-Quebec-France relations. Léger also believed that, once de Gaulle was removed from the centre of political life in France, more sensible elements in the French government would reassert themselves.[31] There was, however, more to their divergent perspectives on Quebec and its international ambitions. Their different personalities – Cadieux the uncompromising, highly principled lawyer and Léger the consummate diplomat (forever seeing shades of grey where Cadieux saw only black and white) – only added to the gulf that divided them.[32]

Cadieux is widely acknowledged to have been a fierce Canadian nationalist, with his nationalism rooted in a firm commitment to a long-standing

French Canadian vision of Canada as a bicultural country.[33] Jules Léger, however, was no less committed than Cadieux to this vision of nationalism. As such, they were both at odds with the emergence of a Québécois nationalism in their home province that threatened to undermine Canadian biculturalism at the very moment in the mid- to late 1960s that it was closer than ever to being realized. They differed, though, in their assessment of how much of a threat Québécois nationalism actually posed to Canada. For Cadieux, the true extent of this threat was summed up by his experience with Claude Morin, the Quebec official at the heart of efforts to expand that government's international identity, who convinced Cadieux that the ultimate goal of Québécois nationalism was the breakup of Canada.[34] Léger, on the other hand, despite the deepening tension between Canada and Quebec in this period maintained a relatively congenial and effective working relationship with Quebec's delegate general in Paris, Jean Chapdelaine, even though this relationship caused a certain amount of unease among their respective colleagues in Ottawa and Quebec City.[35]

For Cadieux, Québécois nationalism was incompatible with his sense of French Canadian nationalism and, since only one of them could prevail, he was committed to ensuring that the one that did preserved the greatest opportunities for French Canadians on the widest possible scale. Léger, though, did not believe that Québécois nationalism and his own sense of French Canadian nationalism were mutually exclusive; they could, in fact, co-exist, although doing so required the Canadian government to be more accommodating of the aspirations of the government of Quebec, among the most notable of which was the desire for its own place in the broader francophone world of *la Francophonie*.

For both Marcel Cadieux and Jules Léger, defending the national interest was a multilayered concern, incorporating the need to protect Canada's national interests as well as French Canadian national interests. Ultimately, these two ardent defenders of both Canada and French Canada agreed that Canada's participation in the international community of French-speaking states was vital for the pursuit of Canadian national interests and an important step towards fulfilling the promise of biculturalism that was central to the French Canadian conception of Canada. That they disagreed about whether the Canadian government could accommodate Quebec's participation in this community without undermining the pursuit of biculturalism in Canada is indicative of the turmoil in Ottawa provoked by the emergence of Québécois nationalism and the related demands for new powers and responsibilities from the government of Quebec in the 1960s. In the end, the governments of Canada and Quebec reached a compromise in 1971–72 enabling Quebec to participate in the international organization later known as *la Francophonie* under a Canadian umbrella.[36] This compromise vindicated Léger's belief that Québécois and French Canadians could in fact co-exist in Canada, and that Québécois nationalism and the more aggressive provincial government that harnessed it for its own purposes were not an irremediable threat to Canada. Moreover, the ongoing commitment to an active role in *la Francophonie* of the Department of External Affairs and the Canadian government as a whole demonstrated the overlapping nature of Canadian and French Canadian interests in this period. Defending the one meant defending the other as well, the fulfillment of a long-standing French Canadian vision of a truly bilingual and bicultural Canadian nation.

NOTES

1 See Robin S. Gendron, *Towards a Francophone Community: Canada's Relations with France and French Africa, 1945–1968* (Montreal and Kingston: McGill-Queen's University Press, 2006), 116.

2 Memorandum, T. Carter to J. George, "Possible Canadian Initiative Regarding a French Commonwealth," 28 January 1966, Department of External Affairs Records (DEAR), vol. 10683, file 26-1, pt. 1, Library and Archives Canada (LAC); and Report, European Division, A French Commonwealth or a Francophone Community, 14 July 1966, DEAR, vol. 10683, file 26-1, pt. 1, LAC.

3 Memorandum, T. Carter to J. George, 28 January 1966, DEAR, vol. 10683, file 26-1, pt. 1, LAC.

4 Telegram 3935, M. Cadieux to External Affairs [DEA], 11 September 1966, DEAR, vol. 10683, file 26-1, pt. 2, LAC.

5 When the Diefenbaker government announced that it would begin extending educational assistance to the French-speaking countries in Africa in November, 1961, Professor Jacques Morin of the Université de Montréal lamented that the government had already been providing scholarships to Commonwealth countries in Africa for over two years. According to Morin, the discrepancy between the two programs only reinforced the degree to which French Canadian interests were of secondary importance in Canada's foreign policy. Jacques Morin, "Scholarships for French-Speaking African Countries," *Le Devoir*, 12 November 1960, DEAR, vol. 5258, file 8260-15-40, pt. 1, LAC.

6 John English, *The Worldly Years: The Life and Times of Lester Pearson, 1949–1972* (Toronto: Vintage, 1993), 149.

7 Ibid.

8 Marcel Cadieux, *Le Diplomate canadien: elements d'une définition* (Paris: Fides, 1962).

9 See, for example, Memorandum, Marcel Cadieux to African and Middle Eastern Division, 3 January 1962, DEAR, vol. 5259, file 8260-15-40, pt. 4, LAC.

10 David Meren, "Antagonism and Engagement: Marcel Cadieux, Jules Léger, and the Department of External Affairs' Response to Canada-Quebec-France Tensions," unpublished paper presented at the Canada and France: A Diplomatic Partnership Conference, Montreal, 31 October 2008, 2.

11 For further information on Lionel Groulx and French Canadian nationalism in the 1920s, see Susan Mann Trofimenkoff, *Action Française: French Canadian Nationalism in the Twenties* (Toronto: University of Toronto Press, 1975). For a brief account of subsequent developments in French Canadian nationalism, see Marcel Martel, *French Canada: An Account of its Creation and Break-Up, 1850–1967* (Ottawa: Canadian Historical Association, 1998).

12 On the emergence of the separatist movement in Quebec, see William Coleman, *The Independence Movement in Quebec, 1945–1980* (Toronto: University of Toronto Press, 1984).

13 As quoted in Louis Balthazar, "Quebec and the Ideal of Federalism," *Annals of the American Academy of Political and Social Science* 538 (March 1995): 43. On the influence of the Tremblay Report, see Donald J. Horton, *André Laurendeau: French Canadian Nationalist, 1912–1968* (Toronto: Oxford University Press, 1992), 167.

14 See Daniel Johnson, *Égalité ou indépendance* (Montreal: Renaissance, 1965).

15 See Robin S. Gendron, "Educational aid for French Africa and the Canada–Quebec Dispute over Foreign Policy in the 1960s," *International Journal* 56, no. 1 (2000–2001): 26–28.

16 See Meren, "Antagonism and Engagement," 2; and English, *The Worldly Years*, 84.

17 J.L. Granatstein and Robert Bothwell, *Pirouette: Pierre Trudeau and Canadian Foreign Policy* (Toronto: University of Toronto Press, 1990), 123–24.

18 In 1964, Jean Chapdelaine left the Department of External Affairs to become Quebec's delegate general in Paris, one of several francophones who left the department in this period. Bitter at being denied the senior position he felt he deserved, Chapdelaine's departure was also partly motivated by the lack of sympathy in the department for Quebec's aspirations, especially after Marcel Cadieux became under-secretary of state for external affairs. See Marcel Cadieux to Jules Léger, 28 September 1964, Jules Léger Papers, vol. 2.3, LAC.

19 In the end, the Canadian government opted for the latter approach. On March 11, 1967, Paul Martin gave a speech to the Junior Chamber of Commerce in Montreal in which he proposed that the Canadian government would sponsor an international conference to foster the birth of an *Association internationale de solidarité francophone*, an umbrella organization to coordinate the activities of non-governmental associations devoted to the development of the French language and culture. See Paul Martin, "Canada and la francophonie," 11 March 1967, DEAR, vol. 10684, file 26-2-CDA, pt. 1, LAC.

20 For numerous, and varied, discussions of the significance and influence of the Gérin-Lajoie Doctrine, see Stéphane Paquin, ed., *Les relations internationales du Québec depuis la Doctrine Gérin-Lajoie (1965–2005): Le prolongement externe des competences internes* (Lévis: Les Presses de l'Université Laval, 2006).

21 Éric Roussel, *Charles de Gaulle* (Paris: Gallimard, 2002), 381–83.

22 Many works have discussed the difficulties in the Canada–France relationship in the 1960s. For some of the most notable, see Eldon Black, *Direct Intervention: Canada-France Relations, 1967–1974* (Ottawa: Carleton University Press, 1996); John Bosher, *The Gaullist Attack on Canada, 1967–1997* (Montreal: McGill-Queen's University Press, 1999); and Dale Thomson, *Vive le Québec libre* (Toronto: Deneau Publishers, 1988).

23 Jean-Daniel Jurgensen, Director of the American section in the French Foreign Ministry, elaborated upon this concern in a conversation with Jules Léger in August 1966. Telegram 1852, Paris to Ottawa, 31 August 1966, DEAR, vol. 10683, file 26-1, pt. 2, LAC.

24 Ibid.

25 Gendron, *Towards a Francophone Community*, 130–33.

26 Granatstein and Bothwell, *Pirouette*, 124–26. Along these same lines see also the legal opinion prepared by the department's legal advisor. See Allan Gotlieb, Memorandum, 27 September 1966, DEAR, vol. 10685, file 26-2-CDA-QUE, pt. 1, LAC.

27 In late December 1967, Cadieux prepared a memorandum for Prime Minister Lester B. Pearson outlining possible responses the Canadian government could take if France engineered an invitation for Quebec to the Libreville Conference in early 1968. These responses included abrogating Canada–France trade agreements, ending the visa waiver for French citizens travelling to Canada, challenging French actions in the World Court, or even breaking off diplomatic relations with France entirely. His own inclination, he wrote, "would be to let the French and the world know that there is still some life left in us, and that we will react with all the vigour and strength at our command to protect ourselves against external intervention [in Canada's internal affairs]." Cadieux to the Prime Minister, 27 December 1967, DEAR, vol. 10689, file 26-4-CME-1968, pt. 1, LAC.

28 See, for example, Jules Léger to Marcel Cadieux, 7 February 1967, DEAR, vol. 10683, file 26-1, pt. 3, LAC. See also Léger's arguments to this effect included in, Memorandum for the Prime Minister, 14 August 1967, DEAR, vol. 10045, file 20-1-2-FR, pt. 7, LAC.

29 Telegram, Paris to Ottawa, 11 January 1968, DEAR, vol. 10685, file 26-2-CDA-QUE, pt. 1, LAC.

30 Marcel Cadieux, Memorandum for the Minister, 30 March 1967, DEAR, vol. 10045, file 20-1-2-FR, pt. 5, LAC.

31 Telegram, Paris to Ottawa, 11 January 1968, DEAR, vol. 10685, file 26-2-CDA-QUE, pt. 1, LAC.

32 English, *The Worldly Years*, 318.

33 See, for example, Granatstein and Bothwell, *Pirouette*, 123.

34 Claude Morin, *Les Choses comme elles étaient* (Montreal: Boréal, 1994), 191–92.

35 Meren, "Antagonism and Engagement," 7.

36 See Granatstein and Bothwell, *Pirouette*, 143–45.

EXTERNAL AFFAIRS AND CANADIAN EXTERNAL TRADE POLICY, 1945-1982[1]

Michael Hart

If the academic literature on Canadian foreign policy is to be believed, trade and economic policy form at best a minor part of Canada's external relations and occupied very little of the time and energy of ministers and officials in the Department of External Affairs during the post-war years.[2] Some will suggest that this changed in 1982, with the integration of the trade components of the former Department of Industry, Trade and Commerce into External Affairs to form the new Department of External Affairs and International Trade, but with the unvoiced suggestion that this was perhaps a retrograde step. To the academic community, foreign policy as practised by Canada's diplomats is largely focused on political and humanitarian issues and only rarely on economic matters.

Nothing could be further from the truth. From the outset, Canadian foreign policy was more a matter of foreign economic policy than anything else, with the political, security, and other dimensions only emerging over time as Canada's role in the world matured and required a broader focus. The economic dimension, however, always remained a critical dimension and never more so than during the postwar years. The Economic Division and later Bureau occupied a large place in the department's activities throughout those years and some of its ablest officials built their careers in trade and economic assignments.

The official on whom many modelled their careers was none other than Norman Robertson. Most people remember Robertson as the successor to O.D. Skelton, as the dominant career official of the 1940s and 1950s, twice under-secretary of state for external affairs, twice high commissioner to the United Kingdom, and ambassador to the United States. His career started and ended, however, as a trade negotiator. In the 1930s, he led the Canadian delegations that negotiated the 1935 and 1938 Reciprocal Trade Agreements with the United States, and, in the 1960s, he initially led the Canadian delegation to the Kennedy Round of General Agreement on Tariffs and Trade (GATT) negotiations, before retiring and becoming the first director of the Norman Paterson School of International Affairs at Carleton University.[3] Those officials who, in later years, sniffed at the dilution of Canadian foreign policy by the dominance of trade considerations were as ignorant of their history as they were of the government's policy priorities. Robertson was succeeded by such able people as Jake Warren, Gerry Stoner, Ed Ritchie, Don McPhail, Frank Stone, Pamela McDougall, Gerry Shannon, John Weekes, and others, a number of whom served the government later as deputy ministers.

Before I go any further, it is important to note that trade policy and trade promotion are – and largely remain – two different branches of government service with remarkably little overlap. Even before there was a Department of External Affairs, Canada employed trade commissioners to promote Canadian exports and assist Canadian exporters in distant markets. The government established the Department of Trade and Commerce in 1892 and employed the first resident trade commissioners in the Caribbean Islands that year. The first Canada-based trade commissioner was posted to Australia in 1894.[4] Over the course of the service's first hundred years, most trade commissioners spent much of their careers at posts abroad and occasionally at home serving, for example, in regional bureaus in Trade and Commerce.[5] Few were deployed in negotiating and implementing trade agreements, although one of the earliest and most distinguished of Canada's trade negotiators, Dana Wilgress, started his career as a trade commissioner assigned to sell farm equipment in Omsk in Russia. In the 1930s, together with Norman Robertson and Hector McKinnon from Finance, he was part of Canada's premier trade negotiating team. In the 1940s, he was head of the Canadian delegation to the negotiations that led to the GATT, and he served for five years as the first chair of GATT's Contracting Parties. He was also, briefly, high commissioner to the United Kingdom, under-secretary of state for external affairs, and ambassador to NATO.

Over the period under review, 1945–82, the making of Canadian trade policy was the preserve of a relatively small group of officials drawn principally from three departments: Finance, Trade and Commerce (after 1968, Industry, Trade and Commerce), and External Affairs. Additionally, because of the historical importance of agriculture in Canadian export trade, Agriculture officials made a large contribution. Other departments and agencies also participated as individual issues demanded, such as Energy, Mines, and Resources, Fisheries and Oceans, and Customs and Excise, but on virtually all issues, the core group was made up of officials from these three departments. Finance officials concentrated on Canadian import policy; their minister was responsible for the tariff and all aspects of customs and related policies and Finance officials were intimately familiar with the vulnerabilities of the Canadian economy to import competition. Trade and Commerce was responsible for export policy and export promotion; its officials were fully up to date on the export interests and capabilities of Canadian industry. External Affairs played a coordinating role, finding middle ground and providing leadership. Its principal instrument was control over communications between headquarters and posts abroad.

Unlike Finance and Trade and Commerce officials, who came armed with legislation and clear ministerial mandates, External Affairs officials participated largely on their personal merits. While they obviously had a sense of broader foreign policy priorities, they rarely injected these into the discussions. They accepted that trade policy had to reflect domestic economic, political, and commercial priorities and international opportunities. Maintaining productive relations with trading partners was also important. But factoring in geopolitical, development, or human rights concerns was definitely far down the list of priorities, no matter what their colleagues in political divisions preferred. Occasionally, broader foreign policy considerations might rise to the top, such as in the consideration of the accession of a number of Eastern European countries to the GATT in the late 1960s and early 1970s, but generally more focused trade and economic concerns crowded out foreign policy considerations and woe the External Affairs official who did not understand this.

To maintain credibility at the trade policy table, therefore, officials from External Affairs had to demonstrate that they were immune to "foreign policy" considerations and were prepared to contribute to the development and delivery of Canadian trade policy on the basis of technical expertise and mastery of the files. As such, the department's trade policy officials were at times treated as aliens in their own ministry and by their colleagues abroad. When I participated in negotiating textile and clothing import restraint agreements in the late 1970s and early 1980s, for example, it was a rare ambassador who was prepared to meet with the Canadian delegation and provide counsel and assistance on local circumstances. More typical were those who got out of town before we arrived, convinced that any association with us would taint their good relations with the locals.[6] They appeared not to comprehend that we might be pursuing the government's policy and Canadian interests, suffering instead from the well-known diplomatic disease of localitis – a tendency to forget that it is the sending government that is a diplomat's employer, rather than the receiving government.

Similarly, when I was responsible for Canadian import policy files at External Affairs in the late 1970s, I was frequently peppered with calls and memoranda from political divisions asking me to do something about those Neanderthals in Finance, Revenue Canada, or elsewhere, who were complicating relations with one of their foreign clients by pursuing, for example, antidumping or countervailing duty investigations. The idea that such investigations were based in Canadian law, were consistent with Canada's international rights and obligations, and reflected legitimate Canadian interests rarely occurred to them. For many such officers, good bilateral relations were an end in themselves rather than a means to serving Canadian interests.[7]

Finally, when I served at Canada's permanent mission in Geneva in the mid-1970s, one of my responsibilities was to represent Canada at meetings developing an Integrated Program for Commodities under the auspices of the United Nations Conference on Trade and Development (UNCTAD). At UNCTAD IV in Nairobi, Kenya, in 1974, governments had adopted a set of resolutions that authorized UNCTAD to explore the parameters of a program that would stabilize world prices, and thus export earnings, for a list of eighteen commodities that were critical to the economic prospects of developing countries. The list included such products as coffee, tea, cocoa, sugar, and jute, all classic developing country exports, but it also included minerals such as copper, iron ore, phosphate, and manganese, and agricultural products such as vegetable oils and tropical timber, products that were of considerable commercial interest to Canadian companies.

It was a fascinating assignment. Officials in Ottawa prepared detailed, helpful briefing material on each of the commodities, allowing me to be well-informed on the issues and participate actively in the discussions. But I also had to wrestle daily with a conundrum: conflicting instructions. Officials in External Affairs responsible for development policy and Canadian participation in UNCTAD wanted me to play a constructive role advancing the conference's goals and objectives, while officials in domestic economic departments were equally firm that I should not support anything that might compromise Canadian commercial interests. In short, my role was to engage in a damage limitation exercise: I had to be seen to be helpful and constructive but make sure nothing serious happened. It was my first introduction to the difference between values-based and interest-based policy-making. In the end, pragmatism and commercial interests trumped ideals.

Juggling conflicting instructions, negotiating textile restraint agreements, and dismissing the immediate concerns of political officers all taught me the truth of what one former under-secretary of state for external affairs, Allan Gotlieb, has characterized as the underlying schizophrenia of much of Canadian foreign policy. Gotlieb traces the tensions in Canadians' desires to satisfy the visionary, romantic, idealistic side of their nature while also attending to the need to deal pragmatically with challenges to their security and prosperity. As he notes, there is no necessary conflict between these two elements, as long as they are kept within a proper balance. But, he adds, if Canada's feet are not planted firmly on the ground of who it is, where it fits, and what it can realistically do, the idealistic side of its nature threatens to descend into bathos. We have seen a lot of evidence along these lines in recent years.[8]

Over the period 1945–82, trade policy was largely immune from this schizophrenia. Despite the different ministers and departments they served, core trade policy officials in the postwar years were remarkably homogenous in their outlook. Many had had some formal education in economics, but their approach was very much based on practical experience and on-the-job training. Over this period, none would have described himself – and they were all men – as free traders. Free trade was an academic concept. Trade negotiations and trade policy were about access to foreign markets and protecting vulnerable Canadian industrial sectors. They lost little sleep worrying about the mercantilist basis for much of the policy they hammered out in their interdepartmental meetings. Progressive liberalization was desirable, but at a pace that was politically sustainable. Their job was to provide ministers with advice that was politically acceptable, expanded opportunities for export-oriented sectors of the economy, and retained scope for Canadian-based manufacturing.

The basic contours of modern Canadian trade policy were set in the 1930s and remained essentially the same until the conclusion of the Canada–United States free-trade agreement in 1987. They were well summed up by Norman Robertson in a 1937 memorandum to the under-secretary of state for external affairs, O.D. Skelton:

> Our stake in world trade and the peculiar degree of dependence of our industries on export markets have identified Canada's real national interest with the revival and liberation of international trade.... It is true that there are a number of important local and sectional interests which in the short run, and perhaps in the longer run, stand to lose rather than to gain from the adjustment in tariffs and preferential margins which our collaboration in new trade agreements with the United Kingdom and the United States would involve. ... this country's general national interest is, for better or worse, bound up with the prospect of freer international trade and that this paramount interest should outweigh special and local interests which may be deriving exceptional advantages from an uneconomic policy.[9]

If he had lived until the 1980s, Robertson might have expressed some regrets about the pace of liberalization, but not about its direction, the central role played by negotiations with the United States, and the declining one of the United Kingdom. These directions were already clear in the 1930s and remained remarkably consistent for the next five decades.

Throughout this period, ministers and their senior officials were generally on the same page, but not always. Indeed, there were a number of celebrated instances in which the prime minister and senior officials were definitely not on the same page. In the spring of 1948, for example, when Prime Minister W.L. Mackenzie King pulled the plug on the secret negotiations between Canada and the United States considering the contours of a possible bilateral free-trade agreement, diplomats Lester Pearson and Norman Robertson both expressed deep disappointment. They accepted King's decision, but regretted it nonetheless.[10] A decade later, when the newly elected Conservative prime minister John Diefenbaker expressed a desire to shift 15 per cent of Canadian trade from the United States to the United Kingdom, officials dutifully prepared their analysis, which indicated the draconian steps required to achieve this objective, and thus buried one of the more quixotic policy impulses in the history of Canadian trade policy.[11]

Although Diefenbaker's impulse was the most dramatic, it was certainly not isolated. Diefenbaker had wanted to change the fundamental character of Canada's trade dependence on the United States by looking to Britain and the Commonwealth. Six years later, Liberal Finance Minister Walter Gordon was equally determined to make the Canadian economy less reliant on American investment capital and international trade in general. As nationalistic as Diefenbaker, Gordon drew on the ideas of the interventionist left rather than on the nostalgic right. The professionals in the bureaucracy found this brand of nationalism just as difficult to translate into practical policy choices. They had seen Diefenbaker's desire to shift 15 per cent of Canada's trade from the United States to Britain as impractical. They found Gordon's desire to make Canada less reliant on United States capital and markets just as foolish.[12]

It is ironic that Gordon found himself presiding as minister of finance over the most important trade policy achievement of the 1960s, the negotiation of the Canada–United States Autopact. The sectoral free trade deal further integrated the Canadian economy into the American one and laid the groundwork for the Canada–United States Free Trade Agreement. Gordon accepted that the alternatives in the automotive sector were politically unacceptable, but even he could not have imagined its success and long-term impact on the evolution of the Canadian economy. Simon Reisman led the autopact negotiations, but his team included two giants from External Affairs: Ed Ritchie and Allan Gotlieb.[13]

The trade policy community was also not convinced that Prime Minister Pierre Trudeau's desire to strengthen Canadian trade ties with the European Common Market and Japan and reduce Canadian dependence on the United States made much sense. This was one of the few significant episodes of a major rift among trade policy officials. External Affairs officials, reporting to Mitchell Sharp and the prime minister, took seriously the ideas of a Canada–Europe contractual link and deepening and broadening Canada–Japan commercial ties. Finance did not. Its deputy at the beginning of the discussions, Simon Reisman, went so far as to claim that the idea had never been approved by Cabinet. He was wrong. I looked up the cabinet memorandum and the related record of decision, but the fact that he continued to hold this view for many years was indicative of the disdain of Finance officials for this dimension of Canadian trade policy.[14]

Trade and Commerce officials were less vocal in their scepticism. Officials in the Western Europe Bureau, for example, were actively engaged in the discussions. The mainline trade officials in the Office of General Relations, on the other hand, devoted their resources to more important matters, such as the ongoing Tokyo Round of GATT negotiations, and ensured that the Canada–Europe and Canada–Japan discussions focused on consultative rather than contractual arrangements. No serious harm was done to existing contractual commitments under the GATT. Years of semi-annual consultations provided wonderful opportunities to eat in Brussels, but proved totally incapable of making a difference to the commercial judgment of both European and Canadian businesses, a lesson today's officials might well keep in mind. Trade policy is most effective when it works with basic market forces, rather than trying to change them.

As with earlier ill-fated impulses to shift Canadian trade patterns, Trudeau's inclinations similarly failed to appreciate that the size, composition, and direction of trade flows result from the decisions of millions of private producers and consumers. These decisions may be influenced by government policy, but major shifts in preferences require heroic or draconian policy measures and run counter to the fundamental values embedded in a democratic polity with a market economy. Such policies are likely to reduce the prosperity of most Canadians and are unlikely to be their conscious choice. Nevertheless, if officials cannot dissuade the government from a course of action that they believe to be quixotic or unproductive, it remains their duty to implement the government's decision, and officials at External Affairs dutifully did so in negotiating new agreements with Europe and Japan aimed at diversifying Canadian trade and investment patterns. Little came of these agreements, but they became an important part of the Trudeau legacy, parts of which continued to be invoked by departmental officials long after their lack of impact had become clear.[15]

For Canada, trade policy has always been one of the most important components of its foreign policy. Canadian trade negotiator Rodney Grey once observed that "for a small country surrounded by larger countries and heavily dependent on trade with one of them, foreign policy should, in major part, be trade relations policy. Of course, other policy issues are also vital to Canadians, but if a small country dissipates its foreign policy bargaining power on issues that concern it primarily as a member of the international community, it might not have the resources, the credibility, or the leverage to protect its trade policy interests."[16] Grey was right, and for most of its history Canadian governments accepted this reality – but not always. Grey made his observation not long after retiring in 1980, following more than a decade of experience with a prime minister who did not see matters that way.

The legacy of the postwar years was the establishment of a rules-based international trade order as a universally accepted part of both intellectual and intergovernmental discourse. The success of that order proved critical in integrating national economies into a global economy. In terms of orders of magnitude, the value of international trade nearly tripled in real terms from 1950 to 1980.[17] Even in a trade-dependent country like Canada, the value of trade measured as a share of total production nearly doubled. Trade stimulated increasing specialization and competition, and contributed importantly to the rise in prosperity in the countries of the Organization for Economic Co-operation and Development (OECD).

For a relatively small economy dependent on trade with larger economies, it is not difficult to identify what became the hallmarks of "good" trade policy. Nevertheless, as in so many areas, the conjunction between good policy and good politics often proved narrow, difficult to find, and hard to implement.[18]

As the postwar generation would have described it, good trade policy involved the careful integration of economic, business, legal, and political ideas and values into a coherent set of laws, agreements, regulations, policies, and practices, attuned to the circumstances of the moment but broad enough to endure. From an economic perspective, it found ways to move towards more open markets. Competitive markets and consumer choice are critical contributors to national and individual welfare and are among the most widely shared values in economics. They are also critical to the goals of the global trade regime.

Governments, of course, pursue more than economic objectives. Policies that distort market efficiencies may serve other important societal goals. Efforts to ensure consumer safety, national security, cultural identity, sustainable environments, or distributive justice may affect the operation of the market and the flow of goods and services across national borders. The challenge, therefore, was to balance competing claims and to design policies that addressed society's most important values and pressing priorities. The trade policy community learned from experience that sound economic policies promoted broad, national interests over narrow, special interests in order to gain benefits for the many rather than for a privileged few. But they also knew that their political masters had very keen noses for the needs of special, particularly local, interests.

From a business perspective, good trade policy establishes a stable and predictable economic climate at home and abroad. It appreciates that business thrives in an orderly setting and stagnates when there is sudden and unpredictable change, and it recognizes that competition only works if everybody plays by the same rules. Canada's business leaders may not always have applauded the benefits of international competition and an open economy, but they never wavered in their commitment to stability and predictability and were quick to criticize policies that undermined these objectives, including policies that required them to adjust to changing and growing international competition. The record shows that, while Canadian officials were sensitive to business interests, they were far from slaves to a corporate agenda.

The legal contribution was to insist on a rules-based order built around the fundamental precepts of non-discrimination, transparency, and due process. Only by establishing rules that treat all traders the same, that are widely known and uniformly applied, and that provide for the orderly and equitable resolution of disputes will entrepreneurs have the confidence to compete, invest in the future, and look beyond their own shores. Transparency, non-discrimination, and due process are the basis not only of domestic law but also of international law. Canadian officials were among the staunchest proponents of a rules-based order, even if at times they had to satisfy ministers by finding ways to avoid politically inconvenient rules. In the 1950s, Australian officials were wont to taunt their Canadian colleagues by referring to them as 'halo polishers.'

Canada's active embrace of the GATT and multilateralism during the postwar years, while broadly beneficial to the country, illustrates the enormous role of external factors in shaping Canadian trade policy. The negotiation of the GATT in 1947–48 proved to be a wonderful framework for pursuing gradual liberalization while not abandoning the internally inconsistent policy impulses that ministers had found so congenial ever since the adoption of the National Policy in 1879. GATT brought together the governments of twenty-three countries with similarly contradictory policies and objectives: maximize export opportunities while minimizing import competition. All were fully in thrall to Lord Macauley's famous dictum that "free trade, one of the greatest blessings which a government can confer on a people, is in almost every country unpopular."

GATT's rules and bargaining method turned out to be admirably suited to countries that wanted to have their cake and eat it too. Its policy of gradual liberalization within a framework of general rules was tailor-made for Canada.[19] It relied on export interests to overcome import-competing interests, but only a little at a time. It was not based on academic theories but on pragmatic observation. It relied on the impact of two sets of external factors to gradually refashion the Canadian economy: the impact of broadly agreed rules and procedures and the economic interests of the country's most promising trading partners. The fact that the country most responsive to Canadian trade and policy priorities was the United States reinforced the pull of geography and business judgment, resulting in the growing interdependence of the Canadian and United States economies.

Throughout this period, critics worried that a growing taste for international rules and institutions would undermine Canada's ability to pursue independent domestic and foreign policy objectives. All international agreements, of course, whether aimed at economic, environmental, human rights, military, or other objectives, seek to curb the full expression of autonomous national decision-making. States make the reasonable calculation that their interests are better served if other states are required to behave in a predictable and stable manner, subject to commonly agreed rules and procedures to enforce them. Trade agreements are neither an exception to, nor fundamentally different from, the many other agreements, conventions, and declarations to which Canada is party.

Between 1945 and 1982, Canadian trade officials learned well, if slowly, the lesson that without the constraint of jointly agreed external rules it was difficult to resist domestic protectionist interests. Canadians found it hard to accept that a resource-based economy without secure markets for its products, coupled with an inefficient, import-substitution manufacturing sector, provided a poor basis for sustained growth and prosperity. In the face of stubborn protectionism in the United States and in Europe, however, Canadians found it difficult to reduce foreign barriers to their exports or to resist the call for protection from their own manufacturers. It took many years, starting in the 1930s, to create the conditions that made "good" trade policy politically acceptable. By 1982 the results were firmly ensconced and paved the way for the negotiation of the Canada–United States Free Trade Agreement.

By 1982, Canada had one of the most open economies in the world, next door to the world's largest and most dynamic market. The deployment of sensible trade policies had gradually provided Canadians with the prosperity, the jobs, and the choices that made the best of Canada's comparative advantage and allowed them to reap the benefits of the best that others could offer. By then, Canadians were prepared to accept that their future prosperity depended critically on developing a more outwardly oriented economy.

The government's decision early in 1982 to merge the trade promotion and trade policy elements of the Department of Industry, Trade and

Commerce with the Department of External Affairs to create the Department of External Affairs and International Trade[20] seems an appropriate place to stop this survey, but not without dismissing the notion that Canadian foreign policy became more sensitive to trade considerations as a result, at the expense of political and other considerations. Trade and other economic considerations had always and continued to form an integral part of Canada's external policy. What changed in 1982 was the institutional basis for the development and delivery of that policy. The decision to proceed with the bilateral free-trade negotiations with the United States in 1985 is often cited as proof that trade considerations had trumped broader foreign policy considerations. As a participant in much of the preparatory work and in the delivery of that policy, I saw no evidence of such a change, nor in the subsequent decision to negotiate a broader agreement to include Mexico, nor in subsequent efforts to negotiate other free-trade agreements.[21] Governments make decisions based on political factors and considerations that are persuasive to the prime minister and his colleagues. The advice tendered by the officials has an important bearing on the shape and detail of that policy, but not on its fundamental direction.

With few exceptions, Canada's approach to trade policy-making over the postwar years was incremental, pragmatic, and cautious. More could certainly have been done, or done more boldly, but radical departures were, in the view of Canada's trade policy practitioners, neither warranted nor likely to succeed. Officials in External Affairs, Finance, and Trade and Commerce all exhibited a deep appreciation of the basic realities within which Canadian government policies operate, including the capability and interest of Canadian firms. In Canada, trade and investment are primarily private sector activities. Governments can facilitate or frustrate these activities, but ultimately they do not trade or invest. Those areas where governments have engaged directly in economic activity – such as crown corporations – have not provided much comfort that government can do better than the private sector.

The relatively small Canadian market imposed a second limitation. Without access to foreign markets, it is unlikely that much Canadian industrial production could have attained the competitive scale required to finance innovation and other desirable features. Additionally, both business leaders and experienced trade officials developed a clear understanding of the extent to which foreign markets offered real rather than potential opportunities. In the case of Japan, for example, Canadian exporters long faced some formidable barriers involving, not only market access, but also costs, consumer interests and preferences, and institutional barriers. Even large, well-financed firms in the United States and the European Union, backed up by the muscle of their much bigger governments, found the Japanese market tough sledding in areas other than those for which there are no Japanese suppliers. European and developing country markets offer their own difficulties. Over time, Canadian firms found niches in these markets, but only after earning enough from Canadian and United States markets to finance the effort.

Within these realities, Canadian officials used the policy instruments at their disposal to nurture trade and industrial patterns that provided Canada with growing prosperity. The desired pace of adjustment, however, was dependent on both external and domestic factors. Externally, Canada's major trading partners, particularly the United States, had to open up their markets to Canadian suppliers and accept the discipline of international rules to underwrite this market access. Domestically, governments, firms, and workers had to accept increasing levels of foreign competition and to make constant efforts to upgrade and adjust domestic production. The mutually reinforcing impact of these external and domestic dimensions has been key to the incremental nature of this strategy.

The results were impressive. Slowly but steadily, Canada opened its economy to greater competition and became an increasingly adroit practitioner of good trade policy. Although exceptions and challenges remain, the default position for Canada is clearly free trade and open markets. As such, Canada is better placed to tackle the next series of challenges arising from both globalization and deepening bilateral integration. And officials from the Department of External Affairs were important contributors to these policy developments that served to advance the national interest.

NOTES

1. I would like to thank Greg Donaghy and the organizers of the centenary conferences for asking me to participate. This paper draws extensively on two sources: my experience as an official in the Department of External Affairs and its successors from 1974 through 1995, and my subsequent research and writing as a professor at the Norman Paterson School of International Affairs at Carleton University, reflected most importantly in *A Trading Nation: Canadian Trade Policy from Colonialism to Globalization* (Vancouver: UBC Press, 2002) and *From Pride to Influence: Towards a New Canadian Foreign Policy* (Vancouver: UBC Press, 2008).

2. For example, in their otherwise admirable study of the foreign policy of the Trudeau years, *Pirouette: Pierre Trudeau and Canadian Foreign Policy* (Toronto: University of Toronto Press, 1990), Jack Granatstein and Robert Bothwell never mention the Tokyo Round of multilateral trade negotiations (1973–79) at the General Agreement on Tariffs and Trade (GATT), or any other aspect of mainstream trade policy. In his new, even more admirable, study of the postwar years, *Alliance and Illusion: Canada and the World, 1945–1984* (Vancouver: UBC Press, 2007), Bothwell provides good coverage of Canada's role in the formation of the GATT, participation in the Kennedy Round negotiations (1964–67), and the negotiation of the Canada–U.S. Autopact (1965), but loses interest in commercial policy once he gets to Trudeau. This mindset is even evident in the Department's official two-volume history, John Hilliker, *Canada's Department of External Affairs: The Early Years, 1909–1946* and Hilliker and Donald Barry, *Canada's Department of External Affairs: Coming of Age, 1946–1968* (Montreal and Kingston: McGill-Queen's University Press, 1990 and 1995).

3. His career is well chronicled in Jack Granatstein's biography, *A Man of Influence: Norman A. Robertson and Canadian Statecraft, 1929–1968* (Toronto: Deneau, 1981).

4. See O. Mary Hill, *Canada's Salesman to the World: The Department of Trade and Commerce, 1892–1939* (Montreal and Kingston: McGill-Queen's University Press, 1977).

5. While most trade commissioners were foreign service officers, they were part of a separate service with headquarters in the Department of Trade and Commerce, and a rather loose reporting relationship to the head of post at missions abroad. It was not until the rationalizing impulses of Prime Minister Trudeau and his clerk, Michael Pitfield, in the early 1970s, that efforts were made to integrate the three foreign services (political, trade, and immigration) with the establishment of the Interdepartmental Committee on External Relations and greater financial, administrative, and managerial control over missions abroad by the head of post. See Bothwell, *Alliance and Illusion*, 372–80.

6. My colleagues and I were, of course, well aware that our efforts served narrow, protectionist interests rather than broader, longer term economic welfare. As officials, however, it was our role to implement the policy preferences of ministers rather than our own. The urge to improve on the government's policy preferences, while widespread among some officials, often proves career limiting.

7. This mindset is not limited to foreign service officers trying to ward off unpleasant or complicating problems. It is also evident in such recent semi-popular laments on the decline of Canadian foreign policy, such as Jennifer Welsh, *At Home in the World: Canada's Global Vision for the 21st Century* (Toronto: Harper Collins, 2004) and Andrew Cohen, *While Canada Slept: How We Lost Our Place in the World* (Toronto: McClelland & Stewart, 2003). In their view, Canadian diplomats should strive harder to ensure that Canada is well-liked and doing

good works, rather than being focused on pursuing the national interest.

8   See Allan E. Gotlieb, "Romanticism and Realism in Canada's Foreign Policy," *C.D. Howe Benefactors Lecture, 2004* (Toronto: C.D. Howe Institute, November 2004). I develop this theme in greater detail in Hart, *From Pride to Influence*, chap. 2.

9   Quoted in Granatstein, *A Man of Influence*, 66–67.

10 See Michael Hart, "Almost But Not Quite: The 1947–48 Bilateral Canada–U.S. Negotiations," *American Review of Canadian Studies* 19, no. 1 (1989): 25-58.

11 For more detail, see Hart, *A Trading Nation*, 206–8.

12 See Stephen Azzi, *Walter Gordon and the Rise of Canadian Nationalism* (Montreal and Kingston: McGill-Queen's University Press, 1999).

13 For more detail, see Hart, *A Trading Nation*, 234–47 and Greg Donaghy, *Tolerant Allies: Canada and the United States 1963–1968* (Montreal and Kingston: McGill-Queen's University Press, 2002).

14 I am relying here on memory. I called up the memorandum and the record of decision when I was part of Reisman's Trade Negotiations Office during the Canada–U.S. Free Trade Agreement talks. Over the course of the negotiations, Simon educated us with many an entertaining lecture on the development of Canadian trade policy, much of it featuring Simon Reisman and some of it prompting me to check whether they were corroborated by the files. Simon's memory proved remarkably accurate, but not on this occasion. See Michael Hart and Bill Dymond, "A Life Well Lived – Simon Reisman," *Policy Options* 29, no. 4 (2008): 23, for a summary of his contribution to Canadian public policy. More generally, on the pursuit of the so-called third option, see Hart, *A Trading Nation*, 288–98.

15 In 1982–83, when I was part of the team reviewing Canadian trade policy, officials in the European Branch and the Policy Planning Bureau complained that the drafts of documents we were preparing for cabinet consideration did not sufficiently reflect the orthodoxy of the third option. Derek Burney, at that time assistant undersecretary for trade and economic policy, had to explain to them that the purpose of the review was, well, to review the past and offer options for the future, and to do so critically. They were not satisfied that this should extend to a critical assessment of the shortcomings of the third option. To their chagrin, ministers did not share their sense of impending doom if the third option were not further enshrined in Canadian policy. Nevertheless, like Banquo, its ghost continues to wander the halls of the Pearson Building. See Michael Hart and Bill Dymond, "A Canada–EU FTA is an awful idea," *Policy Options* 23 (July–August 2002): 27-32.

16 Rodney de C. Grey, *Trade Policy in the 1980s: An Agenda for Canadian–U.S. Relations* (Montreal: C.D. Howe Institute, 1981), 3.

17 The World Trade Organization calculates that the ratio of world trade in goods and services to output increased from 7 to 15 per cent over the period 1950 to 1974, and from 15 to 28 per cent between 1974 and 2004, i.e., it has quadrupled since 1950. It grew most rapidly in the first two decades, slowed perceptibly during the 1970s and 1980s, and again grew rapidly since. This is consistent with, first, the impact of postwar recovery, and second, the impact of regional and global integration. See World Trade Organization, *International Trade Trends and Statistics* (Geneva: World Trade Organization, 1996 and 2006); accessed at www.wto.org.

18 Bill Dymond and I explore the intellectual and political bases of postwar trade policy as embedded in the GATT in "Navigating New Trade Routes: The Rise of Value Chains, and the Challenges for Canadian Trade Policy," *C.D. Howe Institute Commentary*, no. 259 (Toronto: C.D. Howe Institute, 2008).

19 I develop this theme in more detail in *Fifty Years of Canadian Tradecraft: Canada at the GATT, 1947–1997* (Ottawa: Centre for Trade Policy and Law, 1998).

20 Subsequent mythmaking has obscured the prime motive that prompted Prime Minister Trudeau and his clerk of the Privy Council, Michael Pitfield, to make this move. The creation of the Department of Regional Economic Expansion in the 1970s, aimed at promoting economic development in the less advantaged parts of the country, particularly the Maritimes and Quebec, had been at best a qualified success. Trudeau and his advisors were convinced that its impact could be enhanced by integrating its mandate with the broader industrial development programs of the Department of Industry, Trade and Commerce to create a Department of Regional Industrial Expansion. This would have left the trade side of that department as a stand-alone institution. Instead, Trudeau and Pitfield chose what they had long desired: integration of the three elements of the foreign service - political, trade, and immigration. The immigration service proved a poor fit and was soon hived off to the new Department of Citizenship and Immigration, but the trade and political elements found a reasonable bureaucratic accommodation and efforts by Prime Minister Paul Martin to divorce the two partners in 2004 proved ill-fated. Bureaucratic organizational and institutional issues fascinate some analysts but they are on weak grounds when they suggest that the organization of the bureaucracy makes a material difference to the policy officials recommend and implement. As I make clear above, Trade, Finance, and External Affairs officials had always worked together. What changed in 1982 was the extent to which issues were discussed and resolved inter- or intra-departmentally. The integrated department was renamed the Department of Foreign Affairs and International Trade by Prime Minister Jean Chrétien, probably at the behest of his mentor, Mitchell Sharp, who had never liked the convention that relations with Britain and the rest of the Commonwealth, sharing the Queen as head of state, could never be foreign, and thus the long-standing preference for External Affairs.

21 See Michael Hart, with Bill Dymond and Colin Robertson, *Decision at Midnight: Inside the Canada–U.S. Free Trade Negotiations* (Vancouver: UBC Press, 1994), for a detailed account of the decision to proceed with bilateral free trade and the role of officials in that decision.

CONFLICTING VISIONS: PIERRE TRUDEAU, EXTERNAL AFFAIRS, AND ENERGY POLICY

Tammy Nemeth

When the Liberal Party met in April 1968 to choose a successor to Prime Minister Lester B. Pearson they opted for change.[1] Pierre Elliott Trudeau was in many ways the antithesis of Pearson; he was charismatic, energetic, single, bilingual, and, at the comparatively young age of 48, he captured the minds and imagination of the youth of the 1960s. Pearson's bowtie seemed antiquated compared to the rose Trudeau wore in his lapel. Most scholarly works and reflections by contemporaries about the years when Trudeau was in power in Canada have a common theme: a significant aspect of Trudeau's personal philosophy was to challenge conventional wisdom.[2] Or, as Trudeau put it himself, "the only constant factor to be found in my thinking over the years has been opposition to accepted opinions."[3] Both the departments of Energy, Mines and Resources (EMR) and External Affairs were significantly affected by Trudeau's desire to challenge conventional thinking on Canada's energy policy and relations with the United States, as he articulated a new vision of Canada's national interest.

Successive Canadian governments since the end of the Second World War have believed in close cooperation with the United States as the central component of Canada's national interest. Though policy-makers in Ottawa were careful to ensure that these relations were not too close or cozy, they were generally inclined to embrace an informal continentalism that served Canadian interests, especially oil, well. The Trudeau years, however, marked a significant policy reversal from seeking secure export markets in the United States for Canada's oil and gas to ending exports and making Canada "self-sufficient." Two policy decisions had profound effects on Canada–United States relations during the Trudeau period: the decision to phase out oil exports to the United States in 1974, and the implementation of the controversial 1980 National Energy Program. Both policies were intended, not only to disengage Canada from the world oil market, by setting prices internally and being self-sufficient in oil, but also to decouple Canada from its interdependence with the United States in the oil and gas trade. The question remains how and why did Canada's oil policy change during the Trudeau period, and what was the role of the Department of External Affairs in formulating that policy?

Trudeau's View of the National Interest

Prime Minister Pierre Trudeau came to office in April 1968 determined to tie Canada's foreign policy more closely and explicitly to the national interest. For Trudeau and his allies, as historians Jack Granatstein and Robert Bothwell describe, this meant replacing the "helpful-fixer" role of Pearsonian diplomacy with a new focus on "an inward-looking concern for the national interest, for economic growth as the focus of Canadian foreign policy, followed by social justice and the quality of life."[4] Stung by his successor's change, Lester B. Pearson criticized the new direction of Canadian foreign policy for its narrow and traditional conception of the national self-interest, which "merely evokes resistance from other nations, also in the name of national interest, and … leads to confrontation and conflict."[5] Allan Gotlieb, former Canadian ambassador to the United States, explained in a recent interview that "national interest" meant not being crusaders internationally – not overreaching – and, most importantly, having no "special relationship" with the United States.⁶ This meant pursuing relations with countries, such as Cuba and the People's Republic of China, even if Washington considered them beyond the pale; diversifying trade relations in order to reduce Canada's economic dependence on the United States; and increasing Canadian ownership of the economy, which necessarily came at the expense of the United States.

In discussing Trudeau's concept of the "national interest," a close prime-ministerial advisor explained that the government "thought that we could pursue a policy that didn't need to copy the Americans."⁷ Trudeau's view of the national interest vis-à-vis the United States, supported by some key members within the Liberal cabinet (and certain parts of the public), was that "continentalism ... might have gone too far;"⁸ that "exemptionalism" might not necessarily be a good thing; that the existence of a "special relationship" with the United States was questionable; that Canada was too dependent on American trade and investment and therefore diversification was needed; and that Canada's economy was too reliant on staple exports like oil and lumber and needed to be structurally altered to enhance secondary manufacturing. All of these ideas were greeted skeptically by most civil servants, much of the Canadian business community, and by many cabinet ministers. According to Mark MacGuigan, secretary of state for external affairs from 1980 to 1982, "Trudeau was always ready to thumb his nose at the U.S.... [He] projected more anti-Americanism to Americans in the Reagan era than was tolerable to them, and more than was palatable to most Canadians. In this respect, he served neither Canadian interest nor Canadian preferences."⁹

In many ways, as Michael Hart argues in his chapter, Trudeau's view of the "national interest" conflicted with how the Department of External Affairs had managed the Canada–United States relationship in the postwar period, and the rationale behind Canadian oil policy. This is understandable, given that postwar Canadian governments up to Trudeau tended to pursue the type of close relationship with the United States that Trudeau found problematic. In the pre-Trudeau years, and even in the initial years of his first government, the guiding principle behind External Affairs' approach to Canada–United States trade and relations was informal continentalism. Given the importance of oil and gas to a modern economy and the instability of the world market, it was better, in the view of the pragmatic informal continentalists, to have a policy that permitted flexibility if circumstances changed.[10] Most senior diplomats of the 1950s and 1960s, including Norman Robertson, Ed Ritchie, Marcel Cadieux, and Basil Robinson, embraced the informal continental approach and walked the tightrope between economic interdependence with the United States and Canadian economic and political independence.[11] This does not mean that the department's continentalism and its conception of the national interest were unalterable. Indeed, in April 1972, under the direction of the secretary of state for external affairs, Mitchell Sharp, the department developed the idea of reducing dependence on the American market through domestic economic measures and by diversifying Canada's trade, otherwise known as the "third option." Increased economic self-sufficiency was a significant component of the new domestic economic initiative, and the oil industry was at the centre.

As early as 1970, plans were being developed in the Department of Energy, Mines and Resources to enhance Canadian participation in the oil industry and rethink the level of its trade with the United States. However, driven by two key international crises – the 1973 oil crisis generated by the Organization of Petroleum Exporting Countries (OPEC) and the oil crisis that followed the 1979 Iranian revolution, Trudeau's and his inner circle's thinking on energy issues ripened as they sensed an opportunity to set the national agenda. If Canada could have all of its oil supplied internally at a controlled price, well below the world price, then the competitive advantage gained by Canada's industrial base, which happened to be in Quebec and Ontario, would be significant. In order to carry out these changes, officials had to be trusted to develop and implement the appropriate policies. But how did these policies differ from the previous policy direction? How did they challenge the conventional approach to Canadian–American oil policy and reflect Trudeau's conception of the national interest?

Postwar Policies, 1947–1968

In the immediate post-war period, Canadian trade relations with the United States were defined by an informal continentalism.[12] The general strategy involved two stages: first, an exemption was secured from American trade and tariff policies that would normally apply to foreign countries; second, when the exemption began to fail, a more formal sectoral or commodity agreement was often negotiated. A good representative of this view is Mitchell Sharp, who served as deputy minister of trade and commerce for much of the 1950s, before joining Prime Minister Lester B. Pearson's government in 1965.[13] As Sharp describes it in his memoirs, the senior bureaucracy attempted to balance increased economic interdependence with the United States and Canadian political and economic independence.[14] Initially, the Canada–United States oil trade also followed this pattern of informal continentalism. Throughout the 1950s and into the early 1970s, Canada's priority was to secure guaranteed access to the American market for increased oil production surplus to domestic requirements. In due course, Canadian exports, like all other oil imported into the United States, invited American trade restrictions.

Although the onset of the Cold War hastened the development of the Canadian oil and gas industry, it was also responsible for raising U.S. fears about America's reliance on foreign oil supplies.[15] During the 1950s, American domestic producers, concerned that cheap oil imported from the Middle East was flooding the American market, depressing prices, and reducing domestic exploration and development, argued that oil imports jeopardized American national security. Although United States president Dwight Eisenhower delayed as long as possible, he eventually succumbed to the pressures of the independent oil producers and their Congressional supporters and enacted the Voluntary Oil Import Program (VOIP) in 1955. As reliable suppliers during World War II and the Korean War, Canada and Venezuela were exempted from the protectionist program for defence reasons. However, when the first phase of the VOIP unravelled in 1957 because some American companies chose not to comply with the voluntary limits, the program was altered and exemptions were no longer granted. When mandatory controls were introduced on 9 March 1959, Canada and Venezuela vigorously protested. Much to Venezuela's dismay and ire, Canada eventually succeeded in securing an exemption to the mandatory program while Venezuela did not. External Affairs played a key role in securing this exemption through a "diplomatic blitz" and the efforts of Canada's ambassador to the United States, Arnold Heeney, and the embassy's energy counsellor, Norm Chappell.

Heeney was Canada's ambassador to Washington from May 1953 until May 1957, and again from early 1959 until April 1962, and he was well regarded and respected in Washington.[16] Chappell had come to the embassy in the early 1950s to deal with oil and gas and other resource issues, first as a representative from the Department of Defence Production, and then, as the first energy counsellor. His job was to attend technical discussions and help convey the Canadian position to those decision-makers who determined energy policy in the United States government and industry. Confident in his abilities and in the personal networks he had developed, Heeney, with Chappell's invaluable support and assistance, set about to persuade the American executive of the importance of an exemption for Canada.[17]

The exemption under the Mandatory Oil Import Program (MOIP) immediately became a fundamental component of Canadian oil export policy, and, in 1961, after much discussion and debate within cabinet, Canada adopted a National Oil Policy designed around it.[18] External Affairs, represented by A.E. Ritchie, was part of the *ad hoc* committee established to develop a national oil policy and provided welcome advice on the potential American reaction to the various policy options put forward.[19] An important provision of the National Oil Policy, one designed to preserve Canada's MOIP exemption, precluded Alberta oil pipelines from extending east of the Ottawa River. Thus Ontario would have its foreign supplies replaced by slightly more expensive Canadian oil from Alberta, while the eastern part of Canada, particularly the important refining area of Montreal, continued to import foreign oil, mainly from Standard Oil production in Venezuela. Oil exports to the United States were in turn increased to compensate Western producers for the loss of the Montreal market. Instead of embarking upon a policy of national self-sufficiency in oil, this policy represented a commitment by the Conservative government of Prime Minister John Diefenbaker – generally seen as one of the more nationalist Canadian governments – to sanction the emergence of a continental oil relationship.

Concerned about relations with other oil exporting countries that resented the Canadian exemption, particularly Venezuela, the administration of American president John F. Kennedy insisted on an informal understanding with Canada to prevent oil exports from becoming "unreasonable." Between 1963 and 1968, officials in Ottawa and Washington negotiated regularly on agreed levels of Canadian exports. Through the efforts of Chappell and officials at the National Energy Board, Canada often managed to exceed the limits that American officials determined were reasonable. The president, nonetheless, had the power to revoke Canada's exemption from the MOIP at any time, which almost happened at the end of 1962.[20] During most of the 1960s, however, strong personal links and networks between Canadian and American officials prevented minor disagreements over the exemption and Canadian oil exports from becoming major bilateral irritants. Diplomats A.E. Ritchie, ambassador to the United States from 1966 to 1970, and Chappell played a key role representing Canada's national interest in managing oil relations with the United States in order to preserve the National Oil Policy. Working closely with officials from the National Energy Board, the centre for Canadian oil policy until the creation of the Department of Energy, Mines and Resources in 1966, External Affairs helped negotiate and maintain Canadian oil export levels to the United States and deflect American pressure on Canada to build an oil pipeline to Montreal. Although the significance was not immediately evident, a turning point for Canadian–American oil relations and the role of External Affairs came in 1968.

Oil Export Phase Out, 1968–1974

When Trudeau secured his majority government in the 1968 election, he immediately set about restructuring the bureaucracy and initiating extensive policy reviews for every department. During Trudeau's sixteen years in power, consistent with his personal philosophy of challenging conventional wisdom and accepted practices, the policy-making process and structure of the bureaucracy were considerably modified. The reorganization of the departments of EMR and External Affairs, and the review of energy policy took place in two phases. The first phase began in 1968, and lasted until 1974; the second phase began in 1977–78. As part of Trudeau's reorganization of government, a host of standing interdepartmental committees were established to review and develop policy. The problem with such committees was that they were cumbersome; it often took a long time to come up with policies, and they tended to be diluted. Thus, by 1978, a two-tiered policy-making system had evolved whereby the prime minister's "pet" projects could bypass the normal interdepartmental committees.[21] One such "pet" project was the National Energy Program, and, by circumventing the normal process, External Affairs was completely excluded from its development. But in 1968 the policy reviews and the restructuring of the policy-making process and the bureaucracy were just beginning, and Canadian–American oil relations were still moving towards some kind of formal continental agreement.

These existing arrangements on oil exports to the United States were threatened by the discovery of Alaskan oil fields at Prudhoe Bay in 1968.[22] With the future of Canadian oil exports in question, Mitchell Sharp, now secretary of state for external affairs in Trudeau's new government, began discussions with Washington for a broad continental energy agreement in April 1969. Negotiations were scaled down in October 1969 to focus solely on a continental oil policy and these talks continued sporadically into 1973 before eventually dying out.[23]

Although the two governments initially approached the idea of increased continental interdependence with some vigour, negotiations stalled. The failure rested on Canada's refusal to make the East Coast more secure from supply disruptions by building an oil pipeline to Montreal to utilize Canadian oil. At this point, as Table 1 illustrates, it was still cheaper for Eastern Canada to import oil, most of which came from Venezuela, though that began to change in 1972, and Trudeau would not permit a policy that unnecessarily increased prices to Quebec and Ontario consumers.

Thus, in the initial years of Trudeau's first term of government, despite his claim to challenge conventional thinking and his desire to reduce Canada's economic dependence on the United States, there seemed to be little outward change from previous policy. What accounts for this?

First, Trudeau was still consolidating his power within the Liberal party, of which he was a fairly recent member. He likely did not wish to move too quickly to change things.[25] Second, the extensive policy review and departmental reorganization that was initiated in 1968 was still in progress. As long as Canada was willing to *talk* about a continental agreement, it might prevent the Americans from taking drastic action against rising Canadian exports of oil and pre-empting possible policy options that

Table 1. Canadian and World Oil Prices, 1968–74[24] (price/barrel)

Year	Canadian Oil (C$)	World Oil (C$)
1968	3.13	2.59
1969	3.14	2.52
1970	3.13	2.45
1971	3.45	3.12
1972	3.46	3.56
1973	3.66	10.50
1974	5.96	10.26

would be in the policy review. Indeed, both the External Affairs and EMR policy reviews and departmental reorganizations would have a significant impact on Canadian–American oil relations.

Much has been written about the foreign policy review undertaken at this time. Six glossy booklets entitled *Foreign Policy for Canadians* were published in 1970 covering six different areas of Canadian foreign policy, though they omitted relations with the United States. During the review, other affected departments were consulted and a broad range of alternatives for Canadian foreign policy was examined. Critics of the review called it incomplete and vague.[26] The Nixon shock of August 1971, when Washington sought to enact a 10 per cent surcharge on imports, compelled Trudeau's cabinet to request from External Affairs a special study on Canada's economic policy with the United States. The result was the "Third Option" white paper in 1972. The main idea of the "Third Option" was to diversify Canada's trade relations, thereby reducing dependence on trade with the Americans. It would seem, then, that External Affairs was moving in step with Trudeau's view of the continental relationship and not in conflict with it. Yet, could Trudeau be sure the new policy orientation would be fully supported by officials in External Affairs?

To ensure a responsive foreign ministry, Trudeau restructured External Affairs and shifted its senior personnel during the first phase of reorganization from 1968 to 1977. From the beginning, Trudeau conveyed a general attitude that he disliked the sense of mission and elitism at the "Dear Department." To strike down this sense of mission within the department, many of the most promising officials – such as Allan Gotlieb and Basil Robinson – were transferred to other departments.[27] Some returned, but others did not. Trudeau also appointed his own foreign policy advisor, Ivan Head, who would serve as a counterpart to President Nixon's national security advisor Henry Kissinger. Despite Head's brief experience as a junior foreign service officer in External Affairs in the 1950s, a position he resigned in favour of teaching law at the University of Alberta, his appointment was seen as a snub to External Affairs because he came from outside the department and had different views.[28] It also sent a signal to other departments that External Affairs was no longer a department of pre-eminent influence. This change can be seen clearly in the government's handling of the 1973 oil crisis. In the crisis days of the first OPEC embargo, EMR left External Affairs out of the discussion with the Americans. As Granatstein and Bothwell point out, the "Canadian response was directed by Donald Macdonald and his officials in EMR. It was pointedly not managed by External Affairs, even though External Affairs made a valiant effort to persuade cabinet to let it coordinate this most important aspect of Canadian foreign policy."[29] The aftermath of this struggle over jurisdiction between Macdonald and Sharp resulted in a cabinet decision in December 1974 stipulating that External Affairs must be consulted in advance on any major issue that could have an impact on Canada–United States relations.[30]

Although External Affairs' influence in oil matters at higher levels was diminished by 1974, the restructuring of the department and the crippling of its personnel had not yet significantly eroded the networks between mid-level Canadian officials and their American counterparts. External Affairs played an important role in preparing the Americans, or at least softening the blow, regarding Canada's decision at the end of 1974 to phase out oil exports. Fortunately, for Canada–United States energy relations, the position of energy counsellor at the Canadian embassy in Washington remained unchanged during the first phase of restructuring.[31] Chappell utilized his lengthy experience and contacts in Washington to send signals through 1973 and 1974 to the American government and refiners that oil exports would be phased out. He provided stability as a constant and familiar voice and advocate of Canadian energy policies to different American administrations and industry representatives. Chappell finally retired in

1979 after more than twenty years at the embassy, underlining the end of the first phase of restructuring in External Affairs.

The restructuring of EMR, as with External Affairs, took place concurrently with its policy review. However, where the alterations at External Affairs weakened a department on the wane, the changes at EMR were designed to strengthen a department on the rise. After five years of drafting, and three years into the first phase of departmental reorganization that altered personnel and shifted policy-making from the National Energy Board to a new unit in EMR, the energy policy review was published in June 1973. External Affairs, along with many other affected departments, was included in the review process. Its role was to review the document and provide advice on how items might affect Canada–United States, or international, relations. During one of the final meetings in 1973, the Department of Finance, represented by Assistant Deputy Minister T.K. Shoyama, along with officials George Tough, E.A. Ballantyne, and H.L. Tadman, wanted to discuss an option to phase out oil exports. The idea was met with some coolness, though the informal minutes suggest that External Affairs, represented by A.E. Ritchie, D.S. McPhail, and D.W. Fulford, did not openly criticize the idea. The no-export option was not included in the final draft, yet was quietly inserted into the published document.[32] The notion of phasing out oil exports so challenged conventional thinking on Canada–United States oil and energy relations that it would require a whole-scale restructuring of personnel in EMR before it would be properly considered and eventually implemented as policy.

Concerned that his plans to phase out oil exports might flounder on the opposition of officials mired in the certitude of informal continentalism, Trudeau restructured the bureaucracy.[33] He used the Prime Minister's Office and the Privy Council Office to recruit his own people to government service and promoted from within those who shared his way of thinking. For example, during the first phase of restructuring in EMR, Claude Isbister, the career civil servant who had worked his way up to deputy minister, was replaced in 1970 by an outsider, Jack Austin. Austin was personally chosen by Trudeau because he "was concerned about developing a state presence in the oil and gas industry" and he agreed with Trudeau's vision of enacting social change through energy policy.[34] A power struggle ensued between Austin and National Energy Board chairman Robert Howland over whether the board would maintain a policy function or simply become a "rubber stamp" for EMR decisions.[35] As a result of this struggle, Howland, who had been with the board since its inception in 1959, "retired" in August 1973, two years before his term was to end. He was replaced by Marshall Crowe. Crowe, a long-time civil servant, served in the Department of External Affairs from 1947 to 1961. He then worked for six years as an economic adviser to the Canadian Imperial Bank of Commerce before returning to government. Under Trudeau, Crowe held various positions in the Privy Council Office and the Prime Minister's Office, as well as serving as chairman of the Canada Development Corporation.[36] He was also a member of the "non-group," a team assembled by Head in 1969 to provide Trudeau with an alternate perspective on Canadian defence policy.[37] Crowe's membership on this team and his appointment as the head of the Canada Development Corporation underlined Trudeau's trust in Crowe's commitment to the prime minister and his alternative policies. Despite his civil service career, there is evidence suggesting that the National Energy Board under Crowe, during public hearings on oil exports, deliberately disregarded testimony and data that did not coincide with the Government's goal to phase out exports.[38] Perhaps then, one of the reasons for Crowe's appointment was to ensure that the board fulfilled Austin's unwritten mandate: decisions and reports would reflect and support EMR policies.[39]

Austin left EMR in 1974 to work in the Prime Minister's Office, hoping to become president of the new state-owned oil company, Petro-Canada, but ultimately ended up in the Senate.[40] He was replaced in EMR by career civil servant Tommy Shoyama from Finance. Shoyama, like Crowe managed to maintain a senior position because he had a similar ideological disposition to Trudeau and solid credentials: he was a "left-leaning Keynesian" and had been an advisor to Premier Tommy Douglas in the heady days of the socialist Co-operative Commonwealth Federation in Saskatchewan.[41] Shoyama then left EMR to become the deputy minister of Finance after Simon Reisman, another career civil servant, "retired" in protest over Trudeau's economic policies. Before leaving EMR, Shoyama supported the decision to phase out oil exports, a policy he had supported as an assistant deputy minister of finance during the 1973 energy policy review.

Four months after the energy policy review was published, OPEC flexed its muscles and the world was hit with a shocking rise in oil and gas prices, making the policy review seem obsolete. Yet, there was a sense of opportunity among many left-wing supporters in Trudeau's cabinet and in EMR. Indeed, some of the ideas contained in the review, like the creation of a state oil company or the phasing out of oil exports, seemed ready-made for the current crisis. The New Democratic Party, which held the balance of power in the minority parliament elected in 1972, along with consumers feeling the pinch in Eastern Canada, argued that now was the time to have a more active federal oil and gas policy.[42]

Responding to the crisis, Ottawa moved to control prices and increase its revenue through taxation and eventually announced the end of the 1961 National Oil Policy. The price controls meant oil produced and sold in Canada would receive prices significantly lower than the world price. The oil export tax, called the Oil Import Compensation Program, initially levied a flat rate of 40 cents per barrel, which evolved into the equivalent of the difference between the controlled price of Canadian oil and the world price. For example, in September 1973, the federal government received 40 cents for every barrel of oil that was exported, and a year later they collected upwards of $6.40 for every barrel sold to the United States. The Trudeau government suggested that these controls and taxes were temporary, but prices remained controlled and a variation of the export tax continued to exist until after 1984.

Both Alberta, Canada's largest oil producing province, and the United States were vexed by these changes. Nevertheless, despite American agitation over Canada's export tax, Canada and the United States were in constant contact during the crisis. Then, on 6 December 1973, Trudeau announced a new National Oil Policy. The new policy included provisions regarding pricing, continuation of the oil export tax, the creation of a state oil company (Petro-Canada), and support for the immediate construction of an oil pipeline to Montreal, among other initiatives. Although it was not specifically stated that oil exports would be discontinued, the stated principle behind the new policy was to "create a national market for Canadian oil" and seemed to suggest that Canadian oil would be preserved for Canadians.[43]

Preceding the announcement of the new national policy were a National Energy Board oil supply and demand study released in December 1972 and an EMR supply and demand study circulated internally in January 1973. Energy board hearings on Canada's oil export policy followed in the spring of 1974. The reports and hearings all seemed to indicate that Canada was running short of oil. All, that is, except the numbers from the Alberta government. The Alberta Energy Resources Conservation Board submitted data to the National Energy Board hearings that indicated over the next thirty years, there would be an exportable surplus of between 700,000 and 1.8 million barrels a day. After some consideration, the Trudeau government nonetheless announced in December 1974 the decision to phase out oil exports to the United States.[44] The American response to this incredible policy reversal was rather benign. Why?

There is little mention of the phase-out in the archival record around the time of its announcement, except for a brief comment made during Trudeau's visit to Washington in December 1974, when President Gerald Ford expressed his disappointment, but also said that he understood the reasons for the policy. Other documents indicate that by the time of the announcement the United States was already resigned to Canada's policy. In subsequent talks with the Canadians, American authorities sought to ensure that northern United States refineries dependent on Canadian supplies would be given time to adjust.[45] The most compelling reason for this calm response was that there were lengthy advance consultations and "signals" that these changes would be taking place. In the initial restructuring of the policy-making process and the bureaucracy, the traditional system of consultation with other departments still existed. Officials from External Affairs, particularly Chappell, worked diligently to ensure that their American counterparts received the appropriate "signals" that the policy was going to be changed. The Americans were prepared for the Canadian policy shift because they had been warned several times, even once by the prime minister himself, at least a year in advance.[46] Although the Americans were disappointed at Canada's decision to phase out exports, they understood its desire to conserve resources.[47] A similarly benign response was not forthcoming six years later when, after the second phase of restructuring at External Affairs and EMR, the National Energy Program (NEP) was announced.

The National Energy Program, 1977–1984

During the second phase of restructuring, Allan Gotlieb returned to the Department of External Affairs in 1977 as its under-secretary, determined to restore some of its fading power and influence. Part of the perceived weakness of External Affairs was its lack of expertise in economic issues. Supported by Trudeau and the clerk of the Privy Council, Michael Pitfield, who were anxious to rationalize government operations, Gotlieb endeavoured to turn External Affairs into a central agency, eventually incorporating within it parts of the departments of Industry, Trade and Commerce, and Immigration.[48] Gotlieb claimed that Trudeau supported the resurgence of External Affairs partly to respond to the growing separatist threat that followed the election of Premier René Lévesque and his Parti Québécois government in 1976. Obviously, it was not in the national interest for External Affairs to be weakened with a serious domestic crisis with international implications emerging.[49] But the reorganization was also designed to transform External Affairs into a central agency, like the Privy Council Office or the Treasury Board, giving it the authority to coordinate the international activities of other departments.

Under this restructuring, the United States Division became a bureau during the 1970s, and then, in 1983, an entire branch headed by an assistant deputy minister, whose goal was to be the office responsible for consolidating "all the elements of the Government's relations with the United States."[50] Presumably, energy issues would be included, especially after the 1979 Iranian revolution initiated a second international oil crisis and a spike in oil prices. Yet, this is not what happened when the National Energy Program was developed and implemented in 1980. External Affairs was not included in the process. Indeed, despite comments by Pitfield to the contrary, Gotlieb says unequivocally that he only found out about the energy program the night before it was announced "and was instructed to develop a plan to sell it in the United States after it was cast in concrete (that is, after it was unsaleable)."[51] Selling it became part of his job in 1981 when he was appointed ambassador to the United States, where he worked assiduously to defend the program even though he believed it was badly misguided. Derek Burney, assistant deputy minister in the new United States Branch in 1983 and a future ambassador to the Washington, agrees that External Affairs was left out of the process and that this made it hard for officials to respond to American complaints because "it is difficult to defend what you do not know."[52] Here too was a message to External Affairs: despite the reorganizations, the department could not be trusted to advise on and assist in the development of a policy that reflected Trudeau's vision of the national interest and which he thought might conflict with the view in External Affairs. What was it about the National Energy Program that was such a profound source of conflict?

The primary goal of Trudeau's National Energy Program was to achieve energy self-sufficiency by 1990. While this sounds like a worthy goal, several elements in the program were particularly objectionable. Energy security was to be attained by increasing Canadian ownership and participation in the oil and gas industry at the expense of the mostly American-owned multinational companies. Following exploration, any production on federal lands (Arctic and offshore areas especially) had to be undertaken by a firm with a minimum of 50 per cent Canadian ownership. In addition, for every development, past or future on the federally controlled Canada Lands, a 25 per cent interest, or "back-in," to be controlled by Petro-Canada or another crown corporation was required without compensation. Prices were still controlled, as they had been since the first energy crisis in 1973, but this time, as indicated in Table 2, they represented a more concerted effort to disengage Canada from the world energy market structure.[53] In 1980, for example, when world oil prices were the equivalent of C$44.66 per barrel, oil produced and sold in Canada received $17.30 per barrel. For Canadian oil exported to the United States, the federal government claimed through taxation the difference between the Canadian price and world price.

From a diplomatic perspective, the American response, when it came, was blistering.[55] Gotlieb describes in his Washington diaries the judgment of Republican president Ronald Reagan and his advisors: "They hate it. They regard it as confiscation."[56] What concerned the United States most was that the energy program was "blatantly discriminatory with reference to the operations of American companies in Canada."[57] If Canada wanted to preserve its resources for itself, Washington officials argued, the United States would be disappointed but would not object strenuously. Discrimination against American companies, however, was a whole other matter as it set a dangerous precedent for other countries in the world with American

Table 2. Canadian and World Oil Prices, 1974–81[54] (price/barrel)

Year	Canadian Oil (C$)	World Oil (C$)
1974	5.96	10.26
1975	7.44	11.35
1976	8.72	12.14
1977	10.45	14.81
1978	12.53	17.12
1979	13.94	26.23
1980	17.30	44.66
1981	26.91	43.49

investments. Contrary to some popular Canadian accounts, which charged American diplomats with heavy-handed and bullying tactics, the Reagan administration (at the president's behest) pursued a form of high-pressured but restrained "quiet diplomacy" throughout 1981 and early 1982 in order to underline the program's unfair treatment of American interests.[58] As time wore on, changes were made to the National Energy Program that addressed some American complaints, although many of its interventionist aspects remained and would not be effectively dismantled until 1985 under a different government. Part of the reason for Washington's initial negative reaction to the introduction of the National Energy Program can be attributed to shock and a lack of communication beforehand about the policy. There had been no forewarning, no softening of the blow.[59]

In contrast to the potentially controversial phase-out of oil exports in 1974, External Affairs was excluded from the energy policy process in 1979–80. This was due to the second phase of restructuring of the policy-making process and the bureaucracy that had begun in 1978. While EMR's earlier restructuring was relatively gradual and somewhat diffuse, the second phase of restructuring had a different dynamic: the changes were more focused and more comprehensive. Initiated in March 1978 by Marc Lalonde and the clerk of the Privy Council, the "Pitfield shuffle," as it was soon dubbed, shifted several ambitious bureaucrats from Finance to EMR in preparation for a large policy initiative.[60] It can be surmised that Lalonde anticipated taking over the portfolio after the next election.[61] The new deputy minister of finance was Ian Stewart, who had been a close Trudeau energy advisor in the early 1970s. Similarly, a completely new policy-making division was created in EMR under the guidance of Trudeau-loyalists Mickey Cohen, George Tough, and Ed Clark. All three had been recruited and trained by the Prime Minister's Office and the Privy Council Office before they went to Finance and then onto EMR. These three men personally selected their new employees and reassigned those who did not meet their standards or reflect their views.[62] The cumulative effect of these personnel changes was that the ideological complexion of EMR was gradually altered in order to reduce resistance to Trudeau's vision of how Canada relations with the United States might be arranged.[63]

When Lalonde finally became minister of EMR in 1980, after Prime Minister Joe Clark's brief Tory interregnum, the department was ready and willing to tackle the creation of a comprehensive left-leaning energy program that would encompass the principles of energy self-sufficiency, changes to pricing and revenue sharing, and "Canadianizing" the industry. The prospect and intellectual challenge of "redesigning an entire industry's dynamics" was exciting, dramatic, and appealing.[64] Lalonde and his colleagues were motivated and buoyed by their unwavering faith in the ability of technocracy and planning to address and solve pressing and troublesome economic issues. Gotlieb later recalled that there was also an arrogant and cocky attitude emanating from EMR officials because "they were running the world." With the surge in international oil prices and the decline in American production, he explained, there was a euphoric feeling that the tables were turned in Canadian–American energy relations: Canada would be strong and the Americans were going to be weak. Now Canada had the upper hand and would be able to set policy and define the terms of trade.[65] Under Lalonde's direction, the policy these officials developed, reflecting this new attitude, was the National Energy Program. Conventional wisdom on Canadian oil and gas policy was definitely going to be challenged.

A small group of handpicked people within the departments of EMR and Finance, as well as the Privy Council Office developed the National Energy Program in great secrecy and announced it as a *fait accompli* in the October 1980 budget. At roughly the same time, External Affairs recognized that there ought to be some coordination between EMR and External Affairs on international energy issues. Thus, in 1979–80, during the period of the second OPEC oil price shocks, Gotlieb, then under-secretary of state for external affairs, "lobbied the Cabinet to combine an energy policy with overall foreign policy concerns."[66] In the spring of 1980, the new deputy minister of EMR, Mickey Cohen, responded to Gotlieb's pressure by creating an International Energy Relations Branch within EMR. Knowledgeable officials from External Affairs were seconded to EMR in order to organize the new branch. D.R. Whelan came over from External Affairs in August 1980 to help prepare the ground for the new branch, while Don Campbell arrived right around the time the NEP was announced in October 1980.[67] However, this new branch was not included in the policy process for creating the NEP, nor was it asked to provide advice on the NEP before it was announced. The Department of External Affairs was also excluded from the process; thus, it did not have the opportunity to advise on questions that would affect Canada's relations with the United States. In twelve short years, External Affairs went from contributing a respected perspective on Canada–United States energy issues, to being excluded from a policy that had significant ramifications for the bilateral relationship and Canada's national interests.

Conclusion

Trudeau had a view of the national interest and continental relations that challenged traditional postwar thinking on Canada's economic and trade relations with the United States. This vision encompassed the following: reducing Canada's dependence on the United States, increasing Canadian control of the economy, reducing American investment, increasing Canadian manufacturing, and reducing Canada's reliance on staples. The effect on oil and gas policy was a shift away from informal continentalism to a form of economic nationalism, or from maintaining access to the American market to phasing out oil exports and becoming "self-sufficient." Such controversial policies could not have been developed and implemented without the significant changes in the policy-making process and the restructuring of the bureaucracy that took place during the Trudeau years.

Trudeau desired to alter the policy and decision-making processes ostensibly to make government more "efficient," but the changes were also designed to reduce resistance to his more interventionist policies that reflected his conception of the national interest. While EMR was buoyed by its increase in power and importance to the prime minister, External Affairs was destabilized and suffered low morale from its reorganization. It lost its influence as a voice in the development of policies that affected foreign relations, particularly Canada's relationship with the United States. By 1980, the traditional lines of communication between Canadian and American officials were either ignored or no longer existed; and the stronger the U.S. reaction, the more the Canadians believed they had taken the right action.

The role of External Affairs in all of this is a good example of Trudeau's suspicion of the department as it had been before he took power. Perhaps he feared that there was a conflict of visions: that External Affairs' sense of mission and its conception of the national interest would interfere with his repudiation of the informal continentalism that the department and its diplomats had traditionally supported. Trudeau had little faith in the department's professionalism and its willingness to adapt to and implement the policies of the government – no matter how controversial. Therefore, External Affairs had to be marginalized and restructured in such a way as to extinguish any independent sense of mission. Ultimately, Canadian energy policy, Canada's relations with the United States, and Canada's interests suffered for this lack of faith.

NOTES

1. The author would like to thank the following individuals who were gracious enough to grant their time and insight during interviews: Allan Gotlieb, Stan Gooch, Don Campbell, Joseph Stanford, and Kathleen Deutsch.

2. See, for example, Robert Bothwell, *Alliance and Illusion: Canada and the World, 1945–1984* (Vancouver: UBC Press, 2007), 278; J.L. Granatstein and Robert Bothwell, *Pirouette: Pierre Trudeau and Canadian Foreign Policy* (Toronto: University of Toronto Press, 1990), 382. For accounts from contemporaries, see: Mitchell Sharp, *Which Reminds Me...* (Toronto: University of Toronto Press, 1994), 164, 171; Jeremy Kinsman, "Who is My Neighbour? Pierre Trudeau and Foreign Policy," *London Journal of Canadian Studies* 18 (2002/2003): 106–7; Gordon Robertson, *Memoirs of a Very Civil Servant* (Toronto: University of Toronto Press, 2000), 250–68.

3. Thomas Axworthy, "'To Not Stand So High Perhaps but Always Alone': The Foreign Policy of Pierre Trudeau," in *Towards a Just Society: The Trudeau Years*, ed. Thomas S. Axworthy and Pierre Elliott Trudeau (Markham, ON: Viking, 1990), 16.

4. Granatstein and Bothwell, *Pirouette*, 33.

5. Granatstein and Bothwell, *Pirouette*, 34. Charles Ritchie wrote in his diary after a meeting with Trudeau in October 1968 that "Trudeau has got it into his head that the Department is divorced from the real interests of Canada and is embarking on international projects which have no firm basis in Canadian needs, and that this has been characteristic of the Pearson era." Charles Ritchie, *Storm Signals: More Undiplomatic Diaries, 1962–1971* (Toronto: Macmillan of Canada, 1983), 114.

6. Allan Gotlieb, interview by author, telephone tape recording, Toronto/Toulouse, 3 July 2008.

7. Confidential interview, 30 November 1987, B1988-0094/006, Robert Bothwell Papers, University of Toronto Archives.

8. Granatstein and Bothwell, *Pirouette*, 63.

9. Mark MacGuigan, *An Inside Look at External Affairs during the Trudeau Years*, ed. P. Whitney Lackenbauer (Calgary: University of Calgary Press, 2002), 16, 18.

10. Michael Hart, *A Trading Nation* (Vancouver: UBC Press, 2002), 267.

11. Allan Gotlieb, interview by author, telephone tape recording, Toronto/Toulouse, 3 July 2008.

12. Stephen Clarkson, "Continentalism," *The Canadian Encyclopedia*, online version, http://www.thecanadianencyclopedia.com/continentalism.htm. See also, Hart, *A Trading Nation*, 168–71. Hart argues that Canada had little choice but to become more interdependent with the United States in economic terms because "the markets of Europe, Latin America, and Asia had all been virtually closed to Canadian exporters in the decade after the Second World War." The American market was somewhat accessible for Canadian commodities and products, and American capital was available to "help develop Canada's resource and manufacturing sectors."

13. Sharp, *Which Reminds Me...*, 180–81, 183, 185.

14. Ibid. See also, MacGuigan, *An Inside Look at External Affairs*, 18.

15. See, Tammy Nemeth, "Canada–U.S. Oil and Gas Relations, 1959–1974" (PhD diss., University of British Columbia, 2007), chaps. 1 and 2.

16. The U.S. ambassador to Canada, Richard Wigglesworth, sent Heeney an editorial from the *Washington Post*, 21 January 1959, with the headline, "Return of a Friend" referring to Heeney's appointment. See, Arnold Heeney Papers, vol. 1, file: United States Ambassador to Washington, 1958, 1959, Congratulations, Correspondence,

Memoranda, Library and Archives Canada (LAC).

17   See, Telegram to External from WashDC, Subject: Presentation of Credentials to President, 2 March 1959, Heeney Papers, vol. 1, file: United States Ambassador to Washington, 1958, 1959, Congratulations, Correspondence, Memoranda, LAC.

18   For a detailed discussion of these events see, Tammy Nemeth, "Consolidating the Continental Drift: American Influence on Diefenbaker's National Oil Policy," *Journal of the Canadian Historical Association* 13 (2002): 191–215.

19   See, for example, Cabinet Committee on Oil Policy, 7 October 1960, Donald Fleming Papers, vol. 128, LAC; Cabinet Committee on Oil Policy, 22 December 1960, National Energy Board Records (NEBR), vol. 167, file 22, LAC. The two officials involved most consistently on oil issues in the late 1950s and into the 1960s were A.E. Ritchie and Norm Chappell.

20   Nemeth, "Canada–U.S. Oil and Gas Relations, 1959–1974," 172–222.

21   The development of the two-tiered policy-making system is well-documented in Colin Campbell and George Szablowski, *The Superbureaucrats: Structure and Behaviour in Central Agencies* (Toronto: Macmillan of Canada, 1979); and Jeffrey Simpson, *Faultlines: Struggling for a Canadian Vision* (Toronto: Harper-Collins, 1993). For a discussion of the PMs' "pet" projects, see Donald J. Savoie, *Governing from the Centre* (Toronto: University of Toronto Press, 1999), 134–35, 254–59, and chap. 10.

22   For Canadian fears on new limits to Canadian access to the American market, see, Memorandum Oil Matters, 17 March 1969, NEBR, vol. 73, file 56F, LAC; Memorandum to Cabinet from Otto Lang (Acting Minister of Energy, Mines and Resources), Oil Policy Review, 15 May 1969, NEBR, vol. 64, file 9K, LAC. For the American statement to Canada that "the large oil discoveries in Alaska introduced a new factor into the situation," see Memorandum of Conversation, Subject: Canadian Oil, E-1613, 25 March 1969, RG 59, CEPF (Central Foreign Policy Files), Subject-Numeric – Economic 1967–69, box 1350, file "PET 17-2 CAN 1/1/67," 1–2, National Archives and Records Administration (NARA).

23   Telegram 031468 from State Department to Amembassy Ottawa, Subject: Canadian Oil, E-1613, 28 February 1969, RG 59, CEPF (Central Foreign Policy Files), Subject-Numeric – Economic 1967-1969, box 1349, file "PET 11-2 CAN 1/1/69," NARA. This was a copy of an *aide-mémoire* delivered to the State Department by Canadian Ambassador A. E. Ritchie, suggesting that oil talks begin. What is interesting is that a comprehensive energy agreement is not specifically mentioned, phrases such as "broad review" of policies were used instead. See also, Canada [Briefing Paper], file "Booklet – Papers for November 9, 1972 Meeting of the Energy Subcommittee [III]," John F. Schaefer Files, box 56, Energy Policy Office, Staff Members Office Files (SMOF), White House Central Files (WHCF), Nixon Project, USNA.

24   The data in this table is taken from, Earle Gray, *Forty Years in the Public Interest: A History of the National Energy Board* (Vancouver: Douglas & McIntyre, 2000), 140.

25   Ramsay Cook, *The Teeth of Time: Remembering Pierre Elliott Trudeau* (Montreal and Kingston: McGill-Queen's University Press, 2006), 84.

26   Granatstein and Bothwell, *Pirouette*, 39.

27   Bothwell, *Alliance and Illusion*, 372–80. See also, Sharp, *Which Reminds Me …*, 170–73; Allan Gotlieb, interview by author, telephone tape recording, Toronto/Toulouse, 3 July 2008.

28   Ivan Head and Pierre Trudeau, *The Canadian Way: Shaping Canada's Foreign Policy, 1968–1984* (Toronto: McClelland & Stewart, 1995), 5.

29   Granatstein and Bothwell, *Pirouette*, 87.

30   Cabinet Conclusions, 19–20 December 1974, RG 2, vol. 6436, series A-5-a, LAC.

31   On the importance of good people to help make things work, and the effect of

personalities on the Canada–U.S. relationship, see Derek H. Burney, *Getting It Done: A Memoir* (Montreal and Kingston: McGill-Queen's University Press, 2005), 65, 188–89.

32   Memo to Dr. Dickie from D. M. Fraser, Subject: E.P.R., 28 February 1973, NEBR, vol. 77, file "57S – EP12 – NEB Notes – Feb '73," LAC.

33   For an extensive account of the dramatic changes to the policy-making process and the restructuring of the bureaucracy, see Nemeth, "Canada–U.S. Oil and Gas Relations, 1959–1974," 248–345.

34   Austin was also a former Liberal candidate. He was given a great deal of liberty by the prime minister to strengthen and consolidate the policy-making power in the department. This meant the capacity for policy-making had to be taken away from the National Energy Board. See James A. Desveaux, *Designing Bureaucracies* (Stanford, CA: Stanford University Press, 1995), 69; Peter Foster, *The Sorcerer's Apprentices: Canada's Super-Bureaucrats and the Energy Mess* (Toronto: Collins, 1982), 57–59.

35   For fears on the NEB becoming a "rubber stamp," see Airgram A-111 from Amembassy Ottawa to Department of State, Subject: Oil and Gas: Transmittal of Memorandum of Conversation, 23 February 1972, RG 59, Subject-Numeric – Economic 1970–1973, box 1494, file "PET 18-1 CAN-US 1970," NARA.

36   In a history of the National Energy Board, the Canadian Development Corporation, established in 1971, is described as "a government agency established to increase Canadian ownership of resource firms." Gray, *Forty Years in the Public Interest*, 69.

37   Granatstein and Bothwell, *Pirouette*, 20.

38   Memorandum to William E. Simon, John C. Sawhill, Gerald L. Parsky from William C. Calkins thru William A. Johnson, Subject: Oil Policy Review in Canada – A Trip Report, 12 April 1974, job 1418, box 1, folder 11 "Johnson, Bill Memos and Bass," United States Department of Energy (US DOE). See also, Gray, *Forty Years in the Public Interest*, 58.

39   Political scientist John Bridger Robinson suggests that throughout the 1970s, the NEB tailored its energy supply and demand forecasts to reflect "the direction of contemporary policy ... and major project proposals of the time." John Bridger Robinson, "Pendulum Policy: Natural Gas Forecasts and Canadian Energy Policy, 1969–1981," *Canadian Journal of Political Science* 16, no. 2 (June 1983): 299–301. Although Robinson focuses mainly on natural gas forecasts, he does explore to some degree the oil forecasts as well.

40   Foster, *The Sorcerer's Apprentices*, 66.

41   Clarkson and McCall, *Trudeau and Our Times*, vol. 2, 122; John Richards and Larry Pratt, *Prairie Capitalism: Power and Influence in the New West* (Toronto: McClelland & Stewart, 1979), 182–87.

42   See, for example, Editorial, "Time to control the tap," *Globe and Mail*, 17 February 1973, 6. See also, Granatstein and Bothwell, *Pirouette*, 72, 84.

43   Ralph Toombs, *The Canadian Energy Chronology* [book on-line], available from http://www2.nrcan.gc.ca/es/es/Energy-Chronology/index_e.cfm; accessed 17 August 2009, 1973–1976.

44   For the American view of the proceedings at the NEB hearings, see, Memorandum to William E. Simon, et al thru William A. Johnson, Subject: Oil Policy Review in Canada – A Trip Report, 12 April 1974, job 1418, box 1, folder 11, "Johnson, Bill Memos and Bass," US DOE. For internal documents regarding the development of the initial NEB study and the internal EMR study, see, NEBR, vol. 76, file "57L – EPR '72 II," LAC.

45   Briefing Memorandum for the President from Henry A. Kissinger, Meeting with Pierre Elliott Trudeau Prime Minister of Canada Wednesday, December 4, 1974, WHCF, CO 28, box 11, file "CO 28 Canada, 12/1/74-12/31/74 (Executive)," Gerald R. Ford Library (GRFL). See also, Memorandum to ERD/IEA Task Force from Robert G. Sands, Subject: Northern

Tier Refineries Dependency Upon Canadian Crude Which is Being Phased Out of Exports, 13 December 1974, job 1401, box 2, folder 6, Canada, US DOE.

46 There are numerous documents between 1972 and 1974 that demonstrate the Americans expected some kind of oil export controls and had been forewarned by March 1973 that oil exports might be phased out completely. See, for example, Telegram 1110 from Amembassy Ottawa to SecState WashDC, Subject: Policy: U.S. Oil Import Policy and Canada's Role in U.S. Supply, 20 June 1972, box 1055, file "FT CAN-US 1/1/70," NARA; Memorandum of Conversation, Subject: U.S.-Canadian Oil Talks, 27 June 1972 Ottawa, RG 59, CFPF, Subject-Numeric – Economic 1970–1973, box 1494, file "PET 4 CAN-US 1972," NARA. For Trudeau's forewarning see, Letter to the President from Prime Minister Trudeau, E-1613, 7 November 1973, RG 59, Subject-Numeric – Economic 1970–1973, box 1490, file "PET 1 CAN 6/1/70," NARA.

47 Even so, one American official commented that, despite being in constant contact with the Canadians on the issue, it still felt like a "kick in the gut," when the announcement came. Kathleen Deutsch, interview by author, Washington, D.C., 5 February 2003.

48 Granatstein and Bothwell, *Pirouette*, 222–33. The authors suggest that Pitfield realized that External Affairs had been weakened too much and needed to be built up again.

49 Allan Gotlieb, interview by author, telephone tape recording, Toronto/Toulouse, 3 July 2008.

50 Stan Gooch, interview by author, e-mail, October 2008.

51 Allan Gotlieb, interview by author, telephone tape recording, Toronto/Toulouse, 3 July 2008. See also, Allan Gotlieb, *Washington Diaries, 1981–1989* (Toronto: McClelland & Stewart, 2006), 29.

52 Burney, *Getting It Done*, 69.

53 Government of Canada, Department of Energy, Mines and Resources, *The National Energy Program* (Ottawa: Supply and Services, 1980). For an examination of the relations between the producing province of Alberta and the Trudeau government on the NEP see, Tammy Nemeth, "1980: Duel of the Decade," in *Alberta Formed, Alberta Transformed*, ed. Michael Payne, Donald Wetherell, and Catherine Cavanaugh (Edmonton/Calgary: University of Alberta Press/University of Calgary Press, 2006), 676–700.

54 The data in this table are taken from Gray, *Forty Years in the Public Interest*, 140.

55 When the NEP was first announced on 30 October 1980, the United States was in the middle of an election. The Carter administration did put forward its objections to the NEP, the first bilateral consultation taking place a week after the NEP was announced, but a determined response did not arrive until after the election. For initial discussions of American concerns about the NEP, see Memorandum for Denis Clift from Christine Dodson, Subject: Vice President's Meeting with Ambassador Towe of Canada, 26 November 1980, WHCF, Subject Files, CO-28 (Canada), box CO-14, file CO28 1/20/77-1/20/81, Jimmy Carter Library. See also Edward Wonder, "The U.S. Government Response to the Canadian National Energy Program," *Canadian Public Policy* 8, supplement 1 (Oct. 1982): 484–85.

56 Allan Gotlieb, *Washington Diaries*, 16; see also 4–5. For a brief description of the American reaction by the Canadian secretary of state for external affairs see, MacGuigan, *An Inside Look at External Affairs*, 118–21.

57 Memorandum for Richard V. Allen from Norman A. Bailey, Subject: Cabinet Council on Economic Affairs Meeting of July 29, 1981, 30 July 1981, National Security Council, White House Office of Records Management (WHORM), Subject Files, box 15, file FG 010-02 (018919CA), Ronald Reagan Library (RRL). For the view that the NEP was "expropriatory" see, Memorandum to the President from William E. Brock [U.S. Trade Representative], Subject: Status of U.S.–Canada Bilateral

Trade and Investment Issues, 30 October 1981, WHORM, Subject Files, box 17, file FG010-02 (018975CA) [1 of 2], RRL.

58 For exaggerated accounts of the American reaction, see, for example, Stephen Clarkson, *Canada and the Reagan Challenge* (Toronto: James Lorimer, 1985), 33–45; Clarkson and McCall, *Trudeau and Our Times*, vol. 2, chap. 6; and Lawrence Martin, *The Presidents and Prime Ministers* (Toronto: Doubleday, 1982), 280–84. Although elements within the newly elected Reagan Administration advocated retaliatory action, forceful arguments were made with the support of the president, that diplomacy should be employed instead. See, for example, Memorandum for Richard V. Allen from Norman A. Bailey, Subject: Cabinet Council on Economic Affairs Meeting of July 29, 1981, 30 July 1981, National Security Council, WHORM, Subject Files, FG010-02, box 15, file FG 010-02 (018919CA), RRL; Memorandum to the President from William E. Brock [U.S. Trade Representative], Subject: Status of U.S.–Canada Bilateral Trade and Investment Issues, 30 October 1981, WHORM, Subject Files, FG010-02, box 17, file FG010-02 (018975CA) [1 of 2], RRL.

59 For a clear enunciation of the philosophical differences between the two governments with respect to economic policy, see Memorandum to the President from William E. Brock [U.S. Trade Representative], Subject: Status of U.S.–Canada Bilateral Trade and Investment Issues, 30 October 1981, WHORM, Subject Files, FG010-02, box 17, file FG010-02 (018975CA) [1 of 2], RRL.

60 Desveaux, *Designing Bureaucracies*, 75.

61 Clarkson and McCall in *Trudeau and Our Times*, vol. 1, discuss the anticipation of an election in 1978, which was delayed until 1979. See also Christina McCall-Newman, *Grits: An Intimate Portrait of the Liberal Party* (Toronto: Macmillan, 1982), 318–19. Lalonde's involvement in the shuffle of EMR and Finance personnel suggests that he had already shifted his focus to a new priority – EMR.

62 For a comprehensive examination of the evolution of EMR in this period see, Desveaux, *Designing Bureaucracies*.

63 Desveaux, *Designing Bureaucracies*, 67–73. Desveaux observes, "Austin, as deputy minister, was able to effect more change in both organizational [*sic*] structure and decision-making than his predecessor, Claude Isbister, because he had the ear of the prime minister."

64 Clarkson and McCall, *Trudeau and Our Times*, vol. 2, 199.

65 Allan Gotlieb, interview by author, telephone tape recording, Toronto/Toulouse, 3 July 2008.

66 Desveaux, *Designing Bureaucracies*, 139.

67 Ibid.; Don Campbell, interview by author, e-mail, August 2009. Campbell says he was shown the NEP document about two weeks before it was announced but was "given no opportunity to comment on it. External Affairs was not asked for any advice and indeed we were kept completely in the dark as was the rest of the government with the exception of a group in the Department of Finance and the Privy Council until the policy was announced."

SETTING THE CANADIAN FOREIGN POLICY AGENDA, 1984–2009: PRIME MINISTERS AS PRIME ACTORS?

Nelson Michaud

In Canada, the prime minister is traditionally very involved in the shaping of the country's foreign policy. Promoting and defending the national interest, the prime minister plays a vital role as one of its managers, at times in tandem with the minister of foreign affairs, at times as the key actor. This is due, in large part, to the parliamentary system in which Canadian policies are set. The principle of responsible government, which is at the heart of the Canadian system, solidly anchors the leadership and the authority that the prime minister exercises, especially in the realm of foreign relations.[1] In addition, some observers may argue that foreign policy offers prime ministers glamour and exposure, but they overlook the fact that, unlike the United States where a foreign affairs role has an important impact on domestic perception of the leader, politics in Canada is essentially "local." What is of importance is that these relations are conducted with the prime ministers' counterparts around the world, which helps to explain why foreign affairs fall more easily under the leaders' purview, a phenomenon accentuated by summit diplomacy.[2] This prominent role is reinforced by a bureaucratic and political framework that feeds the prime minister with international issues to which attention should be paid.[3]

There is also a historic factor that comes into play. From 1909, when the Department of External Affairs was first formed, until after the Second World War, foreign affairs fell, for the most part, under the purview of the prime minister. It was not until 1946, when Louis St. Laurent took the reigns of the department from an ageing Prime Minister W.L. Mackenzie King, that the position of secretary of state for external affairs was solidified as a separate entity. For a time in the late 1950s, John Diefenbaker acted as both prime minister and his own foreign minister, but by this time a dual command system had already evolved, and he soon returned the portfolio to a minister, with whom he nevertheless worked closely.

The last quarter of the twentieth century presented unique challenges to foreign policy-making as Canada's national interests were reshaped. Geopolitics were redefined with unprecedented changes in the international context; new actors emerged from civil society and stateless advocates of extremism increasingly resorted to violence in attempts to impose their agenda; conflicts often involved factions within a country rather than two belligerents across a disputed border; and new issues emerged at the international level from economic globalization to environmental threats to the obligation to protect vulnerable populations from the abuses of their own government. Do these factors challenge the influence the prime minister has over Canadian foreign policy and the answers the country offers in line with its national interest? Or is foreign policy "governed from the center" as is the case in so many other policy fields?[4]

This analysis belongs to a body of literature that aims at understanding the role of individuals in policy-making processes,[5] the control of individuals over "uncertainties,"[6] and how personal characteristics influence the content of foreign policy stances.[7] The first section offers a closer look at how the international and domestic contexts were reshaped between 1984 and 2009. It will subsequently explore how prime ministers Brian Mulroney, Jean Chrétien, Paul Martin, and Stephen Harper answered this challenge.[8]

A Context Redefined

Not so long ago, foreign policy was the absolute expression of regalia powers. As late as 1985, Canada's minister of national defence, Erik Nielsen, strongly opposed issuing a defence green paper – to which Canadians could react – on the sole basis that foreign and defence policies were not matters to be discussed with the general public.[9] Today, with the democratization of foreign policy, public diplomacy, and the internet, it is hard to conceive of such a stance. In itself, this bears witness to a new era in foreign policy-making.

The transformation is even starker when evaluated in the longer term. When Louis St. Laurent was sworn in as secretary of state for external affairs in 1946, the Cold War had just ushered in a new environment characterized by the emergence of multilateral institutions. In Canada, the postwar economy was flourishing and foreign policy-making was in the hands of people who would leave a lasting imprint, a practice today known as Pearsonian internationalism.

The last twenty-five years has seen the collapse of a Manichean world and the redefinition of international values as the Berlin Wall collapsed, the eastern block imploded, new countries emerged, and political uncertainty undermined global stability. United States president George H.W. Bush hoped to redefine a "New World Order" in the early 1990s where a hyperpower would dominate and provide guidance and stability for world affairs.[10] Although this geopolitical realignment ended the possibility of a multi-polar world, it was soon followed by the recognition of new emerging players: Brazil, Russia, India, and China. Their suddenly perceived strength forced many countries to re-evaluate policies on several accounts, taking into consideration the foursome as new producers, new markets, and as new potential security threats. At the start the new millennium another American president, George W. Bush, called for a war on terror as security dominated the foreign policy agenda. As part of the United States' security perimeter, however, Canada had very few options at hand to deal with these weighty matters. The Canadian government nevertheless does its best to ensure that neither at home nor abroad is the country perceived as Uncle Sam's puppet.

One strategy Canada has often used to differentiate, without completely dissociating, itself from the United States is through its increasing involvement in multilateral institutions. Interestingly, most of these international forums are characterized by a regional component, allowing Canada to position itself alongside the United States, rather than behind. In this regard, the North American Free Trade Agreement can be regarded as a key accomplishment. Other regional achievements include Canada's full membership in the Organization of American States, and active role in the Pacific region, where Canada became an Asia-Pacific Economic Cooperation (APEC) member in 1989. From the cultural perspective, *la Francophonie* emerged in the mid-1980s to offer Canada another international forum, this time without the presence of the United States.

Membership in international organizations has enriched Canada's foreign policy through a diversification of issue areas as well as its partnerships. At the same time, however, Canada's increased participation in multilateral institutions has limited the influence a prime minister has on foreign policy-making. As an example, one need only remember Jean Chrétien's fierce resistance to the North American Free Trade Agreement while on the opposition benches, a treaty which he ultimately signed once in power.[11]

Multilateralism, important as it may be, is not the only demand on the foreign policy-making apparatus. Starting with the Mulroney government in the mid-1980s, the influence of individuals and groups from civil society on foreign policy increased steadily. Be it through parliamentary committees, the short-lived Centre for Foreign Policy Development, ministerial forums under Lloyd Axworthy, *A Dialogue on Foreign Policy* with Bill Graham, and especially with the proliferation of the internet, Canadians' opinions on foreign issues have mattered.[12] As a political consequence, prime ministers have had to show that they have not only heard but they have indeed listened to the public's input, consequently limiting their range of foreign policy options. Since Stephen Harper's election in 2003, however, public input on foreign policy decisions has not been solicited and policy formulation is once again considered by the government to be the prerogative of the prime minister and his inner circle.

Up until the 2009 budget, presented by Conservative Finance Minister Jim Flaherty, all governments since Brian Mulroney have committed themselves to strengthening the economy and fighting the deficit. The subsequent reduction of available resources in the realm of foreign affairs, even under Harper's Conservatives, has been harshly felt. The political price to pay for closing a few legations abroad or cutting policy analyst positions at headquarters in Ottawa was immensely preferable to the political costs associated with cuts that had a direct impact on domestic social, health, or higher education programs.

Against the background of these contextual changes, we must ask ourselves, has the prime minister's role as the ultimate foreign policy-maker diminished? Or has it increased?

Brian Mulroney (1984–1993)[13]

Brian Mulroney can be ranked as one of the most activist Canadian prime ministers in foreign affairs, for as historian Jack Granatstein points out, by "the sheer force of will, Mulroney made himself and Canada matter in world affairs."[14] Mulroney's performance on the world stage, however, was somewhat surprising given his lukewarm attitude towards foreign affairs at the beginning of his first term. Even as a contender to the leadership of his party in 1983, Mulroney remained shy in terms of foreign policy statements. He addressed the commitment capability gap the Department of National Defence then faced, but his speeches did not reflect a major or an enlightened commitment towards international questions.[15] As leader of the official opposition, he was highly critical of Prime Minister Pierre Trudeau's attitude and policies, which sharply increased tensions between Canada and the United States, particularly following Ronald Reagan's swearing in as president in January 1981.[16] Mulroney contended that Canada should embrace a "special relationship" with the United States, promising to "refurbish" relations by introducing a "new era of civility."[17] For Mulroney, however, this was not an issue of foreign policy but rather was crucial for the health of the Canadian economy. These first commitments bear Mulroney's personal imprint: they are clearly related to his own background as a chief executive officer of an American-based multinational company.

Once in power, Mulroney became increasingly sensitive to a wider range of international issues. One of the first crises he faced was the famine that plagued Ethiopia, where the government's actions helped define Canada's reaction.[18] First, the Canadian public's response to the images of horror broadcast nightly on the news – "a quite remarkable demonstration of interest by ordinary Canadians," said then secretary of state for external affairs, Joe Clark – expressed an impulse that the government felt obliged to match.[19] The government responded by appointing David MacDonald, a former Tory cabinet minister, as emergency coordinator to curtail diplomatic red tape that would have slowed down the relief effort.[20] While helping to co-ordinate Canada's relief effort, MacDonald's appointment served to highlight the influence of non-governmental organizations on Canadian foreign policy.

Early in its first term, the Mulroney government established new foreign policy-making ground rules that opened up the decision-making process. Members of Parliament and ordinary Canadians became involved in the shaping of foreign policy white papers through the work of the parliamentary committee that toured the country to hear citizens' concerns. Hence, if a "birthday" can be associated with the democratization of the foreign policy-making process in Canada, it lies within these years. These new paths, while explored under Joe Clark's stewardship, were nonetheless the fruit of Mulroney's commitment and leadership.

The prime minister's interest in African questions grew from the East African famine and relief efforts, and culminated with his efforts to shoulder the fight against apartheid in South Africa. On this issue, Mulroney was able to persuade both Ronald Reagan and British prime minister Margaret Thatcher to support the transition to a more democratic society.[21] Mulroney also intervened personally to help African leaders find common ground from where they could solve problems of mutual interest.[22]

These personal relationships with world leaders were a prominent aspect of Canada's foreign policy in this decade, a process where the prime minister's direct influence came to the forefront. Given the importance of the Canada–United States relationship, both in terms of the economy and in matters of security, and considering the weight this question represented when Mulroney led the opposition, it is not surprising that the rapport that

Mulroney established with both American presidents, Ronald Reagan and George H.W. Bush, was especially visible.

One of the major legacies that came out of the relationship between the American presidents and the Canadian prime minister is the Canada–United States Free Trade Agreement that was signed in 1988, as well as its extension to include Mexico five years later. At first, while advocating the importance of trade for the prosperity of Canada,[23] Mulroney was sensitive to the potential political backlash such a proposal could generate and was not eager to involve his country in such a deal.[24] The Macdonald Commission report of 1985, which strongly advocated the implementation of a continental economy, nonetheless impressed Mulroney. It was the prime minister's personal contact with Reagan, however, that got discussions started and took care of the president's last reluctance about an issue that raised concerns in Congress.

This personalization of diplomatic relations was another major change in the conduct of Canadian foreign policy. Although other Canadian leaders have established good personal relationships with their American counterparts in the past (one may think of the Roosevelt–King, or the Kennedy–Pearson exchanges), the establishment of regular summits between the two leaders was an unprecedented move, and in sharp contrast with the much cooler attitude Trudeau had shown towards the American presidency. As a result, during the Mulroney years, the Canadian prime minister enjoyed a level of access and influence at the White House hard to match in Canadian diplomatic history.

This is not to suggest that there were no conflicts in Canadian–American relations during Mulroney's time in power. Bilateral disputes and differences over policy remained a vivid part of the landscape. Trade disputes proliferated, despite the free-trade negotiations that were underway. There was also conflict over American extraterritoriality in Cuba, American unilateralism towards international institutions, American policy in Central America, and American challenges to Canadian sovereignty in the Arctic. Acid rain was also an important source of conflict during most of the Mulroney years as it had been during Trudeau's final term of office.

However, what characterized the Mulroney government's foreign policy is how conflicts tended to be managed during the Conservative era. Policy disagreements with Washington were always conducted with the recognition that, while some aspects of the hugely complex Canadian–American relationship were relatively unaffected by changes in government policy, other aspects were quite fragile and easy to damage. Moreover, relations were conducted with the shadow of the future in mind: how conflicts are played out today shape responses to future disagreements. An excellent example of this approach is how Canada responded to the invitation to join Reagan's strategic defence initiative, commonly known as Star Wars: the Canadian government would not be directly involved but would not prevent Canadian business interests from taking advantage of the contracts associated with the development of the defence shield.

However important the Canada–United States friendship was during the Mulroney years, Canadian foreign policy of the time cannot be summed up solely by these exchanges. It was during this period that Canada became a member of the Organization of the American States, a decision that Mulroney took after hearing the advice of Louise Fréchette, assistant deputy minister for Latin America and the Caribbean, who prevailed over her deputy minister, Raymond Chrétien, who was staunchly opposed to this change in Canadian hemispheric policy.[25] Mulroney's personal involvement with Québec's premiers and French president François Mitterrand led to the establishment of *La Francophonie*, in which some of Canada's provinces – Quebec and New Brunswick – would play a permanent and legitimate role. When the first summit was held in Paris in February 1986, premiers Robert Bourassa of Quebec and Richard Hatfield of New Brunswick attended as virtually equal participants with Mulroney.[26]

During the years Brian Mulroney was prime minister, the international and domestic contexts no doubt influenced the shaping of the Canadian foreign policy. But we cannot ignore the influence the prime minister himself exercised over who was involved in the process, which issues were to take prominence, and how to conduct exchanges with representatives from other countries. Questions related to human rights, good governance, and a redefinition of state sovereignty – heralding the "responsibility to protect" – took on a new importance due to Mulroney's personal interest in these areas.

Jean Chrétien (1993-2003)

Some of Mulroney's diplomatic initiatives, especially the Canada–United States "super-relationship," did not please everybody. Mulroney's political rivals, the Liberals, exploited what they portrayed as a too cozy connection that could jeopardize Canadian sovereignty. In their electoral platforms of 1993, 1997, and 2000, the Liberal party called for a very different foreign policy and Liberal leader Jean Chrétien emphasized the need to base foreign policy on Canadian values, openly linking foreign and domestic policies. His government advocated a "voluntary, independent and internationalist" role for Canada in world affairs and, like Trudeau, insisted on keeping its distance from the American administration. The message raised concerns south of the border and reassuring signals that NAFTA would not be renegotiated had to be sent from Ottawa.[27] In 1997, the Liberals seemed inspired by Mitchell Sharp's Third Option when they talked of a strategic vision that looked beyond North America and towards Europe. And in 2000, the Liberals again promoted Canadian values as the basis of Canada's international leadership.

Chrétien himself had some international experience as he headed, although briefly, both the departments of External Affairs and Industry and Trade, which could have prepared him to play a major role as Canada's prime foreign policy actor. However, contrary to Professor John Kirton's early assessment that saw in Chrétien a "leading definer and often the deliverer of Canadian foreign policy,"[28] my own evaluation reveals that his interest in foreign affairs was limited. Chrétien, like his political mentor Trudeau, was primarily motivated by domestic policy rather than by foreign affairs. The prime minister's attitude vis-à-vis foreign policy is well-illustrated by his decision to abolish the cabinet committee that dealt with foreign affairs, thereby allowing Canada's foreign affairs ministers to promote their own initiatives. As a result, Chrétien's foreign policy inspired many writings and analyses that deplored Canada's declining influence and lack of clout on the world scene.

Experts, both from academia and from the observers' realm, do not conclude that the Chrétien government left a rich foreign policy legacy. Political scientist Kim Nossal deplored Canada's pinchpenny diplomacy.[29] Jennifer Welsh, professor of international relations at Oxford University, called for a more focused role and a redefined foreign policy practice.[30] Michael Ignatieff, then a professor at Harvard University, questioned the value of multilateralism in an article published in *Policy Options*, a piece to which thirty-seven journalists, policy practitioners, and academics reacted.[31] Ignatieff also contributed his own view by delivering the *2004 O.D. Skelton Memorial Lecture* advocating that, based on the values of peace, order, and good government, Canada should acquire "a prevention capability: to strengthen rule of law, improve police, conciliate ethno-religious conflict, create political dialogue; an intervention capability, not just peace-keepers, but civilian police, administrators, water sanitation and humanitarian experts; and, a reconstruction capability: from constitution-writers to contractors and construction engineers."[32] Others reflected on priorities, policy issues, and foreign policy prospects;[33] and journalist Andrew Cohen explored "how we lost our place in the world."[34] These analyses were based on the need to look anew at Canada's role in the world in a context that had dramatically changed, and it is not surprising to observe a perceived weakening of Canada's international stature.

It was under foreign minister André Ouellet that the Chrétien government's foreign policy statement, *Canada in the World*, was issued, taking a sharp turn in the orientation Canada would pursue in its foreign relations. The policy was based on "three pillars" where, clearly, prosperity trumped security, and "the promotion of Canadian values" completed the agenda. Apart from this legacy, Ouellet "made little impact on Canadian Foreign Policy."[35] Under his leadership, trade took precedence over diplomacy. "Team Canada" banners were prominently displayed in the halls of the Pearson building, the headquarters of the Department of Foreign Affairs and International Trade. This trade initiative allowed the prime minister to be portrayed as the captain of a united team – often composed of provincial and territorial premiers, prominent business people, and small business entrepreneurs – travelling abroad to sell Canada's greatness. The appointment of Ouellet and the image of a united country was a way to put foreign affairs at the service of a domestic concern: national unity in the months leading to the 1995 Québec referendum.

After this political storm vanished, things changed, allowing Lloyd Axworthy, who held the foreign affairs portfolio from 1996 to 2000, to exercise a major influence in a new role for Canada in the world. Axworthy, whose tenure was not unanimously applauded,[36] touted a human security agenda for Canada. Human security was defined as an umbrella covering the protection of civilians, peace operations, conflict prevention, public safety, and good governance – that is, the rule of law, human rights, and accountability. Among the many results that came from this approach, one may note the issue of war affected children and child soldiers, a problem that brought together non-governmental organizations and government officials and culminated in an international conference held in Winnipeg. Axworthy's agenda also supported the creation of the International Criminal Court and, while sitting on the United Nations Security Council, Canada promoted the prevention of armed conflicts.

This list of achievements was crowned by the adoption of the ban on the anti-personnel landmines, informally known as the Ottawa Treaty. Perhaps the most visible success in recent Canadian foreign policy history, many saw it as an expression of the purest Pearsonian peace-seeking tradition. Although the Geneva conference that reviewed the UN Convention on Certain Conventional Weapons in 1996 failed to reach an agreement on anti-personnel landmines, Canada, which was not in a position to influence the outcome of the meeting, had aligned itself strongly and clearly in favour of a ban. As early as January 1996, Canada unilaterally declared a total ban on anti-personnel landmines. In the days following this announcement, it held a first meeting where eight countries, later known as "the core countries,"[37] joined thirteen non-governmental organizations and the International Committee of the Red Cross to prepare a course of action. Thus, at the conclusion of the Geneva conference, Canada announced it would host "an international meeting to develop a strategy for achieving a comprehensive ban on AP landmines."[38] When launching the Ottawa Process, Axworthy also made a statement that took most participants by surprise: a treaty would be signed no later than the end of 1997. The following months were used to muster support for the Canadian initiative, including more "like-minded" governments and non-governmental organizations, among them the International Campaign to Ban Land-Mines chaired by Jodi Williams: an effective exercise of the new "public diplomacy." Fourteen months after the first Ottawa meeting, fast-track diplomacy bore fruit when 122 countries returned to Ottawa to sign the convention. Axworthy continuously applied pressure in order to have more countries sign and ratify the treaty before it came into effect on 1 March 1999.[39] The whole episode was presented as an unmitigated success. Chrétien himself may have contributed "countless hours"[40] to support the effort, but nowhere – not even in his memoirs – do we see traces that this was his initiative.

Axworthy also instructed the Department of Foreign Affairs and International Trade to work with a host of non-governmental organizations as a means of implementing Canada's foreign policy agenda. This was true throughout the Ottawa Process but was also used to gain support for, and contribute to, the short-lived Centre for the Development of Foreign Policy. Axworthy also organized a series of meetings, allowing Canadians from coast to coast to discuss foreign policy issues. For Canadian foreign policy officers, this was an abrupt cultural change in how to deal with foreign policy questions. Grassroots activists, not the prime minister, provided direct input.

The model of remote prime-ministerial influence survived Axworthy's days. When Canada tried to improve its relationship with the United States in early 2001, it was the newly sworn in foreign minister, John Manley, who led the way to Washington, and not Jean Chrétien. Strengthened by his successful stint as minister of industry, Manley was convinced of the importance of a powerful United States–Canada commercial relationship as a tool to achieve economic well-being and prosperity. Moreover, it was Manley who sat behind the minister of foreign affairs' desk on the fateful morning of 11 September 2001, when Islamic terrorists attacked New York and Washington. No doubt that concepts such as the "intelligent border" and other aspects directly related to the new American sensitivity towards territorial security needed to be addressed, and it was Manley, more than Chrétien, who provided Canada's input to solve these sensitive questions.

Manley's successor, Bill Graham, was a cabinet rookie who stepped into his ministerial shoes, having chaired the House of Commons Standing Committee on Foreign Affairs and International Trade. In contrast to both Manley and Axworthy, Graham's agenda embraced large chunks of policy with no clearly defined priorities; though this was partly due to the context in which he had to operate. In his key speeches, Graham walked on a tight rope: on the one hand, he tried to defend Canada's multilateralist tradition; on the other, he had to respond to newly defined post-9/11 challenges, without leaving the impression of taking marching orders from Washington. No doubt it was an uncomfortable situation. As a result, criticism about Canada's role in the world grew louder and the prime minister recognized the need to finally exert direct leadership. This being said, Graham did leave an important imprint on the department and on Canada's foreign policy as a whole. Through his *Dialogue on Foreign Policy* and the use of internet forums, the Department was more than ever open to different forms of policy-making democratization.

It was on questions related to Africa that Jean Chrétien left his mark on Canada's foreign policy agenda. Gravely impressed by television reports of the turmoil in the Great Lakes region of Eastern Africa, Chrétien made Africa his top foreign policy priority. In doing so, he included the New Partnership for Africa's Development (NEPAD) on the G8 summit agenda at the Kananaskis meeting in 2002. NEPAD was a successful recognition-based partnership between the G8 and African states that aimed at consolidating democracy, encouraging sound economic management, and promoting peace and development. Canada's commitment, leadership, and traditional "honest broker" role were put to work in the attainment of this collective commitment, despite a lukewarm reception from the United States. According to former New Democratic Party member of parliament Steven Langdon, Canada's efforts were "so energetic … that African civil society groups and parliamentarians became suspicious that this was really a Canadian set of proposals being circulated through key African leaders" and not a locally supported attempt to enhance economic, political, and security environments on the continent.[41]

Even though the prime minister seemed to enjoy being involved in foreign affairs related questions,[42] his apparent lack of interest in foreign policy was emphasized in a series of diplomatic gaffes: misstatements in the Middle East by the prime minister himself, inappropriate remarks about the American president by his staff, and the sending of his minister to a head of state's funeral. All of this eroded Canada's reputation abroad and diminished its middle power status. It is only slightly surprising then that, in the wake of the tragic events of 11 September 2001, President Bush forgot to thank Canada when he listed allies supporting the United States, even though Canadians had graciously hosted thousands of stranded American airline passengers on 9/11 and in the days that followed.[43] Political scientist

Tom Keating's portrait adequately sums up Chrétien's influence on foreign policy: "While the rhetoric and the spirit were unequivocally internationalist, the tangible commitment of resources reflected a passivity not seen for many decades."[44]

Paul Martin (2003–2005)

One cannot think of Paul Martin's leadership in foreign affairs without having in mind the ungenerous nickname *The Economist* gave him: Mr. Dithers. This came after the Martin government sent mixed signals while simultaneously avoiding a concrete decision, before eventually declining Washington's invitation to take part in an anti-missile shield initiative. Perhaps it was also his indecision or the lack of leadership that let interdepartmental exchanges continue before ultimately settling on the move of Canada's troops from Kabul to Kandahar. Depending on the sources one consults, the answer varies. Yet one thing remains clear: despite the fact that Paul Martin took excessive time to weigh issues, his contribution to foreign policy was more active than his predecessor's or, as we will see in the next section, his successor's.

Expectations were high. The experts who were critical of the Chrétien government's foreign policy performance expected a lot from the incoming government, and prominent academics offered their recommendations to the incoming prime minister in an issue of the *International Journal*.[45] Martin came to office ready to face this foreign policy challenge. At home as minister of finance, he had contributed to revitalizing Canada's finances and economy, providing room for new initiatives. The need for a new policy was not disputed, the only question that remained was how strong the prime minister's leadership would be in conducting the foreign policy review. In hindsight, what we witnessed was a return of the strong role played by the prime minister in the shaping of foreign policy. Janice Gross Stein and Euguene Lang in their book, *The Unexpected War: Canada in Kandahar*, do not hesitate in their evaluation of the foreign policy review: "The Prime Minister wanted this done and done quickly."[46]

Martin was indeed quite sensitive to foreign policy issues. His father's legacy as secretary of state for external affairs was dear to him and, as minister of finance, he was at ease playing in international circles, meeting his counterparts at gatherings of the G8, the Organization for Economic Co-operation and Development (OECD), and other multilateral forums.[47] More importantly, Martin sensed an urgent need to invest in foreign policy issues. As he reported himself: "Our foreign policy should reflect our own interests and values.... In order to show leadership, however, we have to back up our rhetoric with resources. The real problem with our foreign policy [is] that we talk a good game but don't deliver."[48]

Martin made it clear that, while "Canada's role in the world is not simply to support a great power,"[49] it was necessary to recognize the importance of Canada's relationship with the United States; and he did so in a more open manner than his predecessor. Martin brought back a foreign policy unit around the cabinet table and his key ministers, Bill Graham and Pierre Pettigrew, were not preaching from Lloyd Axworthy's gospel of anti-Americanism. Moreover, the appointment of Rick Hillier as chief of defence staff sent a strong signal in terms of like-mindedness with Canada's southern neighbour. Hillier quickly introduced to Canada the "three block war," where armed forces must be prepared to support humanitarian aid and reconstruction, patrol a ceasefire line, and engage in combat in the same theatre of operations. At a time when Washington conducted the most offensive and realist foreign policy[50] of its history, it was a message White House officials appreciated.

Martin's commitment towards a renewed foreign policy was admittedly among his top priorities when he became Canada's twenty-first prime minister in December 2003 and, in April 2005, it would bear fruit with the publication of *Canada's International Policy Statement*. This multifaceted foreign policy statement covered diplomacy, defence, aid, and trade issues in separate booklets that were presented as one policy. The existence of an overarching policy that did in fact unify the silo-designed approach was questioned by most observers. In short, many initiatives were suggested, but the means to reconcile all of the objectives were few.

The statement nevertheless presented a new face to Canadian foreign policy at large. The prioritizing that characterized the three pillars option advocated in Chrétien's *Canada in the World* was put to rest and the government embraced a much larger approach that tackled all aspects of Canada's role abroad. The government advocated a "3D approach" with diplomacy, defence, and development working together – much to the dismay of trade officials who insisted on referring to a 3D+T strategy. The key objectives of the policy were to help failed and failing states, to improve Canada's relationship with the United States, and to increase the capability of Canada's armed forces; all elements that were music to Washington's ears following the Chrétien government's distant stance. To keep the usual sovereignty concern in check, Prime Minister Martin made sure to add the appropriate Canadian touch in the foreword to the policy statement: "We want to make a real difference in halting and preventing conflict and improving human welfare around the world; [this] is a doctrine of activism that over decades has forged our nation's international character."[51]

The policy received mixed reviews. Some academics argued that it brought nothing new, simply listing actions to which Canada was already committed. Tom Axworthy, a former Trudeau policy advisor, described this as "new bottles for old wine,"[52] while Professors David Bercuson and Denis Stairs offered a more nuanced, but just as biting, analysis.[53] It was perhaps political scientist Kim Nossal who advanced the most overarching critique. Taking his cue from the "responsibility agenda"[54] outlined in the policy statement, he called for the "responsibility to be honest."[55] Yet despite the criticism, some aspects of the policy had a longer life than the Martin government itself. Parts of the statement were still referred to by officials after the Harper government was sworn in, as was the case with the defence policy to which Chief of Defence Staff Rick Hillier had heavily contributed.

Despite his short tenure as prime minister, Paul Martin was personally and actively involved in shaping Canada's foreign policy. Martin wanted to distance himself as much as he could from the Chrétien years, and, in terms of foreign policy-making, there is no doubt that he succeeded. His practice was consistent with the active role Canadian prime ministers have usually played. If Martin swung the pendulum the other way, its course was to continue much farther with Stephen Harper coming to power.

Stephen Harper (2005-2009)

Although he has twice been elected by Canadians, Stephen Harper's record in foreign affairs is still to be written, and it is in this context that the analysis of his role must be understood. First indications, however, reveal that, since January 2006, Harper has shaped Canada's foreign policy with what some have called a one-dimensional approach. This is revealed in terms of his foreign policy priorities as well as his foreign policy management.

Much of the inspiration for crafting the Harper government's foreign policy apparently came from Roy Rempel's book, *Dreamland*. The work claims that Canada's foreign policy has eroded its sovereignty and pushed the country into the status of an American protectorate. Rempel suggests this is "because the country's leaders have had a poor sense of the national interest and an ideologically skewed approach to international relations."[56] It is not only a matter of size or power; Canadian leaders have simply lived in a dreamland. Rempel calls for better involvement of the public to build a national consensus reflecting "the interests of all Canadians rather than the view of a select few," to remove ideology in the building of a strategic culture, to make international policy "as non-partisan as possible," and consider the building of a close partnership with the United States as a first priority.

In line with what Paul Martin had started, Harper has fully recognized the United States as Canada's first ally. Harper and President George W. Bush got along well, though the prime minister did not trumpet this friendship. However, there was still little evidence of any overt influence by Canada in Washington, as opposed to the Mulroney years. Issues such as the Security and Prosperity Partnership of North America, implemented in 2005, continued to be among the key topics referred to in terms of Canada–United States relations. However, there were no definite indicators of Canada's priorities in this relationship. Given the dismal state of the Canadian armed forces resources, reinvestment in military equipment cannot be, in itself, an indicator of an American driven agenda. Rather, the purchases serve the domestic *Canada First* policy.

The quiet friendship with Washington is characteristic of the Harper government's attitude towards foreign policy in general. This can be explained, in part, by the prime minister's view of foreign policy which is, by his own admission, not high, and by the narrow width of foreign policy topics that interest him.[57] After years of perceived neglect followed by a slight revival of foreign policy under Martin, observers expected to see clear signals coming from the new government. None came. Not only did the Conservative government refuse to publish a foreign policy statement of its own, but speeches by key ministers often provided little in the way of new information. Speaking before Canadian diplomats posted in Asia, Maxime Bernier, minister of foreign affairs from August 2007 to May 2008, declared: "Canada's foreign policy is anchored in the pursuit of Canadian interests of security and prosperity and in our respect for the values of freedom, democracy, human rights and the rule of law."[58] Any minister of any Canadian government over the past twenty-five years could have said the same.

Where then does Canada stand? Given the one-dimensional aspect of Stephen Harper's foreign policy, peace and security are priorities that immediately come to mind. As deputy minister Len Edwards mentioned in Canada's remarks at the UN General Assembly in 2008: "Today Canada is contributing to peace and security – and making sacrifices – in places as diverse as Afghanistan, Haiti and Sudan. Each of these Canadian engagements flows from a UN mandate."[59] Of these, Afghanistan takes precedence, both in terms of resources and in terms of the government's policy agenda. This engagement encompasses the need for a rapprochement with the United States while the ever-present Canadian call for multilateral action is satisfied.

Canada's role in Afghanistan also serves to illustrate foreign policy decision-making under Harper. It was reported that the first extension of the mission was decided without the input of his ministers of national defence and foreign affairs.[60] Here again, we observe a one-dimensional apparatus where important decisions are concentrated in the hands of experts within the Prime Minister's Office and the Privy Council Office. Officials in the Department of Foreign Affairs and International Trade are ill at ease with this way of making policies, their expertise often disregarded, or simply not solicited. This general malaise is amplified by the lack of support given to public input at home and public diplomacy abroad.[61]

This concentration of power in the hands of a select few goes sharply against Rempel's call for consensus building based on wider input into key national interests and foreign policy priorities. It could be explained, in part, by the weakness of ministers who were appointed to foreign affairs related portfolios. At Foreign Affairs, neither Peter Mackay nor Maxime Bernier were considered stars. Similarly, as minister of national defence, Gordon O'Connor failed to fulfil the expectations he created among the attentive public, the serving military, and foreign policy analysts as an opposition critic and author of the Conservative defence platform. General Hillier's resignation underlines how top strategists found themselves isolated and felt a lack of support from their political masters.[62] The resulting vacuum left plenty of room for the prime minister and his close advisors to have a direct influence on the shaping of Canadian foreign and defence policy. What are the results of this influence?

It is too early to provide a final assessment of the Harper government's contribution to Canadian foreign policy. Heading a minority government and facing a major economic crisis, however, there are few incentives for the government to modify its attitude. A resurgence of foreign policy as a key topic on the government's political agenda before the next election would be surprising.

Different Styles that Matter?

Over the last twenty-five years, prime ministers have been influential in the shaping of Canadian foreign policy. How and to what extent they have been involved is of import as the context in which foreign policy is set has dramatically changed in response to external pressures on the national interest. Theoretically, Canada's institutional framework gives a huge advantage to the prime minister who can dominate the policy-making process. Is this advantage strong enough to curtail these contextual pressures? To answer the question we have reviewed the mandates of Brian Mulroney, Jean Chrétien, Paul Martin, and Stephen Harper.

The first finding is that, indeed, despite changes in the political environment, prime ministers matter in foreign policy formulation and decision-making. Even when Jean Chrétien showed a lesser degree of involvement, he simply left room for strong ministers to capably manage foreign affairs. A second point worthy of note is that there is no consistency in the prime ministers' role and influence on foreign policy-making. To illustrate and explain these differences, it might be useful to use a typology that relates the interest (high or low) of a prime minister towards foreign policy questions and his foreign policy managerial style (hands off – that is, leaving ample room to his ministers – or hands on – that is, controlling as much as possible of the content and of the process). Table 1 offers a portrait of the four types that result:

This typology brings to light an interesting reading of the period studied. First, one can see that prime ministers do not follow a unique pattern when they get involved in setting their foreign policy agenda and work in defence of the national interest: Mulroney was generally of the captain style; most of the time Chrétien was lenient; Martin was a commander; and Harper, in his first years of government, appears as a shackler. Each of these leaders corresponds to a type, but of course to varying degrees.

Prime ministers also tend to move from one type to another when they stay for some time in power. This is something Martin, with his short time as prime minister did not experience: he came in and stayed a commander, though he appeared hesitant at times. Harper has steadily shown the characteristics of a shackler. Both Mulroney and Chrétien, however, came in as lenient and, with time – a short time for Mulroney, but much longer for Chrétien – moved towards forms of captainship. These categories may help us better understand the type of influence a prime minister exercises on foreign policy-making; however, it is possible to imagine two prime ministers falling within the same type, but at sharply different levels. More studies are needed to refine the categories in order to better depict the range of possible behaviours adopted by prime ministers.

This research demonstrates that it is not only the prime ministers' personalities that influence their foreign policy behaviour. It undoubtedly plays a role, but external factors are also part of the equation, as we have seen with Jean Chrétien and NAFTA. This enriches the basis of political scientist Margaret Hermann's frame of analysis which, with further research, could enlighten our understanding of the prime ministers' role on foreign policy-making.

Table 1. Styles of influence.

		Interest	
		Low	High
Management style	Hands off	*Lenient*	*Captain*
	Hands on	*Shackler*	*Commander*

The last twenty-five years have confirmed the importance of the role played by the prime minister in serving the national interest. This role has changed according to who was holding it and, to a lesser extent, a changing environment. Prime ministers of the future will demonstrate how this trend will evolve.

NOTES

1. The principle of responsible government means that the ministers of the government must receive, individually and collectively, the support of a majority of the elected members of parliament.

2. John J. Noble, "Serving the Prime Minister's Foreign Policy," in *Canada among Nations, 2007: What Room for Manoeuvre?* ed. Jean Deaudelin and Daniel Schwanen (Montreal: McGill-Queen's University Press, 2007).

3. Nelson Michaud, "The Prime Minister, PMO and PCO: Makers of Canadian Foreign Policy?" in *Handbook of Canadian Foreign Policy*, ed. Nelson Michaud, Patrick James, and Marc J. O'Reilly (Lanham, MD: Lexington Books, 2006), 21–48.

4. Donald J. Savoie, *Governing from the Centre: The Concentration of Power in Canadian Politics* (Toronto: University of Toronto Press, 1999).

5. Graham Allison, "Conceptual Models and the Cuban Missile Crisis," *American Political Science Review* 43, no. 3 (1969): 689–718. Among others, also see Graham Allison, *The Essence of Decision* (Boston: Little Brown, 1971), and Graham Allison and Philip Zelikow, *Essence of Decision: Explaining the Cuban Missile Crisis* (New York: Rowman and Littlefield, 1999).

6. Michel Crozier and Erhard Friedberg, *L'acteur et le système. Les contraintes de l'action collective* (Paris: Éditions du Seuil, 1971).

7. On this, see works led by Margaret Hermann, for instance: Margaret Hermann, Thomas Preston, Baghat Korany, and Tim Shaw, "Who Leads Matters: The Effects of Powerful Individuals," *International Studies Review* 3, no. 2 (2001): 83–132.

8. I deliberately left Kim Campbell off the list, whose short tenure (June–November 1993) did not allow her to leave a lasting imprint on Canadian foreign policy, despite her interest in the question.

9. Erik Nielsen, *The House is Not a Home: An Autobiography* (Toronto: Macmillan of Canada, 1989).

10. Hubert Védrine, *Face à l'hyperpuissance* (Paris: Fayard, 2003).

11. To get an interesting outsider's view of this change in policy stances, see James J. Blanchard, *Behind the Embassy Door: Canada, Clinton and Quebec* (Toronto: McClelland & Stewart, 1998).

12. On this, see Gerald Schmitz and James Lee, "Split Images and Serial Affairs: Reviews, Reorganizations and Parliamentary Roles," in *Canada among Nations, 2005: Split Images*, ed. Andrew F. Cooper and Dane Rowlands (Montreal: McGill-Queen's University Press, 2005).

13. For a complete analysis of the period, see Nelson Michaud and Kim Richard Nossal, ed., *Diplomatic Departures: The Conservative Era in Canadian Foreign Policy, 1984–1993* (Vancouver: UBC Press, 2001).

14. J.L. Granatstein, *Whose War Is It: How Canada Can Survive in the Post-9/11 World* (Toronto: Harper Collins, 2007), 205.

15. Brian Mulroney, "Canada in the World: Notes for a Speech," 10 June 1983, author's archives; Brian Mulroney, *Where I Stand* (Toronto: McClelland & Stewart, 1983).

16. Stephen Clarkson, *Canada and the Reagan Challenge: Crisis and Adjustment, 1981-85*, rev. ed. (Toronto: James Lorimer, 1985); Adam Bromke and Kim Richard Nossal, "Tensions in Canada's Foreign Policy," *Foreign Affairs* 62 (Winter 1983-84): 335-53.

17. David Taras, "Brian Mulroney's Foreign Policy: Something for Everyone," *The Round Table* 293 (1985): 39.

18. An interesting account of the Ethiopian crisis is in David R. Morrison, *Aid and Ebb Tide: A History of CIDA and Canadian Development Assistance* (Waterloo: Wilfrid Laurier University Press, 1998).

19 Cited in Maureen Appel Molot and Brian W. Tomlin, "The Conservative Agenda," in *Canada among Nations, 1985: The Conservative Agenda*, ed. Maureen Appel Molot and Brian W. Tomlin (Toronto: James Lorimer, 1986), 9.

20 Brian Mulroney, *Memoirs* (Toronto: Douglas Gibson Books, 2007), 399.

21 David R. Black, "How Exceptional? Reassessing the Mulroney Government Anti-Apartheid 'Crusade'," in *Diplomatic Departures*, 173–93.

22 J.H. Taylor, "The Conservatives and Foreign Policy-Making: A Foreign Service View," in *Diplomatic Departures*, 211–19.

23 See Mulroney, *Where I Stand*.

24 Mulroney, *Memoirs*, 280.

25 Louis Bélanger and Nelson Michaud, "Canadian Institutional Strategies: New Orientations for a Middle Power Foreign Policy," *Australian Journal of International Affairs* 54, no. 1 (2000): 97–110.

26 John Kirton, "Shaping the Global Order: Canada and the Francophone and Commonwealth Summits of 1987," *Behind the Headlines* 44, no. 3 (1987): 1-17.

27 Blanchard, *Behind the Embassy Door*.

28 John Kirton, "Foreign Policy under the Liberals: Prime Ministerial Leadership in the Chrétien's Government Foreign Policy-making Process," in *Canada among Nations, 1997: Asia Pacific Face-Off*, ed. Fen Osler Hampson, Maureen Appel Molot, and Martin Rudner (Ottawa: Carleton University Press 1997), 27.

29 Kim Richard Nossal, "Pinchpenny Diplomacy: The Decline of Good International Citizenship in Canadian Foreign Policy," *International Journal* 54, no. 1 (1998–99): 88–105.

30 Jennifer Welsh, *At Home in the World: Canada's Global Vision for the 21st Century* (Toronto: Harper Collins, 2004).

31 Michael Ignatieff, "Canada in the Age of Terror – Multilateralism Meets a Moment of Truth," *Policy Options* 24, no. 2 (February 2003): 14–18; Graham F. Walker, ed., *Independence in an Age of Empire: Assessing Unilateralism and Multilateralism* (Halifax: Centre for Foreign Policy Studies, 2004).

32 Michael Ignatieff, *Peace, Order and Good Government: A Foreign Policy Agenda for Canada* (Ottawa: Department of Foreign Affairs and International Trade, 2004).

33 Norman Hillmer, David Carment, and Fen Osler Hampson, *Is Canada Now Irrelevant?* (Calgary: Canadian Defence and Foreign Affairs Institute, 2003).

34 Andrew Cohen, *While Canada Slept: How We Lost Our Place in the World* (Toronto: McClelland & Stewart, 2003).

35 Graham Fraser, "Liberal Continuities: Jean Chrétien's Foreign Policy 1993–2003," in *Canada among Nations, 2004: Setting Priorities Straight*, ed. David Carment, Fen Osler Hampson, and Norman Hillmer (Montreal: McGill-Queen's University Press, 2004), 173–74.

36 Denis Stairs, "The Changing Office and the Changing Environment of the Minister of Foreign Affairs in the Axworthy Era," in *Canada among Nations, 2004*, 19–38.

37 These countries are: Austria, Belgium, Canada, Denmark, Ireland, Mexico, Norway, and Switzerland.

38 Robert Lawson, "The Ottawa Process: Fast-Track Diplomacy and the International Movement to Ban Anti-Personnel Mines," in *Canada among Nations, 1998: Leadership and Dialogue*, ed. Fen Osler Hampson and Maureen Appel Molot (Toronto: Oxford University Press, 1998), 84.

39 See Christopher Kirkey, "Washington's Response to the Ottawa Land Mines process," in *Canadian–American Public Policy* 46 (Augusta: Canadian–American Center, University of Maine, 2001).

40 Jean Chrétien, *My Years as Prime Minister* (Toronto: Vintage Canada, 2008), 336.

41 The G8 Canadian Sherpa and prime minister's personal representative for Africa, Bob Fowler, outlines the origins of the agreement in "Canada's leadership and the Kananaskis G8 Summit," in *Canada among*

Nations, 2003: Coping with the American Colossus, ed. David Carment, Fen Osler Hampson, and Norman Hillmer (Toronto: Oxford University Press, 2003), 219–41. In the same book, the chapter by Steven Langdon, "NEPAD and the renaissance of Africa," provides a ground-based analysis of the program.

42 See, Chrétien, *My Years as Prime Minister*.

43 Bush finally thanked Canada for its generosity when he visited the country led by a newly elected prime minister, Paul Martin, in late 2004.

44 Tom Keating, "A Passive Internationalist: Jean Chrétien and Canadian Foreign Policy," in *The Chrétien Legacy: Politics and Public Policy in Canada*, ed. Lois Harder and Steve Patten (Montreal: McGill-Queen's University Press, 2006), 139.

45 Canadian Institute of International Affairs, *Foreign Policy for Paul Martin. Eight articles on Canada's International Relations for the new Prime Minister*. Published as an issue of the *International Journal* 58, no. 4 (2003).

46 Janice Gross Stein and Eugene Lang, *The Unexpected War: Canada in Kandahar* (Toronto: Penguin, 2008), 140.

47 Paul Martin, Jr., was sworn in holding tight the Peace Tower flag that flew half mast when the country mourned the passing away of his father, Lester B. Pearson's foreign affairs minister.

48 Paul Martin, Jr., *Hell or High Water: My Life in and out Politics* (Toronto: McClelland & Stewart, 2008), 328–29.

49 Ibid., 330.

50 On this doctrine, see John J. Mearsheimer, *The Tragedy of Great Power Politics* (New York: Norton, 2001).

51 Government of Canada, *Canada's International Policy Statement*, 5 booklets (Ottawa: Supply and Public Works Canada, 2005), 1.

52 Thomas Axworthy, "New Bottles for Old Wine: Implementing the International Policy Statement," in *Canada among Nations, 2005*, 271–82.

53 David J. Bercuson and Denis Stairs, "Canada's International Policy Statement: What's New, What's Old, And What's Needed," in *In the Canadian Interest? Assessing Canada's International Policy Statement*, ed. David J. Bercuson and Denis Stairs (Calgary: Canadian Defence and Foreign Affairs Institute, 2005), 1–4.

54 These responsibilities include: "the 'responsibility to protect,' [which] seeks 'to hold governments accountable for how they treat their people, and to intervene if necessary to prevent a humanitarian catastrophe'; the 'responsibility to deny,' [which] seeks to prevent terrorists and 'irresponsible governments' from acquiring weapons of mass destruction; the 'responsibility to respect,' [which] seeks to 'build lives of freedom for all people' based on 'the fundamental human rights of every man, woman and child on earth'; the 'responsibility to build,' [which] seeks to ensure that Canadian development assistance programs provide 'the tools that ordinary people really need to get on with their own development'; and the 'responsibility to the future,' [which] embraces the goal of sustainable development 'through better management of global public goods.'" Kim Richard Nossal, "The Responsibility to be Honest," in *In the Canadian Interest?*, 40–44.

55 Nossal, "The Responsibility to be Honest," 46.

56 Roy Rempel, *Dreamland: How Canada's Pretend Foreign Policy Has Undermined Sovereignty* (Kingston: Breakout Educational Network and the Queen's University School of Policy Studies released through McGill-Queen's University Press, 2006), 180.

57 John J. Noble, "Serving the Prime Minister's Foreign Policy," 45.

58 Maxime Bernier, *Notes for an Address at a Meeting of the Asian Heads of Mission*, March 12, 2008, http://w01.international.gc.ca/minpub/publication.aspx?publication_id=385946&lang=eng&docnum=2008/4.

59 Leonard J. Edwards, *Notes for an Address on behalf of the Minister of Foreign*

Affairs, to the United Nations General Assembly, September 29, 2008, http://w01.international.gc.ca/minpub/publication.aspx?publication_id=386530&lang=eng&docnum=2008/19.

60 See, Gross Stein and Lang, *The Unexpected War*.

61 Evan Potter, *Branding Canada Projecting Canada's Soft Power through Public Diplomacy* (Montreal: McGill-Queen's University Press, 2009).

62 Nelson Michaud, "Hillier: le refus de tenir un pari rendu impossible," *Le Soleil*, 19 April 2008, 39.

ENGAGING THE UNITED STATES: THE DEPARTMENT OF FOREIGN AFFAIRS AND U.S. POLICY, 1982–2005

Stephen J. Randall

On this the one hundredth anniversary of Canada's Department of Foreign Affairs and International Trade, it is appropriate to review the role that the Department has played in meeting the political, economic, and cultural challenges of dealing with Canada's most important bilateral relationship, the United States. Between the governments of Liberal prime minister Pierre Elliott Trudeau and Conservative prime minister Stephen Harper, it is difficult to imagine any major Canadian policy issue that does not have some degree of relevance to the relationship with the United States. This stands in stark contrast to United States policies where Canada is rarely more than a faint blip on the radar screen. That said, it is remarkable the extent to which the relationship has often been neglected and even mismanaged because of a lack of focus on, or attention to, what has long been Canada's most important, even if uncomfortable, relationship.

On the one hand, it may seem inappropriate to single out one federal department for consideration, since it is evident that virtually every government department and agency, including the Prime Minister's Office

(PMO) and the Privy Council Office (PCO) and even most provincial governments, has direct engagement with its counterpart south of the forty-ninth parallel. The PCO, for instance, has for some time played a direct role in the bilateral relationship. The national security advisor in the PCO provides advice to the prime minister on security issues; the foreign policy advisor in the PCO not only provides a coordinating role among the federal departments and agencies on bilateral relations but also communicates directly with White House officials and the United States embassy in Ottawa.[1] The daily contacts, often at a very personal level, between officials in those departments and agencies with their counterparts in the United States have reinforced the notion articulated by, among others, George Haynal, former assistant deputy minister for the Americas, that relations with the United States are in many respects not foreign relations but rather "inter-mesticity."[2] The role of the federal government in determining bilateral policies is further complicated by federal–provincial relations and the fact that in a number of areas important to the relationship with the United States the provinces are actually sovereign, most notably with respect to natural resources.

The relative importance of the Department of Foreign Affairs and International Trade in shaping the bilateral relationship has varied over the years. In 1982 the Department of External Affairs, as it was called until 1993, underwent a reorganization in part to address the bilateral relationship. The role of the Department in managing these intercontinental relations, however, has to a considerable degree depended upon the importance that the prime minister placed on relations with the United States, the personal relationship between the prime minister and the American president, and the ways in which the prime minister related to the foreign minister and the Department as a whole. In the final analysis it is only the prime minister who "manages" the relationship with the United States; the rest of the actors, important as they are, play only supporting roles, frequently off stage.

Former Canadian Ambassador to the United States Allan Gotlieb captured the complexity of these bilateral contacts most effectively when he wrote in his memoirs: "The relationship is driven by hundreds of institutions and organizations in both the national and provincial capitals, each interacting with points of contact south of the border." Gotlieb also underscored the tendency in External Affairs to try, usually without success, to control all aspects of foreign policy, including the activities of international units in other functional federal departments. His own perspective, Gotlieb suggested, was shared during his time in office by the PCO and Treasury Board; that is that there was a need for more effective management of the bilateral relationship.[3] Thus, the history of DFAIT in shaping and implementing policy toward the United States since the early 1980s is an uneven one. The Department may at times have claimed sovereignty in shaping the policy relationship, but rarely has it succeeded in making that claim a reality.

In 1982, there was no inter-departmental cabinet-level committee responsible for coordinating policy toward the United States. That year, Michael Pitfield, clerk of the privy council, initiated a reorganization of a number of the executive branches that impacted External Affairs. The reorganization included a merger of the Trade Commissioner Service and some policy branches from the Department of Industry, Trade and Commerce into the Department of External Affairs. The result was that External ended with two ministers, one for External Affairs and a new minister of International Trade. The result was considerable confusion over jurisdiction, duplicated reporting structures, and morale problems in the Department. Derek Burney, then assistant under-secretary of the Economic Affairs Bureau, observed in his memoirs that in 1982 there were actually seven separate divisions within the Department that had some responsibility for relations with the United States; and those divisions reported to three different assistant deputy ministers, two different deputy ministers, and two different ministers. Yet, he also observes – and this was crucial for the development of policy during the Mulroney Conservative government – that the reorganization gave the Department of External Affairs sole responsibility for trade policy, even if that sovereignty was at times challenged by the Department of Finance and the Department of Industry.[4]

Between the reorganization in 1982 and September 1983, when he was appointed assistant deputy minister for the United States, Burney and the Economic Affairs Bureau conducted, in consultation with other relevant federal departments, an exhaustive review of Canadian trade policy. Cabinet followed up on this by establishing a task force to cautiously approach the United States on possible sectoral agreements. While this did not achieve any immediate results, it did establish the basis for the more comprehensive free trade negotiations that followed. Once Burney was assistant deputy minister for the United States, he set his mind to bringing together the various divisions that had a U.S. focus to develop a coherent set of policies on trade policy and promotion, and political relations. The bureau also had primary responsibility for the Canadian embassy in Washington, as well as all the Canadian consulates and public affairs in the United States, and had coordinating responsibility with other federal departments on issues such as the environment, of which acid rain was the most contentious concern, and on energy and transportation matters.[5]

The Mulroney Years, 1984–1993

When Brian Mulroney and the Progressive Conservative party came to power in 1984, relations with the United States were clearly under considerable stress. There were differences of perspective between the Canadian and American governments on a range of issues, from energy and acid rain to the extraterritorial application of United States law to Canadian subsidiaries operating in Cuba or selling oil field equipment to the Soviet Union. Once in office, Mulroney also sought to alleviate some of the tensions that had emerged with the United States late in the Trudeau government over the National Energy Program and Trudeau's peace initiative. In addition, the Trudeau government's approach to arms reduction had compromised the good personal relationship between Secretary of State for External Affairs Allan MacEachen and Ronald Reagan's Secretary of State, George Shultz. Mulroney thus had to mend personal as well as policy fences. As a result, his commitment to strengthening the relationship pulled the Canadian bureaucracy in the same direction.[6]

Allan Gotlieb, serving as under-secretary of state for external affairs from 1977–81 and as ambassador to the United States, 1981–89, was one of two individuals who had a remarkable impact over the next decade in refocusing the attention of the Department – and one could also argue the Conservative government of Prime Minister Brian Mulroney – on the United States; the other was Derek Burney. Gotlieb commented at the time of Burney's appointment as the assistant deputy minister in charge of

United States affairs that he would be "more aggressive than his amiable predecessors," and that Burney would also be more effective "provided he restrains himself from rolling over and squashing people."[7] In the fall of 1985 Burney was promoted to deputy minister as one of two deputies at External Affairs. In this new role he had overall responsibility for relations with the United States as well as with Asia. He remained in that position until Prime Minister Mulroney appointed him chief of staff of the PMO in February 1987, where his main task was to bring order out of chaos.[8]

By the time that Burney moved to the PMO, a range of offices in the Department had some degree of responsibility for relations with the United States. At the peak of the free trade debate and implementation, there were no fewer than seven branches and bureaus in the Department dealing directly with United States issues. In addition to the United States Branch, under Donald Campbell as senior assistant deputy minister, there was also a United States Relations Bureau, headed by a director general, and a United States Trade and Investment Development Bureau (established in 1983) also headed by a director general. In 1987, the Department established the United States Trade and Economic Relations Bureau (which replaced the Trade and Investment Development Bureau) and the United States Trade, Tourism, and Investment Development Bureau, headed by a director general. To round out the Department, there was the Free Trade Policy and Options Branch, under an assistant deputy minister, the Free Trade Management Bureau, and the Free Trade Policy Bureau. The two most pressing concerns in the bilateral relationship in the 1980s were free trade and acid rain, and the importance of both issues tended to drive the organizational structure of the Department.

This restructuring within the Department of External Affairs was a clear reflection of the increased emphasis on the United States and the critically important free trade negotiations. It was also, one could argue, a reflection of the fact that relations with the United States had become a political and personal priority for the prime minister. In 1989 Burney succeeded Gotlieb as ambassador in Washington, where he continued to build good personal relations with American lawmakers, the hallmark of the Gotlieb years. As much as one may be reluctant to credit individuals within any complex political and bureaucratic structure with having had a transformational impact, it is arguable that these two men did precisely that in the course of the 1980s and early 1990s. Their success came about in part because they had a clear vision of what needed to be done, how to do it, and who needed to be influenced. Although both were professional civil servants and knew how to work as bureaucrats within the system, they were also political beings who understood the importance of connections in both Ottawa and Washington. They were also confirmed bilateralists and considered themselves foreign policy realists.

The impact of Gotlieb and Burney on policy development toward the United States in the 1980s and early 1990s is particularly remarkable since they differed to some degree from Joe Clark, who served as the secretary of state for external affairs from 1984 until 1991. Clark was hampered by the fact that he did not have the personal connections in Washington comparable to the relationship that had existed between Allan MacEachen and George Shultz, who had been friends at university. Clark also pursued two areas of international relations that were counter to the policies of the Reagan and Bush administrations, in part because he was more closely allied philosophically with the multilateralists in the Department and more sensitive to the views of the NGO community on Canadian policy.[9] One major divergence with the United States was Canada's vocal opposition to the apartheid regime in South Africa, and the imposition of economic sanctions on the South African government, a policy opposed by the Reagan administration. The second issue was Nicaragua, where Clark opposed American military intervention, advocated a negotiated settlement, supported the initiatives of the Contadora Group, and accepted refugees from El Salvador and Guatemala.[10] Canadian policy on both issues was an irritant in Washington at precisely the time that the Mulroney government was seeking to strengthen its relationship with the United States. Clark was also initially seen as cool to the free trade initiative with the United States, which was clearly the main policy initiative of the decade. This set him apart from the direction in which Gotlieb, Burney, and ultimately the prime minister, wanted to go.

Gotlieb expressed concern at the time that Canada appeared to be running a "two track foreign policy," one under Clark, which sought to distance Canada from United States defence policies, and the other under Mulroney, which was more realistic and practical.[11] One result of this disconnect, at least from the perspective of Clark's critics, was that the bilateral relationship was increasingly being managed primarily by the prime minister, who developed a close and effective personal and working relationship with President Reagan. In the 1985 foreign policy review under Clark's leadership, the references to the United States were ambiguous. On the one hand, the document stressed that "there is scarcely an area of Canadian National Life not affected by our relationship with the United States," and the report called for a "new, constructive relationship." At the same time the report contained expressions of concern about the asymmetry of the bilateral relationship, as well as a tendency toward protectionism in the United States and what was considered the "increasingly segmented nature of the U.S. government system."[12] In his memoirs Mulroney is more positive in his assessment of Clark's role than were either Gotlieb or Burney, noting for instance that in late 1986 with the growing concern over the acid rain issue, Clark and trade minister Pat Carney had organized a high level "think in" on Canada–United States relations. The meeting, which included Gotlieb, Burney, and Donald Campbell among others, was the first of this nature to have taken place in some time. The recommendations coming forth advised the prime minister to press President Reagan to include a strong endorsement of free trade in his state of the union address and that the prime minister also send a personal letter to the president on acid rain. Both initiatives proved successful.[13]

In Washington, Ambassador Gotlieb was in the process of revolutionizing the nature of Canadian diplomacy in the Amercian capital with what has come to be known as "public diplomacy." He was convinced that it was imperative to build profile, relationships, and rapport – not just with the executive – but with members of Congress, and especially key committee chairs, if Canada was to achieve its foreign policy goals. He also recognized the extent to which the United States Congress often used "domestic laws to achieve foreign policy goals." "Foreign interests," Gotlieb later wrote, "are often as affected by U.S. domestic legislation as by its foreign policy," and as examples during his years in Washington he cited the Motor Carrier Act of 1980, the Bus Regulatory Reform Act, the ban on asbestos by the Environmental Protection Agency, the 1988 Omnibus Drug Bill, and the limitations on the size of lobsters in interstate commerce. Gotlieb's view was that during the Reagan presidency on issues that were within the clear control of the administration, such as arctic sovereignty or defence procurement, power resided in the National Security Council. For all other issues it was essential for the embassy to work with Congress.[14]

In 1984, Burney's U.S. Branch prepared a comprehensive memorandum for cabinet on the management of the relationship with the United States. The focus of the memorandum was, not surprisingly, a repudiation of the multilateralists and third option advocates in External Affairs, and it highlighted the damage that had been done to the bilateral relationship resulting from the lack of a clear and comprehensive policy framework. The review of Canadian policy toward the United States coincided with what Gotlieb described as "the most exhaustive White House inter-agency review of U.S. policy towards Canada in Washington's memory."[15] With Burney still at External, Prime Minister Mulroney put him in charge of all policy preparations for the official visit of President Reagan to Quebec City in March 1985, what came to be known as the Shamrock Summit. The key issues for the summit from the Canadian perspective were trade and investment, the environment, with a focus on the tensions around acid rain, and defence production. At this stage there was no indication that the Reagan administration was prepared to address the Canadian concern with acid rain, but Gotlieb vigorously lobbied White House officials to turn that around, gaining some support from George Shultz, National Security Adviser Robert McFarlane, and presidential aide Michael Deaver. The announcement at Quebec City of the appointment of two special emissaries to study the issue of acid rain was initially little more than a face-saving gesture, yet it ultimately paved the way for a significant shift in United States public policy with the passage of the Clean Air Act by Congress in 1990.[16]

The Mulroney and Reagan governments struggled to address the issues of acid rain and arctic sovereignty in the mid-1980s but, important as those issues were, it was the free trade initiative that brought the Department to the fore. Clark was appointed to chair a special cabinet committee on trade negotiations, and Simon Reisman was appointed chief trade negotiator in the newly established Trade Negotiation Office, where Michael Hart and Bill Dymond played key roles. This is not the place for a detailed review of the free trade negotiations, but it is evident from the history of this period that it was not only the effective politicking and diplomacy in Washington by Gotlieb and Burney in particular, but also the personal relationship between Mulroney and Reagan that finally resulted in Reagan administration officials moving the American machinery forward. The key players in the final stages not only came from External but also included Michael Wilson from Finance and Pat Carney from International Trade. Donald Campbell played a lead role in External, and Burney, working from the PMO, headed the delegation and also took responsibility for the preparation of the final legal text.[17]

The mid-1980s through the end of Derek Burney's term as ambassador to the United States (1989–93) represented the apogee of United States–Canada relations as well as the influence of the Department of External Affairs on that relationship during the post-1982 years. As ambassador, Burney had the advantage of having developed close personal relationships in the United States administration and Congress prior to his appointment, although by the time he settled into the embassy George H.W. Bush had succeeded Ronald Reagan. Burney also had the advantage of the prime minister's personal confidence. As Burney observed in his memoirs, "access is the lifeblood of diplomacy."[18] Burney indicated that he was also fortunate to have had a number of highly talented External Affairs officers in the embassy, including Len Legault on trade and economic issues, Paul Heinbecker as the first head of the political section, and Jonathan Fried as congressional liaison officer. As with Gotlieb's tenure, Burney focused much of his attention on Congress.[19]

In spite of the major bilateral focus, neither the Department nor the prime minister were exclusively concerned with the United States. There was also increased attention paid to broader hemispheric relations, to some extent a natural extension of closer association with United States interests. It was the Mulroney government that brought the country into the Organization of American States in 1989, after decades of opposition or indecisiveness. Within External Affairs, there also appeared to be interest in exploring new directions in Canadian policy and that transition bridged the Mulroney and Chrétien governments. As engagement with the hemisphere increased, "a small band at external affairs launched a policy review which would provide the rationale for a radical shift in Canada's hemispheric relations."[20] Some, including then-foreign affairs critic Lloyd Axworthy, were concerned that involvement in the OAS would limit Canada's latitude of action and link Canadian policy too closely with American policy. Axworthy lamented: "We're seen as a little red wagon tying itself to the big U.S. engine."[21] When Canada, later that year, was the only OAS member to endorse the American intervention in Panama to remove Manuel Noriega, Axworthy's concerns appeared to have weight. Regardless, by mid-1989, Richard Gorham, Canada's long-time observer to the OAS, and Louise Frechette, a former ambassador to Argentina, had drafted a strategy paper which voiced a radical notion in the nation's strategic history: Canada, it declared, is "a nation of the Americas."[22] The State Department was also turning towards the hemisphere, thus a Western Hemisphere realignment was considered by many in Canada to be a prudent shift.[23]

The Chrétien Years, 1993–2003

The 1980s restructuring of the Department to reflect a more concentrated focus on the United States did not outlast the Gotlieb and Burney years, or for that matter the Mulroney Conservative government. Nor did the triumph of the realists/bilateralists within the Department on the free trade issue endure long beyond the Conservative government. Several factors appear to have accounted for the relative decline in attention to the United States files. One was the fact that the new prime minister, Jean Chrétien, had less interest in the bilateral relationship and fewer personal connections south of the border than had his predecessor. A second factor was that, having criticized the free trade agreement while in opposition, it was politically awkward for the new Liberal government to appear to cozy up to the United States, not least because the newly elected Democratic President Bill Clinton was just as strongly committed to free trade. Once in office, the Chrétien Liberals became silent on the issue and followed Mexico into the trilateral agreement with barely a whimper. Furthermore, as George Haynal has pointed out, following the North American Free Trade Agreement, there was no major issue for DFAIT to rally around. Allan Gotlieb later wrote that the Chrétien government gave strong support to the Canadian ambassador and his staff in Washington during the Liberal years in power, but with free trade a reality and with an agreement already in place on acid rain there did not seem to be the same sense of urgency about getting the relationship right that had characterized the Mulroney years.

While Chrétien did not purposefully set out to antagonize the United States, he simply chose not to make the relationship a priority. The prime minister had a good working relationship with President Clinton but avoided the kind of personal camaraderie of the Mulroney–Reagan and Mulroney–Bush relationships. During the 1993 election campaign, Chrétien vowed that he would not "make friends with the president of the United States" and was determined that relations would be more distant and dignified.[24] In his memoirs Chrétien indicated that his "ambition [was] not to go fishing with the president of the United States" and that he did not want to look as though he was "rushing to ingratiate himself" with Clinton. The former prime minister claims to have told Clinton it would be good for both if the two kept some distance and that "if we look independent enough, we can do things for you that even the CIA cannot do."[25] While many felt the Chrétien era once again reignited tensions between the multilateralists and bilateralists in Canadian foreign policy, others believe this tension is not the most accurate way to categorize philosophical differences within the Department.[26] Regardless, the Chrétien years were not the most harmonious in Canada–United States relations, although the bilateral relationship did not reach crisis levels until after 9/11. Where tensions existed between the two countries, they tended to be at the political rather than bureaucratic level, where normally it was business as usual.

During much of the Chrétien years there appeared to be no single individual with the drive, influence, and focus on the United States of either an Allan Gotlieb or a Derek Burney. Indeed, the dominant figure in Canadian foreign policy during the Liberal years was Lloyd Axworthy, a committed and pro-active multilateralist with a much broader international agenda for Canada than simply minding the bilateral relationship. During his tenure as foreign minister from 1996 to 2000, he pursued policies designed to promote human security and soft power; he also appealed to the international community as a whole to engage in support of a range of multilateral initiatives, some of which ran directly counter to American policies. While many were quick to criticize both Chrétien and Axworthy for alienating the United States, others argued that the prime minister and foreign minister were in fact well-liked and respected in Washington.[27]

Within the first few months of 1997, about a year after Axworthy took over the Foreign Affairs portfolio in a 1996 cabinet shuffle, there was a substantial shake-up to the structure of the Department. The United States Branch, which throughout the 1980s had held court along with other geographic branches, was disbanded and replaced by an Americas and Security Branch, which had responsibility for the entire Western Hemisphere. While there was indeed a United States Bureau within the Americas and Security Branch, it soon became clear that this portfolio was too broad to give due attention to Canada's most important ally. As assistant deputy minister for the Americas Branch from 1998 to 2001, George Haynal turned his attention to the Summit of the Americas process to ensure its success at a time when Canada's influence was high in the western hemisphere and when External Affairs had "become the driving force behind a brisk new hemispheric cheerleading industry."[28] Canada spent a million dollars establishing the Canadian Foundation for the Americas, installed its first military attaché in Mexico City in 1993, began teaching Spanish language courses at the Canadian Forces Staff College, and External Affairs funded a conference in an effort to promote "The Future of the Inter-American Security System."[29] Indeed, the United States was no longer fashionable and, as Haynal describes, "sank back into the mud."[30]

The United States ambassador to Canada during the early years of Chrétien's first term, James Blanchard, suggested that, despite the chill in Canada–United States relations, policy conflicts between the two countries were the exception. Of course there were tensions, but when they did happen, "they tended to get all blown out of proportion."[31] According to Blanchard, who was in Ottawa from 1993 to 1996, Cuba and the controversial Helms-Burton legislation passed in the United States was the only truly divisive bilateral issue. Lloyd Axworthy in his memoirs called the policy decision by the Clinton administration, under pressure from Senate conservative Republican Jesse Helms, a "blatant incursion of American extraterritorial jurisdiction into other countries' economic relations with Cuba." Axworthy was proud of the fact that "[Canada] stood up to American demands and in fact led the international fight against this attempt to impose U.S. policies on the rest of the world."[32] Blanchard recalls how at a Washington dinner for him and his wife, Janet, the Canadian ambassador, Raymond Chrétien, spoke at length and with passion about the "evils of Helms-Burton." Blanchard commented that the two dozen American officials present at the dinner were stunned: "What the hell is he talking about? And why's he ranting about it?"[33] Jean Chrétien, in his memoirs, has suggested that one of Raymond Chrétien's greatest diplomatic achievements as Canadian ambassador in Washington was convincing Bill Clinton to delay the application of American sanctions against Canada over trade with Cuba. Blanchard, however, downplays both the American initiative and the Canadian response to it: "If we didn't have the difference over Cuba, the Canadian government would probably have to invent something else [...] From time to time, Canadian politicians have to show their people that they're overseeing a sovereign nation, not just rubber-stamping the policies made in Washington."[34] This, of course, is at the heart of the ongoing debate between the realists and romantics in Canadian foreign affairs.

Cuba aside, the Canadians concurred that the "number of controversial files [Raymond Chrétien] had to handle each year actually decreased from 120 to 10 during his time in Washington."[35] However, some of those minor tensions became mired in rhetoric and threatened to quickly become rather intractable and tricky to manage, and, as Blanchard stated in his memoirs with respect to ongoing and deeply rooted agriculture and fishing disputes, "nothing was likely to happen, I concluded, if it didn't happen at the top."[36] This statement is reflective of how the relationship between the prime minister and the president dictates the tone of Canada–United States relations.

Canadian political scientist Kim Nossal once stated that "on numerous occasions, Canadian policy has been determined, not directly by the American government, but by Canadian assessments that a divergent policy on an issue would not be worth the damage such a divergence would likely cause Canadian–American relations."[37] Nossal's caution did not appear to be a concern to Lloyd Axworthy while he served at the helm of DFAIT. How senior officials in the Department perceived that orientation, however, is more difficult to determine. Donald Campbell, who served as deputy minister for most of Axworthy's tenure, was well known for his recognition of the importance of Canada's relationship with the United States. The ministers of International Trade, whose appointments overlapped with Axworthy's at Foreign Affairs, were not all bilateralists. Roy Maclaren (1993–96) was Europe-oriented; less so with Art Eggleton (1996–97), Sergio Marchi (1997–99), and Pierre Pettigrew (1999–2003).

Axworthy's interest in hemispheric engagement was reflected in his recruitment of Latin American specialist Brian Stevenson to serve as a special advisor in the Department, first on trade issues and then on foreign policy. Indeed, Axworthy's stances on certain issues, which had a decidedly Pearsonian ring to them, such as Canadian support for the International Criminal Court, were roundly derided in the United States. His January 1999 visit to Fidel Castro's Cuba, despite American efforts to further isolate the Communist regime, and his clear intentions to utilize Canada's seat on the United Nations Security Council in 1999–2000 to attempt to limit the veto powers of the five permanent members, including the United States, also did not make him a universally popular figure with Canada's neighbours to the south. A *New York Times* editorial stated in 1999 that, while Axworthy was "the most successful Canadian Foreign Minister in years," he also made waves and was "the one who has most antagonized Washington" by refusing to declare the United States 'the indispensable nation' and promoting what many considered anti-American initiatives.[38] Of course, denying these charges, Axworthy nonetheless ruffled feathers both in the United States and within bilateral circles in Canada. Senior American diplomats argued that Axworthy lacked an understanding of the different responsibilities each country had on the world stage, and University of Toronto political scientist John Kirton suggested that Axworthy's soft power was really foreign policy "on the cheap" and asked whether it was, "a bit of a Don Quixotic foreign policy?"[39] It was of little surprise when Canada's *National Post* raised the point that Axworthy had "a romantic progressivist vision of Canada as a multicultural coalition against the rich and greedy West, [but] he has forgotten that Canada is a part of the West."[40]

The debate about the change in tone in the Canada–United States relationship aside, Axworthy achieved great success with the Ottawa Treaty to ban anti-personnel landmines, and for his role he was nominated by United States Senator Patrick Leahy for the Nobel Peace Prize. This policy initiative became the hallmark of the much-debated concept of "human security" and is one that diverged from the position of the United States, as well as many other states with key global strategic concerns, such as India along the Pakistani border, China, and Russia. Axworthy's initiative has been lauded as "the story of how a tiny but determined band of outsiders took on and defeated some of the world's great powers at their own game – diplomacy – says a lot about the increasing role of public pressure in world affairs."[41] It also says a lot about Lloyd Axworthy's argument that, although the United States may be the most influential and powerful nation, "countries like Canada can set the pace."[42]

During the Axworthy years as foreign minister, the Department continued to suffer from both budget constraints and a lack of the kind of restructuring that would have given higher profile and attention to the United States agenda. The assistant deputy ministers who directed the Americas Branch between 1996 and 2005, Michael Kergin, George Haynal, and Marc Lortie, were all strong individuals who viewed the United States as critical to Canadian interests, but their portfolio was too broad by any reasonable measure to ensure a focus on relations with the United States. Nor was the focus on the United States that had characterized the Mulroney, Gotlieb, and Burney years any longer reflected in the organizational structure of the Department.

Financial constraints in the 1990s further weakened the Department. While the prime minister came to rely heavily on DFAIT for assistance to prop up the country's flagging economy with its controversial but high-profile "Team Canada" trade missions, which "crossed the globe in search of markets and investments," it was not immune from massive cuts in government expenditures. Between 1988/89 and 1998/99, DFAIT's budget was reduced in ten separate cuts by a total of $292 million.[43] The impact on the Department was far-reaching; however, Lloyd Axworthy still perceived the time as a period of opportunity as rigidities in the alliance system were loosening, and the new administration under Clinton seemed open to multilateral thinking. In his words, "all countries were looking for new markers to steer by" and Canada had an opportunity to make its mark.[44]

With the end of Axworthy's tenure as foreign minister in 2000, there was evident recognition by the Liberal government that it would be prudent to pay more attention to Canada's southern neighbour. John Manley's appointment as foreign minister appeared to represent a shift in focus and was a clear signal to Washington of a more positive Canadian orientation toward the United States. Manley's high-profile political stature, combined with his former role as minister of industry, made him an attractive personality to work with his American counterparts on practical issues. Even in the immediate aftermath of 9/11 and the emergent strains in the bilateral relationship, Manley dealt effectively with both Secretary of State Colin Powell and the newly appointed head of the Department of Homeland Security, Tom Ridge.

The crisis of 9/11 galvanized not only Foreign Affairs but all Canadian federal departments into sharpening their attention on the United States, but some changes were already underway before the terrorist attacks. The departure of Raymond Chrétien (1994–2000) from Washington following George W. Bush's election was inevitable after the ambassador made an indiscreet comment that implied that Canadians would prefer former vice-president Al Gore in the White House. The appointment of career civil servant Michael Kergin (2000–2005) from Foreign Affairs to replace Chrétien as ambassador was another signal that the Canadian government wanted stability in the bilateral relationship, as was the appointment of former Deputy Minister of Industry Peter Harder as deputy minister of foreign affairs and international trade (2003–2007).[45]

Despite all the focus south of the border, as late as 2001–2002, the words "United States" did not appear in the organizational structure of DFAIT. The United States was still subsumed under the responsibility of an assistant deputy minister in the Americas branch, paralleling Asia-Pacific and Africa, Communications, Culture and Policy Planning, and Corporate Services, Passport, and Consular Affairs, all of which reported to the deputy minister for international trade and the deputy minister of foreign affairs. By the following year, the branches also reported to an associate deputy minister of foreign affairs, taking them yet one more step away from the minister and from power. That structure did not change until 2005, when Peter Harder successfully pressed for the establishment of a North American Branch and a North American Bureau, with Peter Boehm as the first assistant deputy minister of the branch and William Crosbie as the director general of the bureau. In 2006 the Department added a North American Commercial Relations Bureau, with Deborah Lyons as director general.

Jean Chrétien's retirement from politics in 2003, to be replaced by Paul Martin in December of that year, brought to the prime ministership an individual with whom both the Canadian business community and the Washington establishment could feel more comfortable. The fact that Martin believed the bilateral relationship needed immediate attention was reflected in his prompt establishment of an interdepartmental cabinet-level committee to coordinate relations with the United States, a committee that met weekly and one that he personally chaired. In addition, the PCO became quite operationally involved in the U.S. relationship, with the result that DFAIT was not the primary driver on policy.

Reflective of the increasing importance of the United States was the release of a guide for Canadian public officials in 2004 entitled, *Action-Research Roundtable on Managing Canada–U.S. Relations*. This report was chaired by the deputy minister for Transport Canada, Louis Ranger, and involved the participation of many other Canadian government departments and agencies, including Foreign Affairs. While not impacting policy specifically, the intent was to better understand the mechanisms and management of the bilateral relationship with the recognition that the United States has often approached Canada–United States relations with a different set of assumptions and priorities. According to the report, Canadians dealing with their counterparts in the United States must recognize, appreciate, and comprehend American perceptions of Canada and its place in its own strategic priorities, as well as the enormity of the United States political machinery and the expansive role played by Congress in policy development. Clearly, the Canadian government realized that it had let its relationship with its southern neighbour falter and that "the growing number of actors involved in the cross-border relationship requires strategic coordination in the pursuit of Canadian interests."[46]

In 2005 the Martin government produced a new International Policy Statement, setting directions for Canadian defence, diplomacy, development, and commerce. In his introduction to the document on diplomacy, Foreign Minister Pierre Pettigrew stated clearly: "Our priorities include the management of our relations with the United States, which are key to the security and prosperity of Canadians." At the same time, the document made the usual genuflection to Canada's global role: "we intend to pursue," Pettigrew wrote, "a new multilateralism that emphasizes effective global governance, to strengthen Canada's regional networks and to reconfigure our representation abroad to reflect the shifting distribution of global power and influence."[47]

The first major section of the document on diplomacy focused on the North American partnership, although that title masked the primary focus on the relationship with Washington. The subheadings included: "Partnership with the United States," "Modernizing Canada–U.S. Security," "Cooperating on Shared Global Objectives," "Environmental Partnership," and "Getting our Message Across," before turning to the third leg in the North American relationship, Mexico. Building on the 2001 Smart Borders Declaration, the security framework that was part of Canada's 2004 National Security Policy, and the 2002 establishment of a bi-national planning group, the 2005 policy document concentrated on modernizing the Canada–United States security relationship in response to the perceived global terrorism threat. The specific initiatives and issues identified included counterterrorism, the renewal of NORAD, and modernizing the bilateral approach to environmental challenges. The policy statement also committed Canada to working with the United States on a range of more global initiatives, including the transformation of NATO to make it a more effective instrument against terrorism and in support of peacemaking operations, promoting democracy through the Summit of the Americas process, supporting nuclear non-proliferation, and addressing new health threats. The statement also identified the goal of advancing Canadian interests in the Arctic, a region that offers opportunities for both collaboration and conflict with the United States.

The Department of Foreign Affairs and International Trade has, over the years, appropriately sought to implement policies designed by the elected officials who have formed a series of Canadian governments. At times, members of the Department have had a significant impact influencing the direction of policy, the most prominent example in the years since 1982 being the free trade negotiations with the United States and subsequently with Mexico. At other times, the Department may have seemed to have been slow to respond to challenges, pushed aside by competing departments, or bypassed completely by the prime minister. Yet, for all the frustration of those who might wish the Department to always be the driving force behind foreign policy, it must be remembered that in the Canadian system of government it is the prime minister and cabinet who are given the mandate to govern.

The debate over the extent to which relations with the United States should be Canada's primary foreign policy focus, however, continues to elude consensus. Writing in *The Globe and Mail* in early 2008, former Foreign Minister Lloyd Axworthy argued that: "Ottawa has been so preoccupied with keeping in sync with these Washington missteps that we have lost sight of the global-sized tectonic changes that are altering power relationships. We have ignored the looming risks of nuclear proliferation and climate change, and abandoned the multilateral diplomacy that gave us a voice and influence on a wide range of significant issues."[48]

On the other hand, Canadian historian Jack Granatstein, in the pages of the same newspaper, has contended: "Above all, given our geographic location, we must have close relations with the United States. The U.S. is our best friend, as a now-forgotten politician said 45 years ago, 'whether we like it or not.' Strong in their anti-Americanism, Canadians took a long time to learn this, and some never have. But unless we can learn to eat grass to survive, we must have access to the American market, the largest, richest in the world. We need Americans' investment, and access to their brainpower and culture. We will need their military support in extremis. And the Yanks aren't going away – Canada is not an island, nor can we hide behind psychological or trade barriers."[49]

The contrast between the Axworthy and the Granatstein perspectives embodies a more general ambiguity or even division in Canadian political culture over the relationship with the United States. The Department of Foreign Affairs and International Trade, as a government department, has historically had the primary responsibility of implementing rather than determining government policies. Yet, to some extent the history of the Department over the past several decades has also mirrored the broader differences in Canadian society.

NOTES

1. See, for instance, John Higginbotham and Jeff Heynen, "Managing through Networks: The State of Canada–U.S. Relations," in *Canada among Nations, 2004: Setting Priorities Straight*, ed. David Carment et al. (Montreal: McGill-Queen's University Press, 2005). See as well Higginbotham and Heynen, *Advancing Canadian Interests in the United States: A Practical Guide for Public Officials* (Ottawa: Canada School of Public Service, 2004), 30.

2. Mr. Haynal has used the term in various of his public statements, and he reinforced this idea in his discussions with the author. The author is very grateful to Mr. Haynal for his reflections and insights. Interview, 22 July 2008.

3. Allan Gotlieb, *I'll be with you in a minute Mr. Ambassador: The Education of a Canadian Diplomat in Washington* (Toronto: University of Toronto Press, 1991), 118.

4. Derek Burney, *Getting It Done: A Memoir* (Montreal and Kingston: McGill-Queen's University Press, 2005), 62–63. Burney indicates that when he was head of the U.S. Bureau he reported to three different officials, to the under-secretary of state for external affairs (Marcel Massé, 1982–85), the deputy minister (political), and the deputy minister for trade (Sylvia Ostry). Michael Hart was the main figure in developing trade strategy from this stage through the free trade negotiations. See Michael Hart, *A Trading Nation: Canadian Trade Policy from Colonialism to Globalization* (Vancouver: UBC Press, 2002).

5. Burney, *Getting It Done*, 63.

6. This paper focuses on the department rather than the prime minister, but it is important to note that PM Mulroney made a particular effort to cultivate not only members of the U.S. executive but also Congress, consistent with the approach taken by the two men who served as his ambassadors in Washington. He also cultivated the U.S. media and key U.S. interest groups. Brian Mulroney, *Memoirs*, (Toronto: McClelland & Stewart, 2007), 485.

7. Gotlieb, *The Washington Diaries*, 173.

8. Burney, *Getting It Done*, 79, 83.

9. In various conversations in previous years with former Prime Minister Joe Clark, he emphasized the extent to which the NGO community, in particular the Church organizations, influenced his thinking on the Central American situation in the 1980s. This is not to suggest that Clark was "wrong" in the policies he pursued. Indeed, his position on apartheid was ahead of its time, and the sanctions worked. His position on U.S. policy in Central America was also much closer to the international consensus. Mr. Clark continued to articulate a multilateral, Pearsonian view of Canadian foreign policy in the years since he left office. Speaking in Toronto in November 2007, he lamented the fact that Canada was "quiet in the multilateral fora which we once animated." "Restoring a Broadly-Based Canadian Foreign Policy," McLaughlin College, Scarborough, November 15, 2007. Mr. Clark left External Affairs in 1991 to deal with the constitutional issues and was succeeded as Secretary of State for External Affairs by Barbara McDougall (1991–93).

10. The Contadora Group was established in 1983 by the foreign ministers of Colombia, Mexico, Panama, and Venezuela in an effort to obtain a negotiated settlement of the Nicaraguan conflict.

11. Gotlieb, *The Washington Diaries*, 538.

12. Canada, Department of External Affairs, *Competitiveness and Security: Directions for Canada's International Relations* (Ottawa: Minister of Supply and Services Canada, 1985), 6ff.

13. Allan Gotlieb has been strongly critical of the Clark approach to Canadian foreign policy. In the Benefactor's lecture to the C.D. Howe Institute in 2004 he noted: "Joe Clark's track did not include the

United States. He barely got involved, so completely did the U.S. become the domain of the prime minister." Allan Gotlieb, "Romanticism and Realism in Canadian Foreign Policy," Benefactor's lecture to the C.D. Howe Institute, 2004, 20. Gotlieb notes that in addition to Clark's position on Central America he also sided with Flora MacDonald, then the Minister of Communications, on the issue of protectionism in the Canadian film industry, a position that threatened the conclusion of the free trade agreement with the United States. On the 1987 Clark visit to Washington see Gotlieb, *The Washington Diaries*, 444; Mulroney, *Memoirs*, 485.

14 Gotlieb, *I'll be with you*, 48, 51–53, 75, 91.

15 Burney, *Getting It Done*, 76; Gotlieb, *I'll be with you*, 68, 73.

16 The two emissaries appointed were William Davis and Drew Lewis.

17 Burney, *Getting It Done*, 117, 121, 122.

18 Burney, *Getting It Done*, 76.

19 Mulroney, *Memoirs*, 658–59.

20 Marci McDonald, "Taking Orders: How Washington Shaped Canada's Foreign Policy in the Mulroney Years," *Special Report, Fifth Annual Atkinson Fellowship in Public Policy* (1993), 7.

21 McDonald, "Taking Orders," 7.

22 McDonald, "Taking Orders," 7.

23 Interview with Peter Boehm. July 2008. Canada was the only one of the twenty-two-member OAS to support the 1989 U.S. intervention in Panama to overthrow the government of Manuel Noriega.

24 *Maclean's*, 6 March 1995, http://www.thecanadianencyclopedia.com/index.cfm?PgNm=TCE&Params=M1ARTM0010399. Accessed November 2008.

25 Jean Chrétien, *My Years as Prime Minister* (Toronto: Knopf, 2007), 87.

26 Interview with Peter Boehm, July 2008.

27 Interview with Peter Boehm, July 2008.

28 McDonald, "Taking Orders," 5.

29 McDonald, "Taking Orders," 5.

30 Interview with George Haynal, 22 July 2008.

31 James Blanchard, *Behind the Embassy Door: Canada, Clinton and Quebec* (Toronto: McClelland & Stewart), 123.

32 Lloyd Axworthy, *Navigating a New World: Canada's Global Future* (Toronto: Knopf, 2003), 68.

33 Blanchard, *Behind the Embassy Door*, 147.

34 Blanchard, *Behind the Embassy Door*, 147–48.

35 Chrétien, *My Years as Prime Minister*, 99.

36 Blanchard, *Behind the Embassy Door*, 125.

37 Kim Richard Nossal, *The Politics of Canadian Foreign Policy*, 3rd ed. (Toronto: Prentice-Hall Canada, 1997), 34.

38 Anthony DePalma, "A Canadian Rousts Diplomacy (and Ruffles the U.S.)," *New York Times*, 10 January 1999, http://query.nytimes.com/gst/fullpage.html?res=9C00E6DB1631F933A25752C0A96F958260. Accessed 15 November 2008.

39 Randall Palmer, "Foreign minister treads softly, raises Canada's profile," *Reuters*, 6 January 1999, http://www.cubanet.org/CNews/y99/jan99/07e8.htm. Accessed 15 November 2008.

40 DePalma, "A Canadian Rousts Diplomacy."

41 Raymond Bonner, "How a Group of Outsiders Moved Nations to Ban Land Mines," *New York Times*, 20 September 1997, http://query.nytimes.com/gst/fullpage.html?res=9E03EFD71F38F933A1575AC0A961958260. Accessed 12 November 2008.

42 DePalma, "A Canadian Rousts Diplomacy."

43 DFAIT history, http://international.gc.ca/department/history-histoire/hp_search_results-en.asp?frm=search.

44 Axworthy, *Navigating a New World*, 45.

45 Gaetan Lavertu preceded Harder as deputy minister (2000–2003). Lavertu was

not a U.S. specialist but rather had previously served primarily in Europe and Latin America. http://www.socialsciences.uottawa.ca/api/eng/glavertu.asp. Accessed 15 November 2008.

46 Jeff Heynan and John Higginbotham, *Action-Research Roundtable – Advancing Canadian Interests in the United States: A Practical Guide for Canadian Public Officials* (Ottawa: Canada School of Public Service, 2007), 8.

47 Canada, Department of Foreign Affairs and International Trade, Canada's International Policy Statement, "A Role of Pride and Influence in the World" (Ottawa: DFAIT, 2005).

48 "Finding Canada's place in the world: We need a new map, Lloyd Axworthy argues," *Globe and Mail*, 16 February 2008, http://www.theglobeandmail.com/servlet/story/RTGAM.20080215.wcomment0216/BNStory/specialComment. Accessed 17 November 2008.

49 J.L. Granatstein, "Finding Canada's place in the world: It's a matter of realizing our national interests," *Globe and Mail*, 17 February 2008, http://www.theglobeandmail.com/servlet/story/RTGAM.20080215.wcomment0218/BNStory/specialComment. Accessed 17 November 2008.

THE DEPARTMENT OF FOREIGN AFFAIRS AND INTERNATIONAL TRADE: INTERDEPARTMENTAL LEADERSHIP AND THE BEIJING CONFERENCE ON WOMEN

Elizabeth Riddell-Dixon

Introduction

In September 1995, the United Nations convened the Fourth World Conference on Women in Beijing. Canada actively participated at the conference – the largest the UN had ever held – and in the preparatory meetings leading up to it.[1] Furthermore, Canada was one of 189 countries that unanimously adopted the *Beijing Declaration and Platform for Action*. The Department of Foreign Affairs and International Trade (DFAIT) exercised a lead role in the interdepartmental process to develop Canada's positions on the *Declaration and Platform for Action*. The process took place in an environment radically different from that of the Pearsonian era, when DFAIT's predecessor, the Department of External Affairs, had exercised a near monopoly over the formulation and implementation of Canadian foreign policy.[2] During the three decades preceding the Beijing conference, a series of factors combined to undermine the department's pre-eminence in foreign policy. Of these factors, the most salient to this case are the expansion of the international agenda to give greater priority to economic and social issues and the increased participation of other branches of the federal government.[3] As the international agenda expanded to include new issues, the definition of Canada's national interest was broadened. The increased involvement of diverse branches of government made the defining of the national interest much more challenging as each had its own particular idea of what constituted the national interest and of how it could best be realized. As a result of these factors, the Canadian foreign policy-making process became much more complex.

The chapter begins by identifying the characteristics that make this case unique and intriguing. Thereafter, it focuses on two themes: the interrelationship of external and domestic determinants, and the interdepartmental process to develop Canada's positions and strategies on the *Beijing Declaration and Platform for Action*. Assessments of the extent to which the expansion of the international agenda and the increased participation of other branches of the federal government affected the role and influence of DFAIT in this case are integrated into these discussions. The themes are interrelated: the broadening of the international agenda has had a profound influence on the interdepartmental decision-making process and contributed to the greatly increased participation by other branches of the federal government. The section on the interdepartmental process briefly describes the actors and the interaction among them, giving particular emphasis to DFAIT. The relative importance of federal government actors, including departments and the central agencies, is assessed, the relevance of the governmental politics approach to explaining the interaction among the key players is examined, and the question of whether DFAIT functioned as a generalist and/or a specialist department is addressed.

In keeping with the general tenets of the literature on Canadian foreign policy, the chapter concludes that the external environment established parameters within which foreign policy-makers operated.[4] Nonetheless, Canada's positions on the Beijing *Platform for Action* exerted some influence on other areas of the country's policies, both domestic and foreign. In terms of the involvement of other government actors, program departments played key roles, while the central agencies had little involvement. Although the governmental politics approach does not rule out collaboration among government officials involved in the foreign policy-making process, it tends to see competition as a more dominant characteristic. Yet, cooperation rather than conflict characterized the interdepartmental work to develop Canada's positions and strategies for the *Beijing Declaration and Platform for Action*. In this process, DFAIT functioned both as a specialist department, which sought to maximize gains on issues most salient to it, and as a generalist department, which advocated compromise on some contentious issues in order to secure international agreement on the best attainable – rather than the ideal – text.

A Unique and Intriguing Case

Canada's policies for the Fourth World Conference on Women must be seen in the context of the country's participation in a long series of conferences and summits that the UN convened in the 1990s. The process of preparing for UN conferences and summits is similar. There are always interdepartmental committees, consultations with the provinces and territories, and the involvement of non-governmental organizations (NGOs). The conferences and summits of 1990s addressed many of the same issues; hence they involved many of the same actors, both governmental and non-governmental. Nonetheless, the process of developing Canada's positions and strategies vis-à-vis the *Beijing Declaration and Platform for Action* is unique and intriguing for a number of reasons: the wide range of issues addressed, the number of actors, and the complexity of the process. The *Platform for Action* dealt with twelve interrelated issue areas: poverty, decision-making, education, human rights, health, media, violence, environment, armed conflict, rights of the girl child, economics, and mechanisms for the advancement of women. Thus the agenda was huge. By comparison, the Copenhagen Summit for Social Development, which was held the same year as the Beijing Conference, focused on only three sets of core issues: poverty, employment, and social integration. Summit participants considered their agenda to be substantial, yet it paled in comparison with that of the Beijing Conference on Women.

In light of the number of issue areas in the *Platform for Action*, over twenty Canadian government departments and agencies participated in the policy-making process. Preparations for the Beijing conference involved an even larger number of government departments and agencies than did preparations for the Group of Seven (G7) Summits held during that time period. The conference also attracted the attention of large numbers of NGOs, including not only women's organizations but also labour, development, education, health, human rights, environmental, peace, and indigenous groups.

The complexity of the policy-making process contributed to making the case unique and intriguing. The development of Canada's positions and strategies was complex because of the number of governmental and non-governmental actors, the number of issue areas and their interrelatedness, and the controversial nature of many of these issues. The tone and substance of the negotiations was very much affected by the macro-level dichotomy between religious/conservative forces and those who took a pro-feminist approach.

At the state level, the religious/conservative forces comprised the Holy See[5] and its allies (most notably Guatemala, Ecuador, Honduras, Argentina, and Malta), as well as fundamentalist[6] Islamic states (in particular, Iran, Sudan, Algeria, and the Gulf states). Their anti-feminist stances were supported by conservative NGOs, such as Catholic Campaign for America, Focus on the Family, and Canada's REAL Women. On the other side, taking pro-feminist positions, were the European Union, Canada, Australia, and the Caribbean countries. The vast majority of the Canadian NGOs involved in the Beijing process were also pro-feminist in their orientations. Needless to say, this polarization rendered the process of reaching consensus on the *Platform for Action* much more arduous.

When the Beijing Conference on Women began, 25 per cent of the *Platform for Action* remained in square brackets, meaning that agreement had yet to be reached on one quarter of the text. Participants at the Copenhagen Summit for Social Development thought they faced a daunting task when 10 per cent of the text remained in square brackets at its onset. While significant, 10 per cent is still a great deal less than 25 per cent.

Interrelationship of External and Domestic Determinants

The Beijing case exemplifies how intertwined the external and the domestic realms can be. As is usual in Canadian foreign policy-making, the process in this case was largely reactive. Negotiating texts were drafted by UN officials and sent out to countries for their reaction – often only a few weeks before the negotiations began – leaving little time for developing positions and strategies. Such tight time lines are the norm for UN negotiations.

Canada's positions and strategies apropos the *Beijing Declaration and Platform for Action* were influenced by its experience at previous UN meetings. The most salient of these negotiations were the three preceding conferences on women: the 1993 Conference on Human Rights, the 1994 Conference on Population and Development, and the 1995 Summit for Social Development. The UN had convened the First, Second, and Third World Conferences on Women in 1975, 1980, and 1985, respectively. Each had produced documents addressing the themes of women's equality, development, and peace. Over time, the documents became more sophisticated and more analytical. In 1985, the Third Conference on Women adopted the *Forward-Looking Strategies for the Advancement of Women to the Year 2000*, which examined obstacles to women's advancement and recommended strategies for overcoming them. The 1993 Vienna Conference on Human Rights declared women's rights to be human rights and called for the mainstreaming of gender analysis within human rights regimes. The 1994 Cairo Conference on Population and Development recognized women's empowerment as a prerequisite for population control and economic development, while the 1995 Copenhagen Summit for Social Development recognized gender equality as a crucial component of sustainable development. Canadian officials planning for the Beijing conference sought to build on and further strengthen the language pertaining to women's rights that had been negotiated at these previous UN meetings.

There were both advantages and disadvantages to the Beijing conference's placement in a long line of UN conferences and summits. On a positive note, the lead departments – DFAIT, Status of Women Canada (SWC), and the Canadian International Development Agency (CIDA)

– had already established patterns of cooperation to promote women's issues before the Beijing conference and its preparatory meetings were convened. The negative consequences included conference fatigue, and often inadequate preparatory time. For example, the final and most important preparatory meetings prior to the Beijing conference were convened in March 1995, immediately following the Copenhagen Summit for Social Development. As a result, there was no time to incorporate provisions agreed to in Copenhagen into the draft *Platform for Action*. Furthermore, many of the delegates came straight from the Summit to attend the preparatory meetings; negotiations had been difficult and, among most participants, there was a certain amount of physical and mental exhaustion.[7] The Group of 77, in particular, had not had time to prepare its joint positions on the *Platform for Action*, with the result that the preparatory meetings were delayed while their members met behind closed doors trying to reach a consensus.

Thus Canada's positions were influenced by external developments. At the same time, Canada's preparations for the Beijing Conference on Women influenced its policies and positions in other forums as well. At home the need to develop positions on the *Platform for Action* served as leverage for developing umbrella policies for advancing women's rights. During the Beijing process, cabinet approval was sought, and received, for a formal mandate to promote women's equality and to mainstream gender-based analysis.[8] The policy applied not only to the *Platform for Action* but also to subsequent domestic and international policies. Preparations for the women's conference provided the impetus and the justification for seeking cabinet approval for the mandate, but its effects were much further-reaching.

In some cases, decisions were taken apropos the Beijing conference that had implications for Canada's positions at other conferences. For instance, when planning for the Beijing conference began, the lead departments agreed on objectives, not only for that venue, but also for addressing women's issues in other international negotiations, including the 1993 Vienna Conference on Human Rights and the 1995 Copenhagen Summit for Social Development.

While external developments very much influenced Canada's positions on the *Beijing Declaration and Platform for Action*, the country's positions had to be consistent with Canadian legislation. The Canadian delegation worked to get gender-based persecution recognized as grounds for claiming refugee status because such provisions were enshrined in Canadian law. Canada led this campaign because its legislation offered greater protection to women refugees than did that of other countries. In short, Canada was the field leader in terms of its legislation; hence, it took the lead role in the negotiations on this issue.

Questions have been raised regarding whether or not Canada is exerting sufficient influence in the world.[9] Has it lost its status as a significant player on the international stage? In this case, Canada can be said to have punched above its weight. The Canadian negotiators achieved some major successes, both at the preparatory meetings and at the Fourth World Conference in Beijing. At the 1995 New York Preparatory Meetings, for example, the Canadian delegation was instrumental in having the Health Section in the draft *Platform for Action* expanded beyond a preoccupation with sexual and reproductive rights to include a more holistic approach that took into account the effects of poverty. Canada also played an important role in ensuring that a gender perspective was incorporated into the *Platform for Action*. In Beijing, Canadian delegates chaired a majority of the working groups that were established to negotiate particularly contentious issues such as parental rights, unpaid work, and sexual rights. Furthermore, several of the major precedent-setting advances in the *Platform for Action* resulted from Canadian initiatives. They included the definition of rape as a war crime and as a crime against humanity, the requirement to develop international, gender-sensitive classifications for measuring unpaid work, and the stipulation that violence and gender-related persecution are grounds for claiming refugee status.

Having noted the considerable gains made by the Canadian negotiators, it is time to examine the interdepartmental process by which Canada's positions and strategies were formulated. This process was very much affected by developments in the international environment.

Interdepartmental Policy-Making Process

As mentioned earlier, the environment in which DFAIT operated in the 1990s was quite different from that of the Pearsonian era, when its predecessor, the Department of External Affairs, had been pre-eminent in the formulation and implementation of foreign policy. A series of developments in the 1960s served to erode the pre-eminence of the Department of External Affairs. Military security was still deemed critical but the international agenda was increasingly concerned with economic and social issues. As a result, the mandates of far more federal departments were affected by foreign policy. Each of these departments sought to advance its own objectives by exerting influence over the direction and substance of Canada's foreign policies. For instance, the Department of Trade and Commerce and the Department of Manpower and Immigration participated in the formulation and implementation of foreign policies relating to their respective mandates. As Tammy Nemeth has detailed in chapter 9, the primacy of the Department of External Affairs was further challenged when Prime Minister Pierre Trudeau took office in 1968. In an effort to open up the policy-making process, he created coordinating mechanisms, such as interdepartmental committees, to ensure that a broad range of government actors was included in policy debates and that competing policy options were presented to cabinet. Trudeau relied heavily on the central agencies, in particular the Prime Minster's Office and the Privy Council Office, for foreign policy advice. Thus, the Department of External Affairs' iron grip over foreign policy was eroded of the increased participation by domestic departments and the central agencies. Such trends were accelerated in the post-Cold War era, when the forces of globalization intensified and economic and social issues became the priorities on the international agenda.

Although more than twenty government departments and agencies were involved in formulating Canada's positions for the Beijing Conference on Women, three were pivotal throughout the process: Status of Women Canada; the Department of Foreign Affairs and International Trade; and the Canadian International Development Agency.[10] SWC was the lead department and served as the secretariat for the interdepartmental policy-making process. Its public servants began preparations for the conference in 1992. In August 1994 – just over a year before the conference began – the position of Executive Director of the UN World Conference on Women Secretariat was created within SWC. Valerie Raymond, the former director of DFAIT's Human Rights, Women's Equality and Social Affairs Division, was seconded to SWC to fill the position. Raymond had extensive experience, both in international negotiations and with women's issues, and had already been working closely with SWC on the preparations for the Beijing conference.[11] Having a Foreign Affairs official serving as the lead negotiator and as the chair of the interdepartmental negotiations at the bureaucratic level was not unusual. Such was also the case for the Copenhagen Summit for Social Development, for which Marius Bujold, another DFAIT official, was appointed Canadian Coordinator. The difference was that Bujold remained in DFAIT and was never seconded to one of the other lead departments.

Legally and operationally responsible for conducting Canada's foreign policy, DFAIT is also tasked with negotiating international agreements and representing Canada at international conferences. Thus, it was not surprising to see it exercising a leadership role in the Beijing process. Furthermore, DFAIT assumed the lead on matters regarding international human rights and peace and security, as these were areas in which it had established expertise and they involved international treaties and covenants.

Within DFAIT, the Human Rights, Women's Equality and Social Affairs Division was pivotal, and it coordinated the department's preparations for the Beijing conference. No formal mechanisms for consultations were established within the Department. Instead the individuals involved consulted informally as the need arose, which meant at least bi-weekly discussions between the Director of the Human Rights, Women's Equality, and Social Affairs Division, and the Director of the Refugee, Population, and Migration Division. Regular contact was also maintained with the Legal Operations Division. Although Valerie Raymond was formally seconded to SWC in 1994, her Foreign Affairs colleagues continued to regard her as one of their own.

The Fourth World Conference on Women was also important to the Canadian International Development Agency on several scores. The conference's three themes (equality, development, and peace) coincided with CIDA's mandate, which is "to support sustainable development in developing countries, in order to reduce poverty and to contribute to a more secure, equitable and prosperous world."[12] Furthermore, advancing the well-being of women in development comprised one of CIDA's key priorities. In particular, it had a commitment:

- To increase women's participation as decision-makers in the economic, political, social and environmental spheres;
- To improve women's economic conditions, basic health, education and human rights;
- To promote activities aimed at eliminating discrimination against women;
- To support developing country partners in voicing their concerns on gender issues in development.[13]

Hence the Beijing conference, which addressed many issues directly related to women and development, was important to the agency.

SWC, CIDA, and DFAIT were all key players in the Interdepartmental Committee on the World Conference on Women, which began meeting in August 1992 and was chaired by SWC. The committee functioned collaboratively to develop Canada's positions. Its recommendations were then given to the Secretary of State for the Status of Women and the Minister of Foreign Affairs for approval. The full cabinet never became involved because the committee's recommendations were in keeping with existing policy guidelines; thus, further cabinet approval was not required. Public servants on the Interdepartmental Committee nevertheless kept their respective ministers apprised of its work. While their ministers were generally supportive, none was directly involved in the formulation of positions and strategies.

The governmental politics approach provides a framework for analyzing the nature of the policy-making process within government. According to the approach, public policies result from a bargaining process in which diverse governmental actors interact to affect outcomes.[14] Issues often come within the jurisdictions of several government departments and agencies; hence, they share responsibility for policy formulation. Since each department has its specific areas of interest to protect and promote, they compete to influence policy outputs. As the governmental politics approach contends, issues in the *Beijing Declaration and Platform for Action* came within the jurisdictions of multiple government departments and agencies; hence, developing Canada's policies and strategies involved extensive interdepartmental consultations. Yet, in contrast to the tenets of the governmental politics approach, which predicts actors competing to determine outcome, the decision-making process within federal government circles was for the most part harmonious. In this respect, the case stands in contrast to several others of the same period. For example, during Canada's 'fish war' with Spain, tensions arose between the Department of Fisheries and Oceans, on one hand, and DFAIT, on the other, over which department would assume the lead and over what approach should be used – the "quiet diplomacy" advocated by DFAIT or the more aggressive style taken by the Department of Fisheries and Oceans.[15] Governmental politics also featured prominently during the campaign to ban anti-personnel landmines as the Department of National Defence and DFAIT each wrestled to control the file and assert primary leadership.[16] Interdepartmental wrangling – primarily involving the Department of the Environment, on one hand, and National Resources Canada, on the other – was also very much in evidence when positions for the 1997 Kyoto negotiations for a legally binding protocol to reduce greenhouse gas emissions were being determined.[17]

Three sets of factors account for the interdepartmental collegiality during the preparations for the Beijing conference. First and most importantly, the issues in the *Platform for Action* all fell within existing government policies. Thus, most of the interdepartmental conflicts that these issues might have triggered had already been resolved in interdepartmental negotiations for previously held UN conferences and summits. Secondly, and closely related, government officials shared a high degree of consensus on priorities and objectives. All departments shared the macro-level goal of advancing women's equality globally. Most of the key public servants had been involved in previous conferences and summits; therefore, they understood the precedents that had been set and the parameters within which they had to operate, both at home and at the international negotiations. A third factor contributing to collegiality was the fact that questions of finance had been settled in advance. While finances frequently trigger interdepartmental strife, they did not do so in this case, because Paul Martin, Minister of Finance, André Ouellet, Minister of Foreign Affairs, and Sheila Finestone, Secretary of State for the Status of Women, had agreed in advance that no additional funds would be allocated. There was, therefore, no controversy between the Department of Finance, on one hand, and the lead departments, on the other, over how much new commitments would cost.

Although questions of finance did not cause direct conflict among members of the Interdepartmental Committee on the World Conference on Women, the 1995 federal budget cast a heavy shadow over Canada's participation at the Copenhagen Summit and the final six months of preparations for the Beijing conference. Many of the budget provisions directly undermined the positions that Canada was promoting in these negotiations. For example, the budget dramatically cut funding for social programs vital to the well-being of Canadian women and for foreign aid, which could have been used to help empower women in Southern countries and to enhance their political, economic, and social status. It also slashed funding for Canadian NGOs. The budget clearly illustrated that, when push came to shove, the views of the Minister of Finance prevailed over the concerns of the lead departments. The ascendancy of the Department of Finance is not uncommon in Canadian politics.[18] The department that controls the federal budget exercises a formidable influence over the extent to which Canada can pursue diplomatic activities, military endeavours, and foreign aid programs abroad.

There was some friction between the Minister of Foreign Affairs and the Secretary of State for the Status of Women, largely over questions of jurisdiction, which was at times exacerbated by personality clashes. The rivalry was, however, minor. Although André Ouellet, the Minister of Foreign Affairs, was officially responsible for two of the three key departments involved in this case, he was preoccupied with issues of national unity. He had been appointed by Prime Minister Jean Chrétien as a political move to place a senior francophone from Quebec in a major portfolio, from which he could promote national unity in the period leading up to the Quebec referendum on independence. As a result, Ouellet devoted little time to the Beijing conference and was generally willing to let the secretary of state for the status of women take the limelight. Thus, the preparations for the Beijing conference involved little of the "pulling and hauling" generally associated with governmental politics, at either the bureaucratic or the ministerial levels.

Although DFAIT is traditionally seen as a generalist department, in this case, it also functioned as a specialist department. The latter gives priority to achieving specific negotiating objectives that pertain directly to its mandate. It is reluctant to compromise on these objectives as doing so can result in weak provisions that are of marginal use in attaining its goals. Of the twelve issue areas in the *Platform for Action*, DFAIT gave highest priority to human rights, violence, armed conflict, reproductive rights, economic equality, and the rights of the girl child. As specialists, foreign affairs officials sought to maximize gains in these areas, making as few concessions as possible. A generalist department gives priority to securing the best overall package and as a result, it is willing to compromise on some issues to achieve a degree of unanimity on a negotiated text that reflects many of the country's priorities. Following the March 1995 preparatory meetings for the Beijing conference, where the conservative forces had been particularly active, there were some philosophical differences in approaches among federal departments. For instance, Health Canada sought to broaden the health agenda and to push for further gains – a position that reflected a specialist's focus on maximizing gains in its issue area. At the same time, DFAIT and SWC opposed the introduction of new language and new initiatives for fear that doing so would trigger a conservative backlash aimed at rolling back the progress already achieved. Their approach reflected a generalist preoccupation with securing the best overall negotiating text.

Conclusion

The policy-making process for the Beijing Conference on Women was particularly complex because of the range of issues under negotiation, the controversial nature of many of these issues, and the number of actors.

With so many issues on the agenda – all of which were considered salient to Canada's national interest – one might have expected a rigorous competition among diverse actors to determine whose concerns received priority. Yet, the interdepartmental policy-making process was marked much more by cooperation than conflict. The role of DFAIT in this process was very different from that of the Department of External Affairs in the two decades following the Second World War. The international agenda had changed significantly. Not only was the range of economic and social issues under negotiation in the 1990s hugely expanded from that of the Pearsonian era, but these issues were subjected to far more in-depth analysis in UN meetings. As a result, large numbers of Canadian government actors were involved. In this process, the Department of Foreign Affairs played a lead role – but not *the* lead role – largely because the conference was much more important to the Secretary of State for the Status of Women than for the Minister of Foreign Affairs. SWC's leadership was further solidified when the chief negotiator was seconded from DFAIT. Thus, in the 1990s, it was the department responsible for the well-being of women in Canada – not the department responsible for conducting foreign policy – that assumed the lead in preparing for the Beijing conference. SWC nonetheless received strong and vital support from DFAIT in this endeavour.

Although DFAIT has traditionally been seen as a generalist department, in this case it acted as a specialist department as well as a generalist department. When specific interests in the realm of foreign affairs were at stake, it acted as a strong advocate for them. When the interests of other departments appeared to threaten securing the best overall package in the *Platform for Action*, DFAIT acted as a generalist department to achieve a compromise position. The negotiating skills, expertise, and flexibility of DFAIT officials helped to foster the relatively harmonious working relations among members of the interdepartmental committee and to ensure Canada's success in achieving most of its negotiating objectives at the Fourth World Conference on Women in Beijing. Thus, Canada's national interest was well served.

NOTES

1. The discussion of the case draws on Elizabeth Riddell-Dixon, *Canada and the Beijing Conference on Women: Governmental Politics and NGO Participation* (Vancouver: UBC Press, 2001). Research for the book relied heavily on interviews with a wide range of government and NGO representatives, to whom I extend my heartfelt thanks.

2. For a discussion of the department's primacy in the two decades following the Second World War, and the factors that subsequently challenged it, see Andrew F. Cooper, *Canadian Foreign Policy: Old Habits and New Directions* (Scarborough: Prentice Hall Canada, 1997), 41–70; and Kim Richard Nossal, *The Politics of Canadian Foreign Policy*, 3rd ed. (Scarborough: Prentice Hall Canada, 1997), 239–64. The Pearsonian era refers to the period when Lester B. Pearson was first secretary of state for external affairs and then prime minister of Canada.

3. Other factors include the increased participation of the provinces and territories; and the proliferation of non-governmental actors demanding access to the policy-making process, both of which are discussed in the context of this case in other venues. See: Elizabeth Riddell-Dixon, *Canada and the Beijing Conference on Women*; Elizabeth Riddell-Dixon, "Democratizing Canadian Foreign Policy?: NGO Participation for the Copenhagen Summit for Social Development and the Beijing Conference on Women," *Canadian Foreign Policy* 11, no. 3 (2004): 99–118; and "Organizing for Beijing: Canadian NGOs and the Fourth World Conference on Women," in *Feminist Perspectives on Canadian Foreign Policy*, ed. Claire Turenne Sjolander, Heather A. Smith, and Deborah Steinstra (Don Mills, ON: Oxford University Press, 2003), 185–97.

4. Cooper, *Canadian Foreign Policy*, especially chap. 8, 281–95; Tom Keating, *Canada and World Order: The Multilateralist Tradition in Canadian Foreign Policy*, 2nd ed. (Don Mills, ON: Oxford, 2002), 10; and Nossal, *The Politics of Canadian Foreign Policy*, especially chap. 2, 19–51.

5. The Holy See is the Roman Catholic Church's supreme organ of government whose membership comprises the Pope, the College of Cardinals, and the Church's central government bodies. It is considered by the UN to be a non-member state with permanent observer status. Nevertheless, at most recent UN conferences, including the Beijing Conference on Women, it has been a full participant with a vote. The contrast between the Holy See's status as a full participant and the observer status of the UN Committee on the Elimination of Discrimination Against Women did not go unnoticed. The Holy See did not oppose all provisions in the *Platform for Action*. For example, it supported education for the girl child. On the other hand, it opposed many of the provisions related to sexual and reproductive rights.

6. Marie-Andrée Roy, professor of Religious Studies at the University of Quebec in Montreal, defines fundamentalism as "a religious movement which tries not only to resist modernity, secularity, separation of Church and the state, but also wants to impose its values and belief system on the whole population. Religious Fundamentalism rejects all other interpretations of tradition – in fact it positions itself as the only thinking authorized interpreter." See Canadian Beijing Facilitating Committee, "Fundamentalism at the NGO Forum," *Onward from Beijing* (December 1995): 16.

7. The World Summit for Social Development in Copenhagen focused on three sets of core issues: the alleviation and reduction of poverty, the expansion of productive employment, and the enhancement of social integration, especially of those groups that are most marginalized and disadvantaged. Many of the proposals for achieving these goals involved diametrically opposed, core interests of Northern and Southern countries; thus they were highly controversial. For example, the "20/20 Initiative" in its

original form required rich countries to allocate at least 20 per cent of their foreign aid spending to meet basic human needs and poor countries to spend 20 per cent of their respective national budgets to achieve the same social objectives. Such mandated obligations were vehemently opposed by many participants and, in the final text, the "20/20" allocation of funds was left as voluntary rather than as required policy.

8   The policy was outlined in Canada, Status of Women Canada, *Setting the Stage for the Next Century: The Federal Plan for Gender Equality* (Ottawa: Status of Women Canada, 1995).

9   Andrew Cohen, *While Canada Slept: How We Lost Our Place in the World* (Toronto: McClelland & Stewart, 2003); and Jennifer M. Welsh, "Reality and Canadian Foreign Policy," in *Canada among Nations, 2005: Split Images*, ed. Andrew F. Cooper and Dane Rowlands (Montreal: McGill-Queen's University Press, 2005), 23–46.

10 In addition to SWC, DFAIT, and CIDA, the other major participants included the Departments of Heritage, Justice, Health, Human Resources Development, Environment, Indian Affairs and Northern Development, National Defence, Citizenship and Immigration, and the Privy Council Office.

11 Raymond had also served on the Canadian delegation to the 1985 Nairobi Conference on Women and as the women's rights advisor on the Canadian delegation to the 1993 Vienna Conference on Human Rights.

12 Canada, Canadian International Development Agency, *Engendering Development: Women in Development and Gender Equity* (Hull: CIDA, 1995), 3.

13 CIDA, *Engendering Development*, 4.

14 See Graham Allison, *The Essence of Decision: Explaining the Cuban Missile Crisis* (Boston: Little, Brown, 1971); Kim Richard Nossal, "Allison through the (Ottawa) Looking Glass: Bureaucratic Politics and Foreign Policy in a Parliamentary System," *Canadian Public Administration* 22 (Winter 1979): 610–26; and Elizabeth Riddell-Dixon, "Deep Seabed Mining: A Hotbed for Governmental Politics," *International Journal* 41, no. 1 (1985–86): 72–94.

15 See Cooper, *Canadian Foreign Policy*, 157–72.

16 Brian W. Tomlin, "On a Fast Track to the Ban: The Canadian Policy Process," *Canadian Foreign Policy* 5, no. 3 (1998): 3–23.

17 See Douglas Macdonald and Heather A. Smith, "Promises Made, Promises Broken: Questioning Canada's Commitments to Climate Change," *International Journal* 55, no. 1 (1999–2000): 107–24.

18 See, for example, Duncan Wood, "Canada and International Financial Policy: Non-Hegemonic Leadership and Systematic Stability," in *Handbook of Canadian Foreign Policy*, ed. Patrick James, Nelson Michaud, and Marc J. O'Reilly (Lanham, MD: Rowman and Littlefield, 2006), 265–86.

BIBLIOGRAPHY

Archival Sources

Canada

LIBRARY AND ARCHIVES OF CANADA
Cabinet War Committee Records
Privy Council Office Records
Department of External Affairs Records
Department of National Defence Records
R.B. Bennett Papers
W.L.M. King Papers
Lester B. Pearson Papers
Arnold Heeney Papers
Escott Reid Papers
Hume Wrong Papers
Ian Mackenzie Papers
Jules Léger Papers
O.D. Skelton Papers

Queen's University Archives
John Buchan Papers
Isabel Skelton Papers

University of British Columbia Archives
Alan Plaunt Papers

University of Toronto Archives
Vincent Massey Papers

United Kingdom

National Archives of England, Wales, and the United Kingdom
Dominions Office Records
Foreign Office Records
Maurice Hankey Papers

United States

Herbert Hoover Presidential Library
Herbert Hoover Presidential Papers

Franklin D. Roosevelt Presidential Library
Franklin D. Roosevelt Presidential Papers
Adolf Berle Papers
Raymond L. Buell Papers
Oscar Cox Papers
Sumner Welles Papers

Gerald R. Ford Presidential Library
White House Confidential Files

Ronald Reagan Presidential Library
White House Confidential Files

Library of Congress
Helen Howard Papers
Ernest J. King Papers
William Mitchell Papers

National Archives and Records Administration
Army Air Corps Records
Army Air Force Records
Department of State Records
Department of State Diplomatic Post Records
War Department General and Special Staffs Records

United States Air Force Archives
Billy Mitchell Papers

Duke University Archives
J.J. McSwain Papers

Houghton Library, Harvard University
J. Pierrepont Moffat Papers

Yale University Library
Henry J. Stimson Papers

Newspapers and Periodicals, 1909–2008

External Affairs
Financial Post
Globe and Mail
La Presse
Le Devoir
London Daily Telegraph
Maclean's
Manchester Guardian
Montreal Daily Star
New York Herald
New York Times
Ottawa Citizen
Ottawa Morning Journal
Saturday Night
The Spectator
Toronto Daily Star
Washington Herald
Washington Post
Winnipeg Free Press

Government Publications

Canada

Canadian International Development Agency. *Engendering Development: Women in Development and Gender Equity*. Hull: CIDA, 1995.

Department of Energy, Mines and Resources. *An Energy Policy for Canada: Phase I – Analysis, Summary of Analysis*. Ottawa: Minister of Supply and Services, 1973.

———. *The National Energy Program*. Ottawa: Minister of Supply and Services, 1980.

Department of External Affairs. *Annual Report*. Ottawa: King's Printer/Queen's Printer, various years.

———. *Canada and the United Nations*. Ottawa: King's Printer/Queen's Printer, various years.

———. *Canada and the United Nations, 1945–1975*. Ottawa: Supply and Services Canada, 1977.

———. *Competitiveness and Security: Directions for Canada's International Relations*. Ottawa: Supply and Services Canada, 1985.

———. *Report of the First Part of the First Session of the General Assembly of the United Nations*. Ottawa: King's Printer, 1946.

———. *Report of the United Nations Conference on International Organization Held at San Francisco, 25th April – 26th June 1945*. Ottawa: King's Printer, 1945.

———. *We the Peoples: Canada and the United Nations, 1945–1965*. Ottawa: Queen's Printer, 1966.

Department of Foreign Affairs and International Trade. "A Role of Pride and Influence in the World." Ottawa: DFAIT, 2005.

Donaghy, Greg, ed. *Documents on Canadian External Relations*, vol. 21: *1955*. Ottawa: Canada Communication Group, 1999.

Hilliker, John, ed. *Documents on Canadian External Relations*, vol. 9: *1942–1943*. Ottawa: Minister of Supply and Services Canada, 1980.

———. ed. *Documents on Canadian External Relations*, vol. 11: *1944–1945*, part 2. Ottawa: Minister of Supply and Services Canada, 1990.

———, and Donald Barry, ed. *Canada's Department of External Affairs*, vol. 2: *Coming of Age, 1946–1968*. Montreal: McGill-Queen's University Press, 1995.

Hillmer, Norman, and Donald Page, ed. *Documents on Canadian External Relations*, vol. 13: *1946*. Ottawa: Minister of Supply and Services, 1993.

House of Commons. *Debates*. Queen's Printer, Various years.

Inglis, Alex I., ed. *Documents on Canadian External Relations*, vol. 5: *1931–1935*. Ottawa: Information Canada, 1973.

Lalande, Gilles. *The Department of External Affairs and Biculturalism*. Ottawa: Queen's Printer, 1969.

Ministère de la Défense. *Livre blanc sur la défense*. Ottawa: Information Canada, 1971.

Ministère des Affaires étrangères et commerce international. *Le Canada dans le monde : énoncé du gouvernement*. Ottawa: MAECI, 1995.

Munro, John H., ed. *Documents on Canadian External Relations*, vol. 6, *1936–1939*. Ottawa: Information Canada, 1972.

Murray, David R., ed. *Documents on Canadian External Relations*, vol. 8, *1939–1941*. Part II. Ottawa: Information Canada, 1976.

Page, Donald, ed. *Documents on Canadian External Relations*, vol. 12, *1946*. Ottawa: Minster of Supply and Services, 1977.

Status of Women Canada. *Setting the Stage for the Next Century: The Federal Plan for Gender Equality*. Ottawa: Status of Women Canada, 1995.

United States

Hearings before the Committee on Military Affairs House of Representatives Seventy-Fourth Congress, First Session, on H.R. 6621 and H.R. 4130, February 11–13, 1935. Washington, DC: Government Printing Office, 1935.

Books and Articles

Allison, Graham. "Conceptual Models and the Cuban Missile Crisis." *American Political Science Review* 43, no. 3 (Summer 1969): 689–718.

———, and Philip Zelikow. *Essence of Decision: Explaining the Cuban Missile Crisis*. New York: Rowman and Littlefield, 1999.

———. *The Essence of Decision*. Boston: Little Brown, 1971.

Axworthy, Lloyd. "Canadian Foreign Policy: A Liberal Party Perspective." *Canadian Foreign Policy* 1, no. 1 (1992–93): 7–14.

———. *Navigating a New World: Canada's Global Future*. Toronto: Knopf, 2003.

———, and Christine Stewart. *Part of the Americas: A Liberal Policy for Canada in the Western Hemisphere*. Ottawa: Liberal Party of Canada, 1991.

Axworthy, Thomas. "'To Not Stand So High Perhaps but Always Alone': The Foreign Policy of Pierre Trudeau." In *Towards a Just Society: The Trudeau Years*, edited by Thomas S. Axworthy and Pierre Elliott Trudeau. Markham, ON: Viking, 1990.

———. "New Bottles for Old Wine: Implementing the International Policy Statement." In *Canada among Nations, 2005: Split Images*, edited by Andrew F. Cooper and Dane Rowlands, 271–82. Montreal: McGill-Queen's University Press, 2005.

Azzi, Stephen. *Walter Gordon and the Rise of Canadian Nationalism*. Montreal and Kingston: McGill-Queen's University Press, 1999.

Balthazar, Louis. "Quebec and the Ideal of Federalism." *The Annals of the American Academy of Political and Social Science* 538, no. 1 (March 1995): 40–53.

Bélanger, Louis, and Nelson Michaud. "Canadian Institutional Strategies: New Orientations for a Middle Power Foreign Policy." *Australian Journal of International Affairs* 54, no. 1 (2000): 97–110.

Bercuson, David J. "Continental Defence and Arctic Sovereignty, 1945–1950: Solving the Canadian Dilemma." In *The Cold War and Defence*, edited by Keith Neilson and Ronald Haycock. New York: Praeger, 1990.

———, and Denis Stairs, "Canada's International Policy Statement: What's New, What's Old, And What's Needed." In *In the Canadian Interest? Assessing Canada's International Policy Statement*, edited by David J. Bercuson and Denis Stairs, 1–4. Calgary: Canadian Defence and Foreign Affairs Institute, 2005.

———. *True Patriot: The Life of Brooke Claxton, 1898–1960*. Toronto: University of Toronto Press, 1993.

Berger, Carl. *The Writing of Canadian History: Aspects of English-Canadian Historical Writing, 1900–1970*. Toronto: Oxford University Press, 1976.

Black, Conrad. *Duplessis*. Toronto: McClelland & Stewart, 1977.

Black, David R. "How Exceptional? Reassessing the Mulroney Government Anti-Apartheid 'Crusade.'" In *Diplomatic Departures: The Conservative Era in Canadian Foreign Policy, 1984–1993*, edited by Nelson Michaud and Kim Richard Nossal, 173–93. Vancouver: UBC Press, 2001.

Black, Eldon. *Direct Intervention: Canada–France Relations, 1967–1974*. Ottawa: Carleton University Press, 1996.

Blanchard, James J. *Behind the Embassy Door. Canada, Clinton and Québec*. Toronto: McClelland & Stewart, 1998.

Boorstin, Daniel J., ed. *An American Primer*. Chicago: University of Chicago Press, 1966.

Bosher, John. *The Gaullist Attack on Canada, 1967–1997*. Montreal: McGill-Queen's University Press, 1999.

Bothwell, Robert. *Alliance and Illusion: Canada and the World, 1945–1984*. Vancouver: UBC Press, 2007.

———. *Loring Christie: The Failure of Bureaucratic Imperialism*. New York and London: Garland, 1988.

———, and J.L. Granatstein, *Pirouette: Pierre Trudeau and Canadian Foreign Policy*. Toronto: University of Toronto Press, 1990.

Brennan, Patrick H. *Reporting the Nation's Business: Press–Governmental Relations during the Liberal Years, 1935–1957.* Toronto: University of Toronto Press, 1994.

Bromke, Adam, and Kim Richard Nossal. "Tensions in Canada's Foreign Policy." *Foreign Affairs* 62 (Winter 1983-84): 335-53.

Burney, Derek H. *Getting it Done: A Memoir.* Montreal and Kingston: McGill-Queen's University Press, 2005.

Burns, James MacGregor. *Roosevelt: The Lion and the Fox.* New York: Harcourt Brace, 1956.

Cadieux, Marcel. *Le Diplomate canadien: elements d'une définition.* Paris: Fides, 1962.

Campbell, Colin, and George Szablowski. *The Superbureaucrats: Structure and Behaviour in Central Agencies.* Toronto: Macmillan of Canada, 1979.

Canadian Institute of International Affairs. *Foreign Policy for Paul Martin: Eight Articles on Canada's International Relations for the new Prime Minister.* Published as an issue of the *International Journal* 58, no. 4 (Fall 2003).

Carroll, Michael. *Pearson's Peacekeepers: Canada and the United Nations Emergency Force, 1956–1967.* Vancouver: UBC Press, 2009.

Chapnick, Adam. *The Middle Power Project: Canada and the Founding of the United Nations.* Vancouver: UBC Press, 2005.

———. "Popular Attitudes towards the United Nations in Canada and the United States: A Study in National Images." Association for Canadian Studies in the United States, *Occasional Papers on Public Policy*, Series 2, no. 1 (2008).

Chrétien, Jean. *My Years as Prime Minister.* Toronto: Vintage Canada, 2008.

Clark, Joe. "Restoring a Broadly-Based Canadian Foreign Policy." McLaughlin College, Scarborough, 15 November 2007, Unpublished paper.

Clarkson, Stephen. *Canada and the Reagan Challenge: Crisis and Adjustment, 1981-85*, rev. ed. Toronto: James Lorimer, 1985.

———, and Christine McCall. *Trudeau and Our Times*, vol. 1: *The Magnificent Obsession.* Toronto: McClelland & Stewart, 1990.

———, and Christine McCall. *Trudeau and Our Times*, vol. 2: *The Heroic Delusion.* Toronto: McClelland & Stewart, 1994.

Coates, Ken, Whitney Lackenbauer, William Morrison, and Greg Poelzer. *Arctic Front: Defending Canada in the Far North.* Toronto: Thomas Allen, 2008.

Cohen, Andrew. *While Canada Slept: How We Lost Our Place in the World.* Toronto: McClelland & Stewart, 2003.

Coleman, William. *The Independence Movement in Quebec, 1945–1980.* Toronto: University of Toronto Press, 1984.

Cook, Ramsay. *Quebec and the Uses of Nationalism*, 2nd ed. Toronto: McClelland & Stewart, 1995.

Cooper, Andrew F. *Canadian Foreign Policy: Old Habits and New Directions.* Scarborough, ON: Prentice Hall Canada, 1997.

Creighton, Donald. *The Forked Road: Canada, 1939–1957.* Toronto: McClelland & Stewart, 1976.

Crozier, Michel, and Erhard Friedberg. *L'acteur et le système : Les contraintes de l'action collective.* Paris: Éditions du Seuil, 1971.

Dallek, Robert. *Franklin D. Roosevelt and American Foreign Policy, 1933–1945.* New York: Oxford University Press, 1979.

Delisle, Esther. *The Traitor and the Jew: Anti-Semitism and Extremist Nationalism in Quebec from 1929 to 1939.* Montreal: R. Davies Publishing, 1993.

Denis Stairs. "The Diplomacy of Constraint." In *Partners Nevertheless: Canadian–American Relations in the Twentieth Century*, edited by Norman Hillmer. Toronto: Copp Clark, 1989.

Desveaux, James A. *Designing Bureaucracies.* Stanford: Stanford University Press, 1995.

Dirks, Patricia. *The Failure of l'action liberale nationale.* Montreal: McGill-Queen's University Press, 1991.

Donaghy, Greg. "Coming Off the Gold Standard: Re-assessing the Golden Age of Canadian Diplomacy." http://www.suezcrisis.ca/pdfs/Coming%20off%20the%20Gold%20Standard.pdf [accessed May 2009].

———. "Pacific Diplomacy: Canadian Statecraft and the Korean War, 1950–53." In *Canada and Korea: Perspectives, 2000*, edited by R.W.L. Guisso and Young-sik Yoo. Toronto: Centre for Korean Studies, 2002.

———. *Tolerant Allies: Canada and the United States, 1963–1968.* Montreal and Kingston: McGill-Queen's University Press, 2002.

———, and Don Barry. "Our Man from Windsor: Paul Martin and the New Members Question, 1955." In *Paul Martin and Canadian Diplomacy*, edited by Ryan Touhey, 3–20. Waterloo: Centre for Foreign Policy and Federalism, 2001.

Dziuban, Stanley. *Military Relations between the United States and Canada, 1939–1945.* Washington: Office of the Chief of Military History, 1959.

Eayrs, James. "Problems of Canadian–American Relations." In *Canada in World Affairs, October 1955 to June 1957.* Toronto: Oxford University Press, 1959.

Elliot-Meisel, Elizabeth. *Arctic Diplomacy: Canada and the United States in the Northwest Passage.* New York: Peter Lang, 1998.

English, John. *Shadow of Heaven: The Life of Lester Pearson*, vol. 1: *1897–1948*. Toronto: Lester and Orpen Dennys, 1989.

———. *Citizen of the World: The Life of Pierre Elliott Trudeau*, vol. 1: *1919–1968*. Toronto: A.A. Knopf Canada, 2006.

Evans, Michael William. "The Establishment of the Distant Early Warning Line, 1952–1957: A Study of Continental Defense Policymaking." M.A. thesis, Bowling Green University, 1995.

Firestone, Bernard J. *The United Nations under U Thant*. Lanham, MD: Scarecrow Press, 2001.

Fowler, Bob. "Canada's Leadership and the Kananaskis G8 Summit." In *Canada among Nations, 2003: Coping with the American Colossus*, edited by David Carment, Fen Osler Hampson, and Norman Hillmer. Toronto: Oxford University Press, 2003.

Fransen, David. "Unscrewing the Unscrutable: The Rowell-Sirois Commission, the Ottawa Bureaucracy and Public Finance Reform, 1935–1941." PhD diss., University of Toronto, 1984.

Fraser, Graham. "Liberal Continuities: Jean Chrétien's Foreign Policy 1993–2003." In *Canada among Nations, 2004: Setting Priorities Straight*, edited by David Carment, Fen Osler Hampson, and Norman Hillmer. Montreal: McGill-Queen's University Press, 2004.

Gallup, George, and Saul Rae. *The Pulse of Democracy: The Public Opinion Poll and How it Works*. New York: Simon and Schuster, 1940.

Gendron, Robin S., "Educational Aid for French Africa and the Canada–Quebec Dispute over Foreign Policy in the 1960s." *International Journal* 56, no. 1 (2000–2001): 19–36.

———. *Towards a Francophone Community: Canada's Relations with France and French Africa, 1945–1968*. Montreal and Kingston: McGill-Queen's University Press, 2006.

Gotlieb, Allan. *I'll be with you in a minute, Mr. Ambassador: The Education of a Canadian Diplomat in Washington*. Toronto: University of Toronto Press, 1991.

———. "Romanticism and Realism in Canada's Foreign Policy." *C.D. Howe Benefactors Lecture 2004*. Toronto: C.D. Howe Institute, November 2004.

———. *Washington Diaries, 1981–1989*. Toronto: McClelland & Stewart, 2006.

Granatstein, J.L. *Canada's War: The Politics of the Mackenzie King Government 1939–1945*. Toronto: University of Toronto Press, 1975.

———. "The Conservative Party and the Ogdensburg Agreement." *International Journal* 22 (Winter 1966–67): 73–76.

———. "Hume Wrong's Road to the Functional Principle." In *Coalition Warfare: An Uneasy Accord*, edited by Keith Neilson and Roy A. Prete. Waterloo: Wilfrid Laurier University Press, 1983.

———. *The Importance of Being Less Earnest: Promoting Canada's National Interests through Tighter Ties with the U.S.* Toronto: C.D. Howe Institute, 2003.

———. *A Man of Influence: Norman A. Robertson and Canadian Statecraft, 1929–1968*. Ottawa: Deneau, 1981.

———. "Mackenzie King and Canada at Ogdensburg, August 1940." In *Fifty Years of Canada–U.S. Defence Cooperation: The Road from Ogdensburg*, edited by J. Jockel and J. Sokolsky, 9–29. Lewiston, NY: Edwin Mellon Press, 1992.

———. *The Ottawa Men: The Civil Service Mandarins, 1935–1957*. Toronto: Oxford University Press, 1982.

———, and R. D. Cuff. "The Hyde Park Declaration 1941: Origins and Significance." *Canadian Historical Review* 55 (March 1974): 59–80.

Grant, Shelagh. *Sovereignty or Security? Government Policy in the Canadian North, 1936–1950*. Vancouver: UBC Press, 1988.

Grey, Rodney de C. *Trade Policy in the 1980s: An Agenda for Canadian–U.S. Relations*. Montreal: C.D. Howe Institute, 1981.

Hampson, Fen Osler, Norman Hillmer, and Maureen Appel Molot. "The Return to Continentalism in Canadian Foreign Policy." In *Canada among Nations, 2001: The Axworthy Legacy*, edited by Fen Osler Hampson, Norman Hillmer, and Maureen Appel Molot, 1–18. Toronto: Oxford University Press, 2001.

Harper, John Lamberton. *American Visions of Europe: Franklin D. Roosevelt, George F. Kennan, and Dean G. Acheson*. Cambridge: Cambridge University Press, 1994.

Harris, John Nicholas. "National Defence and Northern Development: The Establishment of the DEW Line in the Canadian North." MA thesis, Simon Fraser University, 1980.

Harris, Stephen J. *Canadian Brass: The Making of a Professional Army*. Toronto: University of Toronto Press, 1988.

Hart, Michael. "Almost But Not Quite: The 1947–48 Bilateral Canada–United States Negotiations." *American Review of Canadian Studies* 19, no. 1 (1989): 25–58.

———. *Fifty Years of Canadian Tradecraft: Canada at the GATT 1947–1997*. Ottawa: Centre for Trade Policy and Law, 1998.

———. *From Pride to Influence: Towards a New Canadian Foreign Policy*. Vancouver: UBC Press, 2008.

———. "A Life Well Lived – Simon Reisman." *Policy Options* 29 (April 2008): 23.

———. "Navigating New Trade Routes: The Rise of Value Chains, and the Challenges for Canadian Trade Policy." *C.D. Howe Institute Commentary*, No. 259. Toronto: C.D. Howe Institute, 2008.

———. *A Trading Nation: Canadian Trade Policy from Colonialism to Globalization*. Vancouver: UBC Press, 2002.

———, and Bill Dymond. "A Canada–EU FTA is an awful idea." *Policy Options* 23 (July–August 2002): 27–32.

———, with Bill Dymond and Colin Robertson. *Decision at Midnight: Inside the Canada–U.S. Free Trade Negotiations*. Vancouver: UBC Press, 1994.

Heller, Peter B. *The United Nations under Dag Hammarskjöld, 1953–1961*. Lanham, MD: Scarecrow Press, 2001.

Heynen, Jeff, and John Higginbotham. *Advancing Canadian Interests in the United States: A Practical Guide for Public Officials*. Ottawa: Canada School of Public Service, 2004.

Herd, Alexander W.G. "As Practicable: Canada–United States Continental Air Defense Cooperation 1953–1954." MA thesis, Kansas State University, 2005.

Hermann, Margaret, Thomas Preston, Baghat Korany, and Tim Shaw. "Who Leads Matters: The Effects of Powerful Individuals." *International Studies Review* 3, no. 2 (2001): 83–132.

Higginbotham, John, and Jeff Heynen. "Managing through Networks: The State of Canada–U.S. Relations," In *Canada among Nations, 2004: Setting Priorities Straight*, edited by David Carment et al. Montreal: McGill-Queen's University Press, 2005.

Hilliker, John. *Canada's Department of External Affairs*, vol. 1: *The Early Years, 1909–1946*. Montreal and Kingston: McGill-Queen's University Press, 1990.

Hillmer, Norman. "The Anglo-Canadian Neurosis: The Case of O.D. Skelton." In *Britain and Canada: A Survey of a Changing Relationship*, edited by Peter Lyon. London: Frank Cass, 1976.

———. "O.D. Skelton and the North American Mind." *International Journal* 60, no. 1 (2004–5): 93–110.

———, David Carment, and Fen Osler Hampson. *Is Canada Now Irrelevant?* Calgary: Canadian Defence and Foreign Affairs Institute, 2003.

Holmes, John W. *The Shaping of Peace: Canada and the Search for World Order, 1943–1957*, vol. 2. Toronto: University of Toronto Press, 1982.

Horn, Lt. Colonel Bernd. "Gateway to Invasion or the Curse of Geography? The Canadian Arctic and the Question of Security, 1939–1999." In *Forging a Nation: Perspectives on the Canadian Military Experience*. St. Catharines, ON: Vanwell Publishing, 2002.

Horn, Michael. *The League for Social Reconstruction: Intellectual Origins of the Democratic Left in Canada, 1930–1942*. Toronto: University of Toronto Press, 1980.

Horton, Donald J. *André Laurendeau: French Canadian Nationalist, 1912–1968*. Toronto: Oxford University Press, 1992.

Ignatieff, Michael. "Canada in the Age of Terror – Multilateralism Meets a Moment of Truth." *Policy Options* 24, no. 2 (2003): 14–18.

———. *Peace, Order and Good Government: A Foreign Policy Agenda for Canada*. Ottawa: Department of Foreign Affairs and International Trade, 2004.

Jockel, Joseph. "The Canada–United States Military Co-operation Committee and Continental Air Defence, 1946." *Canadian Historical Review* 64, no. 3 (1983): 352–77.

———. *No Boundaries Upstairs: Canada, the United States, and the Origins of North American Air Defence, 1945–1958*. Vancouver: UBC Press, 1987.

———, and Joel Sokolsky. "Lloyd Axworthy's Legacy: Human Security and the Rescued Canadian Defense Policy." *International Journal* 56, no. 1 (2000–2001): 1–19.

Johnson, Daniel. *Égalité ou indépendance*. Montreal: Renaissance, 1965.

Johnson, Gregory Allan. *North Pacific Triangle? The Impact of the Far East on Canada and Its Relations with the United States and Great Britain, 1937–1948*. PhD diss., York University, 1989.

Keating, Tom. *Canada and World Order: The Multilateralist Tradition in Canadian Foreign Policy*, 2nd ed. Don Mills, ON: Oxford University Press, 2002.

———. "A Passive Internationalist: Jean Chrétien and Canadian Foreign Policy." In *The Chrétien Legacy: Politics and Public Policy in Canada*, edited by Lois Harder and Steve Patten. Montreal: McGill-Queen's University Press, 2006.

Keenleyside, H. L. *Memoirs of Hugh L. Keenleyside*, vol. 1: *Hammer the Golden Day*. Toronto: McClelland & Stewart, 1981.

Kennedy, Greg. *Anglo-American Strategic Relations and the Far East 1933–1939*. London: Frank Cass, 2002.

Kinsman, Jeremy. "Who is My Neighbour? Pierre Trudeau and Foreign Policy." *London Journal of Canadian Studies* 18 (2002–3): 103–20.

Kirkey, Christopher. "Smoothing Troubled Waters: The 1988 Canada–United States Arctic Co-operation Agreement." *International Journal* 50, no. 2 (1995): 408–26.

———. "Washington's Response to the Ottawa Land Mines Process." In *Canadian–American Public Policy* 46. Augusta: Canadian–American Center, University of Maine, 2001.

Kirton, John. "Shaping the Global Order: Canada and the Francophone and Commonwealth Summits of 1987." *Behind the Headlines* 44, no. 3 (1987): 1–17.

———. "Foreign Policy under the Liberals: Prime Ministerial Leadership in the Chrétien's Government Foreign Policy-making Process." In *Canada among Nations, 1997: Asia-Pacific Face-Off*, edited by Fen Osler Hampson, Maureen Appel Molot, and Martin Rudner. Ottawa: Carleton University Press, 1997.

Kuklick, Bruce. *Blind Oracles: Intellectuals and War from Kennan to Kissinger*. Princeton, NJ: Princeton University Press, 2006.

Lackenbauer, Whitney. "Right and Honourable: Mackenzie King, Canadian–American Bilateral Relations, and Canadian Sovereignty in the Northwest, 1943–1948." In *Mackenzie King: Citizenship and Community*, edited by John English, Kenneth McLaughlin, and Whitney Lackenbauer. Toronto: Robin Brass Studio, 2002.

Lajeunesse, Adam. "Lock, Stock, and Icebergs? Defining Canadian Sovereignty from Mackenzie King to Stephen Harper." Occasional Paper No. 1. Calgary: Centre for Military and Strategic Studies, 2007.

———. "The True North as Long as It's Free: The Canadian Policy Deficit 1945–1985." MA thesis, University of Calgary, 2007.

Langdon, Steven. "NEPAD and the Renaissance of Africa." In *Canada among Nations, 2003: Coping with the American Colossus*, edited by David Carment, Fen Osler Hampson, and Norman Hillmer, 242–55. Toronto: Oxford University Press, 2003.

Larson, David L. "United States Interests in the Arctic Region," *Ocean Development and International Law* 20 (1989): 183–84.

Lawson, Robert. "The Ottawa Process: Fast-Track Diplomacy and the International Movement to Ban Anti-Personnel Mines." In *Canada among Nations, 1998: Leadership and Dialogue*, edited by Fen Osler Hampson and Maureen Appel Molot. Toronto: Oxford University Press, 1998.

Leeming, J.M. "HMCS Labrador and the Canadian Arctic." In *The Royal Canadian Navy in Retrospect*, edited by James Boutilier. Vancouver: UBC Press, 1982.

Lenarcic, David. *Where Angels Feared to Tread*, PhD diss., York University, 1990.

Liberal Party of Canada. *Bâtir notre avenir ensemble. Préparer le Canada pour le XXIe siècle*. Ottawa: Liberal Party of Canada, 1997.

———. *Pour la création d'emplois pour la relance économique: Le plan d'action libéral pour le Canada*. Ottawa: Liberal Party of Canada, 1993.

Lower, A.R.M. *My First Seventy-Five Years*. Toronto: Macmillan of Canada, 1967.

Lynhiavu, Tou Chu Dou. "Canada's Window on Asia: The Establishment of the Tokyo Legation in 1928–1931." *Journal of Canadian Studies* 31 (1996–97): 97–123.

Lyon, Peyton V. *Canada in World Affairs, 1961–1963*. Toronto: Oxford University Press, 1968.

Macdonald, Douglas, and Heather A. Smith. "Promises Made, Promises Broken: Questioning Canada's Commitments to Climate Change." *International Journal* 55, no. 1 (1999–2000): 107–24.

Mackenzie, Hector. "Recruiting Tomorrow's Ambassadors: Examination and Selection for the Foreign Service of Canada, 1925–1997." In *Diplomatic Missions: The Ambassador in Canadian Foreign Policy*, edited by Robert Wolfe. Kingston: School of Policy Studies, Queen's University, 1998.

Marquis, Dominique. *Un quotidian pour L'Eglise: L'action catholique, 1910–1940*. Montreal: Lemeac, 2004.

Martel, Marcel. *French Canada: An Account of its Creation and Break-Up, 1850–1967*. Ottawa: Canadian Historical Association, 1998.

Martin, Lawrence. *The Presidents and Prime Ministers*. Toronto: Doubleday, 1982.

Martin, Paul, Jr. *Hell or High Water: My Life In and Out of Politics*. Toronto: McClelland & Stewart, 2008.

Massey, Vincent. *What's Past is Prologue: The Memoirs of the Right Honourable Vincent Massey*. Toronto: Macmillan, 1963.

May, Ernest R. *American Imperialism: A Speculative Essay.* New ed. Chicago: Imprint, 1991.

McCall-Newman, Christina. *Grits: An Intimate Portrait of the Liberal Party.* Toronto: Macmillan of Canada, 1982.

McDonald, Marci. "Taking Orders: How Washington Shaped Canada's Foreign Policy in the Mulroney Years." *Special Report, Fifth Annual Atkinson Fellowship in Public Policy*, 1993.

McGuigan, Mark. *An Inside Look at External Affairs during the Trudeau Years.* Edited by P. Whitney Lackenbauer. Calgary: University of Calgary Press, 2002.

Mearsheimer, John J. *The Tragedy of Great Power Politics.* New York: Norton, 2001.

Meehan, John D. "Steering Clear of Britain: Canada's Debate over Collective Security in the Far Eastern Crisis of 1937." *International History Review* 25 (June 2003): 253–81.

Meren, David. "Antagonism and Engagement: Marcel Cadieux, Jules Léger, and the Department of External Affairs' Response to Canada-Quebec-France Tensions." Unpublished paper presented at the Canada and France: A Diplomatic Partnership Conference, Montreal, 31 October 2008.

Michaud, Nelson. "The Prime Minister, PMO and PCO: Makers of Canadian Foreign Policy?" In *Handbook of Canadian Foreign Policy*, edited by Nelson Michaud, Patrick James, and Marc J. O'Reilly, 21–48. Lanham, MD: Lexington Books, 2006.

———, and Kim Richard Nossal, ed. *Diplomatic Departures: The Conservative Era in Canadian Foreign Policy, 1984–1993.* Vancouver: UBC Press, 2001.

Molot, Maureen Appel, and Brian W. Tomlin. "The Conservative Agenda." In *Canada among Nations, 1985: The Conservative Agenda*, edited by Maureen Appel Molot and Brian W. Tomlin. Toronto: James Lorimer, 1986.

Morin, Claude. *Les Choses comme elles étaient.* Montreal: Boréal, 1994.

Morris, Margaret W. "Boundary Problems Relating to the Sovereignty of the Canadian Arctic." In *Canada's Changing North*, edited by Wm. C. Wonders. Toronto: McClelland & Stewart, 1971.

Morrison, David R. *Aid and Ebb Tide: A History of CIDA and Canadian Development Assistance.* Waterloo: Wilfrid Laurier University Press, 1998.

Mulroney, Brian. *Memoirs.* Toronto: Douglas Gibson, 2007.

———. *Where I Stand.* Toronto: McClelland & Stewart, 1983.

Munton, Don, and Don Page. "Planning in the East Block: The Post-Hostilities Problems Committees in Canada, 1943–45." *International Journal* 32, no. 4 (1977): 677–726.

Neatby, H. Blair. *William Lyon Mackenzie King*, vol. 3, *1932–1939: The Prism of Unity.* Toronto: University of Toronto Press, 1976.

Nemeth, Tammy. "Consolidating the Continental Drift: American Influence on Diefenbakers' National Oil Policy." *Journal of the Canadian Historical Association* 13 (2002): 191–215.

———. "1980: Duel of the Decade." In *Alberta Formed, Alberta Transformed*, edited by Michael Payne, Donald Wetherell, and Catherine Cavanaugh. Edmonton/Calgary: University of Alberta/University of Calgary Press, 2006.

———. "Canada–U.S. Oil and Gas Relations, 1959–1974." PhD diss., University of British Columbia, 2007.

Nielsen, Erik. *The House is Not a Home: An Autobiography*. Toronto: Macmillan of Canada, 1989.

Nixon, Edgar B, ed. *Franklin D. Roosevelt and Foreign Affairs*, vol. 2: *March 1934–August 1935*. Cambridge, MA: Belknap Press of Harvard University Press, 1969.

Noble, John J. "Serving the Prime Minister's Foreign Policy." In *Canada among Nations, 2007: What Room for Manoeuvre?*, edited by Jean Deaudelin and Daniel Schwanen. Montreal: McGill-Queen's University Press, 2007.

Nossal, Kim Richard. "Allison through the (Ottawa) Looking Glass: Bureaucratic Politics and Foreign Policy in a Parliamentary System." *Canadian Public Administration* 22, no. 4 (1979): 610–26.

———. "Pinchpenny Diplomacy: The Decline of Good International Citizenship in Canadian Foreign Policy." *International Journal* 54, no. 1 (1998–99): 88–105.

———. *The Politics of Canadian Foreign Policy*, 3rd ed. Toronto: Prentice-Hall Canada, 1997.

Ovendale, Ritchie. *'Appeasement' and the English-Speaking World. Britain, the United States, the Dominions and the Policy of 'Appeasement,' 1937–1939*. Cardiff: University of Wales Press, 1975.

Owram, Doug. *The Government Generation: Canadian Intellectuals and the State, 1900–1945*. Toronto: University of Toronto Press, 1986.

Paquin, Stéphane, ed., *Les relations internationales du Québec depuis la Doctrine Gérin-Lajoie (1965–2005): Le prolongement externe des competences internes*. Lévis, QC: Les Presses de l'Université Laval, 2006.

Pearson, L.B. *Mike: The Memoirs of the Right Honourable Lester B. Pearson*, vol. 1: *1897–1948*. Toronto: University of Toronto Press, 1972.

Perras, Galen Roger. *Franklin Roosevelt and the Origins of the Canadian–American Security Alliance: Necessary But Not Necessary Enough*. Westport, CT: Praeger, 1998.

———. *Stepping Stones to Nowhere: The Aleutian Islands, Alaska, and American Military Strategy, 1867–1945*. Vancouver: UBC Press, 2003.

———, and Katrina E. Kellner. "'A perfectly logical and sensible thing': Billy Mitchell Advocates a Canadian–American Aerial Alliance against Japan." *Journal of Military History* 72 (July 2008): 785–823.

Pharand, Donat. *Canada's Arctic Waters in International Law*. Cambridge: Cambridge University Press, 1988.

Potter, Evan. *Branding Canada Projecting Canada's Soft Power through Public Diplomacy*. Montreal and Kingston: McGill-Queen's University Press, 2009.

Pratt, Lawrence. "The Anglo-American Naval Conversations on the Far East of January 1938." *International Affairs* 47 (October 1971): 745–63.

Preston, Richard A. *Canada in World Affairs, 1959–1961*. Toronto: Oxford University Press, 1965.

Price, John. "The 'Cat's Paw': Canada and the United Nations Temporary Commission on Korea." *Canadian Historical Review* 85, no. 2 (2004): 297–324.

Prince, Robert. "The Limits of Constraint." *Journal of Canadian Studies* 27, no. 4 (1992–93): 129–52.

Pullen, T.C. "What Price Canadian Sovereignty?" *U.S. Naval Institute Proceedings* 113 (September 1987): 66-72.

Reid, Escott. *Radical Mandarin: The Memoirs of Escott Reid*. Toronto: University of Toronto Press, 1989.

Rempel, Roy. *Dreamland: How Canada's Pretend Foreign Policy Has Undermined Sovereignty*. Kingston: Breakout Educational Network and the Queen's University School of Policy Studies through McGill-Queen's University Press, 2006.

Richards, John, and Larry Pratt. *Prairie Capitalism: Power and Influence in the New West*. Toronto: McClelland & Stewart, 1979.

Riddell-Dixon, Elizabeth. *Canada and the Beijing Conference on Women: Governmental Politics and NGO Participation*. Vancouver: UBC Press, 2001.

———. "Deep Seabed Mining: A Hotbed for Governmental Politics." *International Journal* 41, no. 1 (1985–86): 72–94.

———. "Democratizing Canadian Foreign Policy? NGO Participation for the Copenhagen Summit for Social Development and the Beijing Conference on Women." *Canadian Foreign Policy* 11, no. 3 (2004): 99–118.

———. "Organizing for Beijing: Canadian NGOs and the Fourth World Conference on Women." In *Feminist Perspectives on Canadian Foreign Policy*, edited by Claire Turenne Sjolander, Heather A. Smith, and Deborah Steinstra. Don Mills, ON: Oxford University Press, 2003.

Robertson, Gordon. *Memoirs of a Very Civil Servant*. Toronto: University of Toronto Press, 2000.

Robinson, Daniel J. *The Measure of Democracy*. Toronto: University of Toronto Press, 1999.

Roussel, Éric. *Charles de Gaulle*. Paris: Gallimard, 2002.

Roy, Patricia E. *The Oriental Question: Consolidating a White Man's Province, 1914–41*. Vancouver: UBC Press, 2003.

Rutherford, Paul. *Weapons of Mass Persuasion: Marketing the War against Iraq*. Toronto: University of Toronto Press, 2004.

Savoie, Donald J. *Breaking the Bargain: Public Servants, Ministers and Parliament*. Toronto: University of Toronto Press, 2003.

———. *Governing from the Centre: The Concentration of Power in Canadian Politics*. Toronto: University of Toronto Press, 1999.

Sayle, Timothy Andrews. "A Pattern of Constraint: Canadian–American Relations in the Early Cold War." *International Journal* 62, no. 3 (2007): 689–705.

Schmitz, Gerald, and James Lee. "Split Images and Serial Affairs: Reviews, Reorganizations and Parliamentary Roles." In *Canada among Nations, 2005: Split Images*, edited by Andrew F. Cooper and Dane Rowlands. Montreal and Kingston: McGill-Queen's University Press, 2005.

Sharp, Mitchell. *Which Reminds Me....* Toronto: University of Toronto Press, 1994.

Simpson, Jeffrey. *Faultlines: Struggling for a Canadian Vision*. Toronto: Harper-Collins, 1993.

Skelton, O.D. "Canada and Foreign Policy." In *The Canadian Club Year Book, 1921–1922*. Ottawa: Canadian Club, 1922.

———. *Our Generation: Its Gains and Losses*. Chicago: University of Chicago Press, 1938.

Smith, Denis. *Rogue Tory: The Life and Legend of John G. Diefenbaker*. Toronto: Macfarlane Walter & Ross, 1995.

Smith, Gordon. "Sovereignty in the North: The Canadian Aspect of an International Problem." In *The Arctic Frontier*, edited by R.St.J. Macdonald, 194–255. Toronto: University of Toronto Press, 1966.

Soward, F.H., and Edgar McInnis. *Canada and the United Nations*. New York: Manhattan Publishing, 1956.

Stacey, C.P. *Canada and the Age of Conflict*, vol. 2: *1921–1948: The Mackenzie King Era*. Toronto: University of Toronto Press, 1984.

Stairs, Denis. "The Changing Office and the Changing Environment of the Minister of Foreign Affairs in the Axworthy Era." In *Canada among Nations, 2004: Setting Priorities Straight*, edited by David Carment, Fen Osler Hampson, and Norman Hillmer, 19–38. Montreal and Kingston: McGill-Queen's University Press, 2004.

Stein, Janice Gross, and Eugene Lang. *The Unexpected War: Canada in Kandahar*. Toronto: Penguin, 2008.

Strachan, W. R. "The Development of Canadian Energy Policy 1970–1982 – One Man's View." *Journal of Business Administration* 14, no. 1–2 (1983–84): 143–62.

Sutherland, R.J. "The Strategic Significance of the Canadian Arctic." In *The Arctic Frontier*, edited by R. St. J. MacDonald. Toronto: University of Toronto Press, 1966.

Taras, David. "Brian Mulroney's Foreign Policy: Something for Everyone." *The Round Table* 293 (1985): 35–46.

Taylor, J.H. "The Conservatives and Foreign Policy-Making: A Foreign Service View." In *Diplomatic Departures: The Conservative Era in Canadian Foreign Policy, 1984–1993*, edited by Nelson Michaud and Kim Richard Nossal, 211–19. Vancouver: UBC Press, 2001.

Thompson, John Herd, and Allen Seager. *Canada 1922–1939: Decades of Discord*. Toronto: McClelland & Stewart, 1985.

Thomson, Dale. *Vive le Québec libre*. Toronto: Deneau, 1988.

Tomlin, Brian W. "On a Fast Track to the Ban: The Canadian Policy Process." *Canadian Foreign Policy* 5, no. 3 (1998): 3–23.

Trofimenkoff, Susan Mann. *Action Française: French Canadian Nationalism in the Twenties*. Toronto: University of Toronto Press, 1975.

Védrine, Hubert. *Face à l'hyperpuissance*. Paris: Fayard, 2003.

Vigod, Bernard. *Quebec before Duplessis: The Political Career of Louis-Alexandre Taschereau*. Montreal and Kingston: McGill-Queen's University Press, 1986.

Walker, Graham F., ed. *Independence in an Age of Empire: Assessing Unilateralism and Multilateralism*. Halifax: Centre for Foreign Policy Studies, 2004.

Weiers, Margaret K. *Envoys Extraordinary: Women of the Canadian Foreign Service*. Toronto: Dundurn, 1994.

Welsh, Jennifer M. *At Home in the World: Canada's Global Vision for the 21st Century*. Toronto: HarperCollins, 2004.

———. "Reality and Canadian Foreign Policy." In *Canada among Nations, 2005: Split Images*, edited by Andrew F. Cooper and Dane Rowlands, 23–46. Montreal and Kingston: McGill-Queen's University Press, 2005.

Wiltz, John E. *From Isolation to War, 1931–1941*. New York: Thomas Y. Crowell, 1968.

Wood, Duncan. "Canada and International Financial Policy: Non-Hegemonic Leadership and Systematic Stability." In *Handbook of Canadian Foreign Policy*, edited by Patrick James, Nelson Michaud, and Marc J. O'Reilly, 265–86. Lanham, MD: Rowman and Littlefield, 2006.

CONTRIBUTORS

MICHAEL CARROLL is an Assistant Professor of History at Grant MacEwan University.

ADAM CHAPNICK is the Deputy Director of Education at the Canadian Forces College and an Associate Professor of Defence Studies at the Royal Military College of Canada.

GREG DONAGHY is Head of the Historical Section at Foreign Affairs and International Trade Canada.

ROBIN GENDRON is an Associate Professor of History at Nipissing University.

J.L. GRANATSTEIN is Distinguished Research Professor of History Emeritus at York University and was Director and Chief Executive Office of the Canadian War Museum.

MICHAEL HART holds the Simon Reisman Chair in Trade Policy at the Norman Paterson School of International Affairs at Carleton University.

NORMAN HILLMER is Professor of History and International Affairs at Carleton University.

PETER KIKKERT is a Ph.D. Candidate in History at the University of Western Ontario.

P. WHITNEY LACKENBAUER is an Associate Professor and Chair of the Department of History at St. Jerome's University.

HEATHER METCALFE holds a Ph.D. in History from the University of Toronto and teaches at Ryerson University.

NELSON MICHAUD is Vice-Rector (Teaching and Research) at the École nationale d'administration publique.

TAMMY NEMETH holds a Ph.D. in History from the University of British Columbia and is an independent scholar living in Bremen, Germany.

GALEN PERRAS is an Associate Professor of History at the University of Ottawa.

STEPHEN RANDALL is Professor of History and Director of the Latin American Research Centre at the University of Calgary.

ELIZABETH RIDDELL-DIXON is Professor of International Relations at the University of Western Ontario.

INDEX

3D+T approach, 195–96
9/11, 1, 192, 193, 217, 222

A

acid rain, 187, 210, 211, 213, 214, 216
Action Libérale Nationale, 60
L'Action nationale, 60, 67n33
Advisory Committee on Northern Development, 111
Afghanistan, 194, 198
Africa, 6, 123, 124, 125, 126, 127, 128, 186, 193
Agence de coopération culturelle et technique, 128
Alaskan highway, 34–36, 103
Alberta, 160, 167, 168
Alberta Energy Resources Conservation Board, 168
Aleutian Islands, 31
Algeria, 122
Anglo-Japanese Alliance, 28
Anglo-Norwegian Fisheries Case, 113, 115
Antarctica, 113
anti-missile shield initiative, 194
anti-personnel landmines. *See* Ottawa Process
Apartheid, 186, 212
Arctic, 5, 101–16, 187, 213, 224
Armour, Norman, 33, 37, 38, 39, 40
Arnold, H.H., 31
Ashton, E.C., 35, 39–40
Asia, 6, 36, 37, 40, 76, 175n12, 211, 222
Asia-Pacific Economic Cooperation (APEC), 184
Austin, Jack, 165, 177n34
Australia, 34, 123, 138, 232
Axworthy, Lloyd, 1, 78, 184, 190–91, 195, 215–16, 217–21, 225
Axworthy, Tom, 196

B

Ballantyne, E.A., 165
Barry, Don, 85
Baxter, Clive, 108
Beijing Conference on Women. *See* Fourth World Conference on Women in Beijing
Beijing Declaration and Platform for Action, 229, 230, 231, 234, 235, 241
Belgium, 32, 123
Bennett, R.B., 29, 30, 33
Bercuson, David, 102, 104, 196
Berle, Adolf, 37, 38
Berlin blockade, 87
Bernier, Maxime, 198, 199
Blanchard, James, 218–19
Boal, Pierre de la, 30, 32
Boehm, Peter, 222
Bomarc missiles, 75, 77
Borden, Robert, 2, 3, 8
Bothwell, Robert, 81–82, 156, 164
Bourassa, Henri, 125
Bourassa, Robert, 188
Bourguiba, Habib, 121
Brazil, 183

British Columbia, 23, 29, 33, 34, 36, 37, 38, 39, 40, 74
British Commonwealth, 34, 40, 112, 122, 123, 127
British Commonwealth Air Training Plan (BCATP), 72
British Empire, 12, 28, 38, 62, 70
British Foreign Office, 15, 63
British War Office, 31
Bryce, Robert, 72
Buchan, John, 37
Bujold, Marius, 237
Burney, Derek, 152n15, 169, 209–15, 217, 221, 226n4
Burns, James MacGregor, 37
Bus Regulatory Reform Act, 213
Bush, George H.W., 183, 187, 215, 217
Bush, George W., 183, 197, 204n43, 222

C

Cabinet Defence Committee, 107
Cadieux, Marcel, 6, 121–32, 134n27, 158
Cairo Conference on Population and Development (1994), 233
Campbell, Donald, 173, 179n67, 211, 213, 215, 219
Campbell, Kim, 202n8
Campney, Ralph, 107
Canada
   1921 election, 11
   1957 election, 75, 93
   1963 election, 125
   1968 election, 161
   1993 election, 217
   Africa, 123, 124, 133
   Arctic, 101–16
   autopact, 143–44
   defence policy, 37, 40, 70, 199
   economic policy, 70, 73, 185, 240
   energy policy, 7, 155–74, 210
   English Canadian intellectuals, 58–59, 60–61
   French Canadian intellectuals, 59–60
   French-Canadians, 51–52
   House of Commons, 55
   immigration to, 22, 23
   multilateralism, 91, 123, 147, 184, 190, 192, 195, 198, 212, 214, 217, 221, 223, 225, 226n9
   national unity, 3, 5, 52, 70, 123
   oil policy, 156–73
   postwar planning, 83–84
   and Quebec, 129, 130, 131–32, 134n27
   relations with France, 129, 130, 134n27
   relations with the U.K., 12, 13, 38, 53–54, 65, 70, 71, 73, 142–43
   relations with the U.S., 3, 7, 13, 21, 22–23, 27, 31, 34–35, 38, 39, 41, 43, 65, 69, 71–72, 72–73, 75, 76–78, 91, 101–16, 142–43, 144, 147–48, 150, 156–61, 162, 164, 165, 167, 168, 174, 183–84, 186–88, 192–93, 195–96, 197–98, 207–25
   role of prime minister, 181–201
   Royal Canadian Air Force, 108
   Second World War, 64
   sovereignty, 101, 102, 103–6, 187, 189
   tariffs, 139
   territorial waters, 111
   trade policy, 6, 137–50, 190, 221
   United Nations, 81–97
   United Nations Security Council, 86, 87, 191, 220
Canada Development Corporation, 166, 177n36
Canada in the World, 190, 195
Canada Shipping Act, 110
Canada–U.S. Free Trade Agreement, 143, 144, 148, 149, 152n14, 187, 211, 212, 214–15, 216
Canada's International Policy Statement, 195, 223
Canadian Broadcasting Corporation (CBC), 78
Canadian Business, 55
Canadian Club, 11, 12, 13, 14, 16, 22, 24, 59
Canadian Foundation for the Americas, 218
Canadian Institute of International Affairs (CIIA), 41, 59, 72, 130
Canadian International Development Agency (CIDA), 233, 236, 238
Canadian Radio League, 59
Caribbean, 138, 232
Carney, Pat, 213, 215
Carter, Thomas, 122, 123
Centre for Foreign Policy Development, 184, 192
Chamberlain, Neville, 37, 38, 53, 70

Chapdelaine, Jean, 131, 132n18
Chappell, Norm, 159–60, 161, 164–65, 168
China, 36, 37, 38, 90, 157, 183, 221
Christie, Loring, 2, 14, 35, 40, 42
Chrétien, Jean, 77, 78, 153n20, 184, 189–94, 196, 199, 200, 216–23, 240
Chrétien, Raymond, 188, 219, 222
Churchill, Winston, 73
Clark, Ed, 172
Clark, Joe, 120n59, 172, 186, 212–13, 214, 226n9, 226–27n13
Claxton, Brooke, 72
Clean Air Act, 214
Clinton, Bill, 216, 217, 219, 221
Cohen, Andrew, 1–2, 190
Cohen, Maxwell, 92, 93
Cohen, Mickey, 172, 173
Cold War, 4, 5, 6, 75, 85, 86, 89, 91, 102, 104, 106, 115, 159, 183
Commonwealth. *See* British Commonwealth
conscription, 3, 52
Contradora Group, 212, 226n10
Convention on Territorial Waters, 112–13
Copenhagen Summit for Social Development (1995), 231, 232, 233, 234, 237, 240, 243n7
Craig, Malin, 38, 40
Crerar, Harry, 38
Crowe, Marshall, 166
Crowther, Keith, 16
Cuba, 157, 187, 210, 219, 220
Cuban Missile Crisis, 77, 95
Czechoslovakia, 61

D

Dafoe, John, 61
Davis, Norman, 37–39
Deaver, Michael, 214
decolonization, 95
de Gaulle, Charles, 127, 130
Department of Citizenship and Immigration, 153n20
Department of Defence Production, 160
Department of Energy, Mines and Resources (EMR), 155, 158, 161, 163, 165–66, 172, 174
Department of External Affairs (DEA), 2, 5, 6, 13, 15, 16, 19–22, 41, 53, 54, 56, 70, 74, 77, 91, 95, 97, 103, 104, 113, 114, 140, 155, 172, 174, 209, 229, 236
  declining influence of, 164, 173, 174
  foreign policy, 82, 83, 132, 215, 218
  French Canadians, 124–25
  Quebec, 128–30
  reorganization, 137, 148–49, 153n20, 161, 163–64, 165, 169–70, 174, 208, 209, 211, 216
  views on US, 31, 43, 157–58
Department of Finance, 139, 144, 149, 240
Department of Fisheries and Oceans, 239
Department of Foreign Affairs and International Trade (DFAIT), 6, 8, 153n20, 198, 207, 208, 209, 216, 219, 221, 222, 223, 224, 225, 229, 230–33, 236, 237, 238, 239, 241, 242
Department of Industry, Trade and Commerce, 6, 137, 144, 148–49, 169, 209
Department of National Defence (DND), 28, 30, 31, 33, 35, 39, 43, 76, 77, 185, 239
Department of Northern Affairs and Natural Resources, 111
Department of Regional Economic Expansion, 153n20
Department of Trade and Commerce, 138, 151n5
Depression, the, 33, 60, 61
Dern, George, 32
Distant Early Warning (DEW) line, 107–9, 110, 111
Désy, Jean, 15, 17
Dexter, Grant, 61, 67n37
Dialogue on Foreign Policy, 184, 193
Diefenbaker, John, 5, 74, 75, 76, 77, 93, 125, 143, 160, 182
disarmament, 75, 76, 86, 94
Dymond, Bill, 214

E

Edwards, Len, 198
Eggleton, Art, 220
Egypt, 91
Eisenhower, Dwight D., 159
Elliot-Meisel, Elizabeth, 102
El Salvador, 212
Environmental Protection Act, 213
Ethiopia, 34, 186

European Common Market, 144, 145
Evans, Michael, 108–9
External Affairs, 94

F
feminism, 232
Ferguson, George, 61
Financial Post, 108, 116
Finestone, Sheila, 240
Finlayson, Roderick K., 61
First World War, 3, 28, 52, 70
Flaherty, Jim, 184
Ford, Gerald, 168
Foreign Policy for Canadians, 163
Foster, W.W., 103
Fourth World Conference on Women in Beijing, 7–8, 229–42
France, 42, 91
    relations with Canada, 129, 130
    relations with Quebec, 127, 130
Francophonie, la, 128, 131, 132, 184, 188
Fransen, David, 60
Fréchette, Louise, 188, 216
Freedman, Max, 61
free trade. *See* Canada–U.S. Free Trade Agreement
Fried, Jonathan, 215
Fulford, D.W., 165
functionalism, 5, 84, 95, 97, 103, 109, 115, 116, 118n21

G
Gaglione, Anthony, 85
Gallup, George, 55
Gallup Poll; 54–55
General Agreement on Tariffs and Trade (GATT), 138, 139, 140, 144, 147, 151n2
George VI, 51–52, 61
Gérin-Lajoie Doctrine, 127
Germany, 41, 42
Good Neighbor Policy, 33
Gordon, Walter, 143
Gore, Al, 222
Gorham, Richard, 216
Gotlieb, Allan, 141, 144, 156, 164, 169, 170, 172, 173, 208–9, 210, 211–14, 216, 217, 221, 226n13
Graham, Bill, 184, 192–93, 195

Granatstein, Jack, 156, 164, 185, 225
Grant, Shelagh, 102
Great Britain. *See* United Kingdom
Green, Howard, 74, 75, 76, 77, 83, 93, 95
Grey, Rodney, 145
Griffiths, Franklyn, 115
Groulx, Abbé Lionel, 125
Group of 77, 234
Group of Eight (G8), 193, 195, 203n41
Group of Seven (G7), 232
Guatemala, 212
Guinea, 122
Gzowski, Peter, 78

H
Haiti, 198
Hammarskjöld, Dag, 82, 89, 95
Hankey, Maurice, 29
Hanson, R.B., 55–56
Harder, Peter, 222
Harkness, Douglas, 76
Harper, Stephen, 2, 182, 184, 196, 197–99, 200, 207
Harris, Steve, 29
Hart, Grace, 18
Hart, Michael, 69, 214, 226n4
Hatfield, Richard, 188
Haynal, George, 208, 216, 218, 221
Head, Ivan, 164, 166
Heeney, Arnold, 76, 159–60, 175n16
Heinbecker, Paul, 215
Helms, Jesse, 218
Helms-Burton Act, 218–19
Herd, Alexander, 108
Hermann, Margaret, 200–201
Hillier, Rick, 195, 196, 199
Hilliker, John, 85
Hitler, Adolf, 41, 71, 72, 73
HMCS *Labrador*, 110
Hollis, Christopher, 76
Holmes, John, 82, 91
Holy See, 232, 243n5
Horn, Michael, 60
Howland, Robert, 165–66
Hull, Cordell, 36, 37
human security, 1, 191, 220
Hungary, 92
Hyde Park Declaration, 73

I

Ignatieff, Michael, 190
Immigration, 23
Imperial Conference of 1923, 14
Imperial Conference of 1937, 51
India, 183, 221
Institute of Public Opinion, 55
Interdepartmental Committee on External Relations, 151n5
Interdepartmental Committee on the World Conference on Women, 238
International Atomic Energy Agency, 90
International Campaign to Ban Land-Mines, 191
International Conference on the Law of the Sea, 112
International Court of Justice (ICJ), 113, 115
International Criminal Court, 1, 191
International Journal, 130, 194
Iraq, 64
Isbister, Claude, 165
Israel, 91
Italy, 34

J

Japan, 6, 21, 23, 30, 34, 35, 36, 37, 38, 40, 42, 144, 145, 150
Jeune-Canada movement, 59
Johnson, Daniel, 126

K

Keating, Tom, 91, 194
Keenleyside, H.L., 16, 18, 19, 41, 42–43, 53–54, 57, 72
Kennedy, John F., 77, 160–61
Kenya, 141
Kergin, Michael, 221, 222
Khrushchev, Nikita, 94
King, William Lyon Mackenzie, 3, 11, 14, 16, 24, 28, 29, 33, 34, 35, 36, 37, 38, 39, 41, 42, 51, 52–53, 55–56, 58, 62, 69, 71, 72, 73, 74, 84, 85, 105, 106, 143, 182
Kirkwood, Kenneth, 16
Kirton, John, 189, 220
Korean War, 88, 107
Kuklick, Bruce, 58

L

Lalonde, Marc, 171, 172
Lang, Eugene, 194
Langdon, Steven, 193
Lapointe, Ernest, 52
Laurier, Wilfrid, 2
Lavertu, Gaetan, 227–28n45
League of Nations, 3, 34, 37, 62
Leahy, Patrick, 220
Leahy, William, 39, 40
Legault, Len, 215
Léger, Jules, 6, 121–32
Lesage, Jean, 123, 126
Lévesque, René, 169
Liberal Party of Canada, 14, 33, 61, 75, 155, 157, 162, 189, 216, 217, 221
Libreville conference, 128, 129, 134n27
Lie, Trygve, 82, 89
Lindsay, Robert, 38, 39
London Naval Conference, 34
Lord Tweedsmuir. *See* Buchan, John
Lortie, Marc, 221
Lusitania, 39
Lyon, Peyton, 94
Lyons, Deborah, 222

M

Macaulay, Thomas Babington, 147
Macdonald Commission, 187
MacDonald, David, 186
Macdonald, Donald, 164
MacDonald, Flora, 227n13
Macdonald, J. Scott, 15–16
MacDonald, Malcolm, 103
MacEachen, Allan, 210, 212
MacGuigan, Mark, 157
MacKay, Peter, 199
Mackenzie, Ian, 37, 39
Mackenzie River Valley, 30
Maclaren, Roy, 220
Mandatory Oil Import Program (MOIP), 160, 161
Manhattan, 102, 115
Manley, John, 192, 221–22
Marchi, Sergio, 220
Marler, Herbert, 40
Martin, Paul Jr., 2, 78, 153n20, 182, 194–96, 198, 199, 200, 204n47, 240

Martin, Paul Sr., 72, 83, 91, 95–96, 124, 127, 129, 134n19, 194
Massé, Marcel, 226n4
Massey, Vincent, 19–21, 28–29, 61
May, Ernest, 56–57
McCloskey, Agnes, 17, 18
McDougall, Pamela, 138
McFarlane, Robert, 214
McGreer, E. D'Arcy, 16
McKenzie, Marjorie, 17, 18
McKinnon, Hector, 139
McNaughton, A.G.L., 29, 30, 31, 33, 35
McPhail, Don, 138, 165
Meighen, Arthur, 2
Mexico, 149, 218, 224
middle power, 84
Mitchell, William, 28, 33, 34
Mitterand, François, 188
Moffat, J. Pierrepont, 36, 37, 38, 39, 42
Monroe Doctrine, 35, 41
Morin, Claude, 123–24, 131
Morocco, 122
Motor Carrier Act, 213
Mulroney, Brian, 7, 77, 103, 115, 116, 182, 184, 185–88, 199, 200, 210–16, 221, 226n5
Munich Crisis, 41, 52, 53, 63

N
National Energy Board (NEB), 161, 165, 166, 177n39
National Energy Program (NEP), 156, 162, 168–73, 178n55, 179, 179n67, 210
National Oil Policy, 160, 161, 167
National Policy, 147
National Research Council, 35
Nelles, Percy, 40
New Brunswick, 188
New Democratic Party, 167
New Partnership for Africa's Development (NEPAD), 193
New World Order, 183
New Zealand, 34, 123
Nicaragua, 212
Nielsen, Erik, 183
Nine Power Conference, 38
Nixon, Richard, 164
Nixon shock, 163
Nobel Peace Prize, 91, 220

non-governmental organizations (NGOs), 212, 226n9, 231, 232, 240
Non Group, 166
Noriega, Manuel, 216
North American Air Defence Command (NORAD), 75, 77, 224
North American Free Trade Agreement (NAFTA), 184, 200, 216
North Atlantic Treaty Organization (NATO), 89, 107, 112, 224
Northwest Passage, 103, 110, 112, 113, 116
Northwest Staging Route, 103
Nossal, Kim, 189, 196, 219
nuclear weapons, 75–76, 86
Nutt, Jim, 111

O
O'Connor, Gordon, 199
Ogdensburg Agreement, 42
oil, 103, 156–73
Oil Import Compensation Program, 167
Omnibus Drug Act, 213
Ontario, 7, 41, 54, 69, 158, 160, 162
Operation Polaris, 106
Organization for Economic Co-operation and Development (OECD), 145, 195
Organization of American States (OAS), 184, 188, 215–16, 227n23
Organization of Petroleum Exporting Countries (OPEC), 158, 164, 167, 173
Ostry, Sylvia, 226n4
Ottawa Process, 1, 191–92, 239
Ottawa Treaty, 191, 220
Ouellet, André, 190, 240
Owram, Doug, 58, 59, 60

P
Panama, 216
Panama Canal, 113
Parti Québécois, 169
Patry, André, 123
peacekeeping, 91–92, 96
Pearl Harbor, 103
Pearson, Lester B., 4, 5, 16, 61, 63–64, 74, 77, 87–88, 89, 90–91, 92, 93, 95–96, 101, 102, 114, 124, 127, 129, 143, 155, 156
Permanent Joint Board on Defence (PJBD), 42, 72, 73, 106
Petro-Canada, 166, 167, 170

Pettigrew, Pierre, 195, 220, 223–24
Phillips, William, 21, 32
Pickersgill, J.W., 72
Pitfield, Michael, 151n5, 153n20, 169, 171, 209
Poland, 63
Polar Sea, 115
Policy Options, 190
Pope, Joseph, 2, 14
Powell, Colin, 222
Power, C.G., 55
Prime Minister's Office (PMO), 165, 207–8, 211, 215, 236
Privy Council Office (PCO), 165, 207–8, 209, 223, 236
public opinion, 3, 5, 51–65, 71, 73
Pullen, T.C., 110

Q

Quebec, 6, 7, 34, 51–53, 54, 60, 62, 121–32, 158, 162, 169, 188, 190, 240
   1995 referendum, 190
   foreign relations, 128–30, 134n27
   relations with France, 127
Québécois nationalism, 122, 123, 125, 126–27, 129, 131–32
Queen Elizabeth, 51–52, 61–62
quiet diplomacy, 109, 113, 115, 171, 197, 239

R

Ranger, Louis, 222
Raymond, Valerie, 237, 244n11
Reagan, Ronald, 170–71, 185, 187, 213, 215, 217
Reciprocal Trade Agreements, 138
Reed, John E., 16
Reid, Escott, 41, 42, 62–63
Reisman, Simon, 144, 152n14, 166, 214
Rempel, Roy, 197, 199
Renaud, Paul-Emile, 16
responsible government, 181
Revenue Canada, 140
Ritchie, A. Edgar, 138, 144, 158, 160, 161, 165
Ritchie, Charles, 175n5
Robbins, Warren, 31, 33
Robertson, Gordon, 111, 113
Robertson, Norman, 5, 16, 43, 74, 75, 76, 77, 78, 83, 113, 138, 139, 142–43, 158

Robinson, Basil, 158, 164
Roosevelt, Franklin, 27, 28, 32, 33, 35, 36, 37, 39, 41, 43, 69, 72, 73
Ross, Edward, 56–57
Royal Canadian Air Force, 108
royal tour (1939), 51, 61–62, 63–64
Rush-Bagot Agreement, 32
Russia, 139, 183, 221
Rutherford, Ian, 64

S

Second World War, 4, 43, 63, 64, 70, 71–74, 77, 103
sector principle, 103, 105, 106, 115, 117n15
Security and Prosperity Partnership of North America, 197
Senegal, 121, 124
Senghor, Léopold, 121
Shamrock Summit, 214
Shannon, Gerry, 138
Sharp, Mitchell, 144, 153n20, 158, 159, 162, 164, 189
Shoyama, T.K., 165, 166
Shultz, George, 120n59, 210, 212, 214
Sicotte, Gilles, 110
Sino-Japanese conflict, 38
Skelton, Isabel, 13
Skelton, Oskar Douglas, 3, 4, 5, 11–24, 27–28, 29, 30, 31, 32, 33, 35, 36, 39–40, 42, 53, 54, 58, 61, 63, 70–71, 72–73, 74, 77, 78, 106, 138, 142
Smart Borders Declaration, 224
Smith, Gordon W., 115
Smith, Sidney, 74, 93
soft power, 220
South Africa, 34, 186, 212
Soviet Union. *See* Union of Soviet Socialist Republics
Spain, 239
Spry, D.C., 105
St. Laurent, Louis, 4, 93, 104, 107, 182, 183
Stairs, Denis, 196.
Stalin, Joseph, 82, 89
Stanner, H.T., 55
Star Wars. *See* Strategic Defence Initiative
Status of Women Canada (SWC), 233, 236–37, 238, 241, 242
Stein, Janet Gross, 194
Stevenson, Brian, 220

Stewart, Ian, 172
Stimson, Henry, 42
Stone, Frank, 138
Stoner, Gerry, 138
Strategic Defence Initiative (SDI), 188
Sudan, 198
Suez Crisis, 77, 97
summit diplomacy, 181
Summit of the Americas, 218, 224
Sutherland, R.J., 108
Switzerland, 123

T
Tadman, H.L., 165
Tarr, E.J., 61
Thant, U, 82, 95
Thatcher, Margaret, 186
Third Option, the, 144, 145, 158, 163, 189, 214
Tough, George, 165, 172
Trade Commissioner Service, 6, 209
Tremblay Report, 126
Trudeau, Pierre, 6, 7, 77, 78, 81–82, 103, 116, 153n20, 155–74, 185, 187, 189, 207, 236
Tunisia, 121, 124

U
U Thant. *See* Thant, U
Union of Soviet Socialist Republics, 76, 83, 86, 87, 92, 94, 101, 105, 210
  relations with the U.S., 93, 104, 111
United Kingdom, 30, 34, 41, 123
  relations with Canada, 12, 13, 53–54, 73, 142–43
  relations with the U.S., 38–39
  Royal Navy, 72
United Nations, 5, 76, 81–97, 229
United Nations Conference on Trade and Development (UNCTAD), 141
United Nations Convention on Certain Conventional Weapons, 191
United Nations Educational, Scientific, and Cultural Organization (UNESCO), 87
United Nations Emergency Force (UNEF), 81, 97
United Nations Security Council, 86, 87, 191, 220
United States, 55, 86
  Arctic, 106, 111
  Autopact, 143–44
  energy policy, 159
  Free Trade Agreement, 144, 148
  isolationism, 33
  relations with Canada, 3, 7, 21, 22–23, 39, 41, 43, 72–73, 75, 76–78, 91, 101–16, 142–43, 147–48, 156–61, 162, 164, 165, 167, 168, 170–71, 174, 186–88, 192–93, 195–96, 197–98, 207–25
  relations with U.K., 38–39
  relations with U.S.S.R., 93
  State Department, 21, 29, 43, 106
United States Army Air Corps, 29, 30, 31, 32
United States Congress, 32, 159, 187, 213, 214, 215, 223
United States Navy, 32, 37, 42, 110, 112
USS *Panay*, 38

V
Venezuela, 159, 160, 162
Vienna Conference on Human Rights (1993), 233, 234
Voluntary Oil Import Program (VOIP), 159

W
Wang, Eric, 109
Warren, Jake, 138
Weekes, John, 138
Welles, Sumner, 34, 37, 38, 39, 40
Welsh, Jennifer, 189
Whelan, D.R., 173
Wigglesworth, Richard, 175n16
Wilgress, Dana, 138–39
Williams, Jodi, 191
Wilson, Michael, 215
women's rights, 234
World Trade Organization, 152n17
World War I. *See* First World War
World War II. *See* Second World War
Wrong, Hume, 15, 16, 19, 31, 33, 34, 54, 84, 102

www.ingramcontent.com/pod-product-compliance
Lightning Source LLC
Chambersburg PA
CBHW052014290426
44112CB00014B/2242